Overcoming the Retributive Nature of the Israeli-Palestinian Conflict

Thomas L. Saaty • H. J. Zoffer • Luis G. Vargas •
Amos Guiora

Overcoming the Retributive Nature of the Israeli-Palestinian Conflict

Springer

Thomas L. Saaty
University of Pittsburgh
Pittsburgh, PA, USA

H. J. Zoffer
University of Pittsburgh
Pittsburgh, PA, USA

Luis G. Vargas
University of Pittsburgh
Pittsburgh, PA, USA

Amos Guiora
SJ Quinney College of Law
University of Utah
Salt Lake City, UT, USA

ISBN 978-3-030-83957-4 ISBN 978-3-030-83958-1 (eBook)
https://doi.org/10.1007/978-3-030-83958-1

This Springer imprint is published by the registered company Springer Nature Switzerland AG.
The registered company address is: Gewerbestrasse 11, 6330 Cham, Switzerland

We would like to dedicate this book to our beloved friend and mentor Thomas L. Saaty (1926–2017) for his untiring efforts, enthusiasm, and encouragement during the project that culminated with this book.

Preface

Overcoming the Retribute Nature of the Israeli Palestinian Conflict reflects a determined effort to address a seemingly irresolvable conflict. While we do not claim to have all the answers on how to untie a seeming Gordian knot stretching over an interminable period of time, we do have concrete recommendations on how to significantly move the ball forward. Our recommendations, presented in detail, are not based on a pipe dream, reflecting half-baked ideas, but rather the results of an extraordinary set of meetings in Pittsburgh, PA, USA, and Spain, over the course of more than a decade.

We are not the first to participate in such an undertaking. However, what distinguishes our effort, distinct from those that came before us, is that our work is predicated on a mathematical, hierarchical model called the Analytic Hierarchy Process (AHP). It is the application of a prioritization-based approach rather than the traditional, zero-sum game model that enables us to state with a fair degree of confidence: implementation of the AHP suggestions will make a remarkably significant contribution to solving the conflict.

There is, of course, an important caveat of which we are well aware: at the end of the day, peace is made by leaders who convene, sometimes for an extended period of time, occasionally with great anger and distrust. The maxim that peace is made among enemies, not friends, is as true regarding this conflict as any other. More than that, we do not—under any circumstances—assert that the AHP comes instead of decision makers, carrying historical, political, religious, and personal baggage. But we do believe the AHP, as discussed at length in this book, gives decision makers tools unlike any other existing model.

The book[1] reflects our distinct disciplines, experiences, and backgrounds. Parts of the book are mathematical in focus; other parts are more conversational. The sum

[1] This book contains excerpts from papers or book chapters previously published in the process of developing the AHP proposed solution, and during the project conducted that yielded the results presented in the book. The following papers and book have been used in the preparation of this book:

total is an accurate barometer of our efforts these past years. For a reader whose orientation is mathematical models and numerical analysis, sections of the book will be familiar and highly relatable. For a reader whose focus is history-law-politics, other sections will be more comprehensible.

This approach is deliberate both because it reflects our own academic disciplines and because it is the most accurate manifestation of our approach to the conflict. To create a way forward for decision makers, traditional methods are not effective and therefore a creative mechanism fills the void. It is in that spirit that we have dedicated years to this project and the reason we have written this book.

The book is intended for a wide range of audiences; while, admittedly, some of the text may be challenging for those not steeped in mathematics, the discussion and explanation are intended to facilitate sufficient understanding to appreciate the applicability of what we propose. We took this into consideration when deciding both how to write the book and how to frame the discussion. We recommend the reader keep a sharp focus on the true objective of this project: to give decision makers tools for their toolbox they otherwise do not have. It is clear that numerous tools are missing from that elusive toolbox; adoption of what to discuss will significantly enrich the possibilities.

While we do not claim to step into the shoes of decision makers, we do note that the proposed resolutions that are at the core of this book reflect the collective wisdom of individuals who are, truly, subject matter experts. While we cannot disclose their identity, the reader will have to take our word that the Israelis and Palestinians we convened over the course of many years, in multiple locations in the world, under an absolute guarantee of anonymity, brought significant knowledge to the discussion.

There was mutual respect among the participants, some who knew each other from previous engagements. For some, the AHP presented a significant challenge; ultimately, all understood its benefit and value. Needless to say, arguments were part and parcel of the gatherings; sometimes, the arguments were loud and vociferous. That should come as no surprise to anyone who has spent time in the region.

However, while occasionally voices were raised and tempers flared, all participants were fully committed to the undertaking. There was, whether directly or tacitly acknowledged, an understanding that the AHP's uniqueness deserved their attention and merited their time and effort. This book, in its distinct voices, seeks to bring that

---

- Saaty, T.L. and H.J. Zoffer (2012). "A New Approach to the Middle East Conflict: The Analytic Hierarchy Process," *Journal of Multi-Criteria Decision Analysis* **19**(5–6): 201–225.
- Saaty, T.L. and H.J. Zoffer (2013). "Principles for Implementing a Potential Solution to the Middle East Conflict," *Notices of the American Mathematical Society* **60**(10): 1300–1322.
- Saaty, T.L., L.G. Vargas and H.J. Zoffer (2015). "A Structured Scientific Solution to the Israeli–Palestinian Conflict: The Analytic Hierarchy Process Approach," Decision Analytics 2(7):1–53.
- Saaty, T.L. and L.G. Vargas (2012). *Models, Methods, Concepts & Applications of The Analytic Hierarchy Process*. Int'l Series in Operations Research & Management Science. Springer, Revised 2nd edition. Springer.

level of commitment to reader and decision maker alike. If the book makes even a sliver of a contribution to resolution of the conflict, no one would be happier than us.

Overcoming the Retribute Nature of the Israeli Palestinian Conflict is structured as follows. Chapter 1 describes the goals and objectives of the project on which this book is based. Chapter 2 lays out the origins, the evolution, and attempts at resolving the conflict. Chapter 3 summarizes the theory of the analytic hierarchy process (AHP) used to model the group decision methodology employed in the analysis of the conflict. Chapter 4 describes how conflicts of a retributive nature can be studied with the AHP. These conflicts involve benefits, costs, perceived benefits, and perceived costs of concessions (trade-offs) made by the parties. The main trade-off mechanism is introduced and illustrated with a basic negotiation case. Chapter 5 describes the hierarchies of benefits, costs, perceived benefits, and perceived costs needed to evaluate concessions (trade-offs) from the parties. Chapter 6 gives a description of the lessons learned in the process of using the AHP up to that point in time in the project. Chapter 7 uses judgments elicited from the participants in the project to evaluate concessions and build the core of a fair and equitable agreement. Chapter 8 develops each of the principles into actionable steps for implementation. Chapter 9 shows in detail how the Palestinian refugee problem could be solved. Chapter 10 describes what is needed to succeed in the implementation of the agreement by drawing from actual situations learned after the Oslo Accords were implemented. Finally, Chap. 11 looks ahead. This is the most difficult chapter due to recent developments as of the time of the finishing of the writing of this book in the spring of 2021.

The agreement developed in this book did not include Gaza as part of the discussions. However, one of the principles (#2) states "…Israel must respect the territorial integrity of the West Bank and Gaza by allowing free and safe passage between the two areas …." So, albeit indirectly, the participants considered the inclusion of Gaza as part of the agreement. We were not concerned with which political party was in power as long as compromise and cooperation are part of the agenda.

Just because the future looks grim now it does not mean there is no path forward in which all parties involved can cooperate to find a fair and equitable solution. The results of this book show that only through cooperation an acceptable solution to both parties is attainable. Extreme positions only lead to radical solutions in which only one party will win, and the zero-sum paradigm will take hold. As we have seen, that is ultimately not a solution and is best defined as "lose-lose."

Pittsburgh, PA — Thomas L. Saaty
Pittsburgh, PA — H. J. Zoffer
Pittsburgh, PA — Luis G. Vargas
Salt Lake City, UT — Amos Guiora

Contents

Chapter 1
Laying the Groundwork

This book introduces a process to address the Israeli–Palestinian conflict. It does so in two ways that are different from past efforts. The first is by formally structuring the conflict, and the second is the way discussions are conducted and conclusions drawn. The effort is to create an objective, rather than subjective, model for resolving the conflict. As aspirational as that sounds, if not improbable as it may be, we believe that we have developed a workable model that is applicable to the conflict. We are confident because we have seen it in action; the model enables decision makers to engage in negotiations dramatically different from the traditional "zero-sum game" approach that has largely defined Israeli–Palestinian negotiations.

That has been the case over the years whether the parties negotiated with or without third parties having a seat at the table. While exceptions exist—the Oslo Peace Process is the obvious example—the reality is that as these lines are written, to suggest peace is in the offing would be an extraordinary exaggeration. While, perhaps, the contemporary stalemate is perceived by current Israeli and Palestinian leadership as beneficial to their specific, narrow tactical calculations, that truculence does not portend well for the years to come. This is despite the fact that there is little, if any, clamoring for resolving the conflict among Israelis and Palestinians. It is as if leadership and public alike have come to accept the status quo as tolerable, if not permanent.

Nevertheless, the model we discuss in this book—reflecting our active engagement in small group settings with Israelis and Palestinians—provides a path forward for resolving the conflict. Our approach provides negotiators with a unique pathway to consider the thorny issues and corresponding concessions underlying the deliberations, together with their implementation. The approach has been successfully applied in both South Africa (Saaty, 1988) and in Northern Ireland (Alexander & Saaty, 1977a, 1977b). The outcomes of this process added valuable dimension to the discussions and resolutions of those conflicts. That is what we set out to do in this book. That is our primary purpose and what drives this undertaking.

This is not a history book in the traditional sense, nor a book about politics and international relations. We do not argue which side is right, which side has suffered

T. L. Saaty et al., *Overcoming the Retributive Nature of the Israeli-Palestinian Conflict*, https://doi.org/10.1007/978-3-030-83958-1_1

more, which side has history in its corner, which side is more effective in the contemporary global arena, which side has more justified claims, or which side is the winner and which side is the loser. Those issues we leave to others for that is neither our purpose nor intent. Similarly, we do not engage in conversation regarding the broader Middle East. We eschew examination of Palestinian relations with the Arab world, Turkey, and Iran; similarly, we do not analyze Israeli relations with the broader Middle East, including the peace agreement with the Emirates and what may follow in its footsteps. In that vein, we avoid discussion of broader geopolitics and trigger points in the Middle East, whether it is Iran's nascent nuclear capabilities, ongoing conflicts in Iraq and Syria, or the complicated roles of the USA and Russia in the region.

We make a committed effort to "drown" out all external noise not specifically germane to the Israel-Palestinian conflict, narrowly defined. There is, however, an important caveat: the historical role played primarily, albeit not exclusively, by the USA to bring the parties together. We will examine that and other foreign involvements in various peace processes—such as the Oslo Peace Process—given their relevance to our narrow focus, but avoid broader discussion regarding foreign engagement, if not intervention, in the Middle East. That is in accordance with our very specific and narrow focus.

What does interest us is presenting to the reader an alternative mechanism to resolve what is widely understood to be an all but intractable conflict between two parties fighting over a small piece of land. The means we suggest are distinct from traditional approaches; they reflect an effort to engage in the conflict from an objective, rather than subjective, perspective. While the reader may look asunder at the notion of such an approach—after all much of the conflict is about emotion—we truly believe that our alternative model deserves an audience who is at the core of this undertaking. Understandably, an alternative model may raise eyebrows and be greeted with skepticism and doubt. We understand that and welcome the challenge of convincing the reader of the viability and validity of a fresh approach distinct from traditional orthodoxies.

At the center of the approach used is the Analytic Hierarchy Process (AHP). We explain it in more detail in Chap. 3. Here is a summary of what the AHP is about. It is a scientific approach used to determine the relative importance of a set of activities or criteria. The novel aspect and major distinction of this approach is that it structures any complex, multi-person, multi-criteria, and multi-period problem hierarchically. Hierarchies are used to decompose the problem from the general to the particular. For example, the top level could be the goal, the next level could comprise the criteria to reach the goal, and the third level contains the alternative courses of action to be compared according to the criteria. Using a method for scaling the weights of the elements in each level of the hierarchy with respect to an element (e.g., a criterion or property they share) of the next higher level, comparisons of the activities in pairs can be elicited from decision makers. Each comparison indicates the strength with which one element dominates another with respect to a given criterion. Structurally, the hierarchy is broken down into a series of comparisons. For example, given a criterion and two alternatives, which alternative is more important according to that criterion and by how much? The answer to this question is a judgment translated into a numerical value using Table 3.1.

This scaling formulation yields a unique vector of priority weights for each level of the hierarchy (always with respect to the criteria in the level above), which in turn results in a single composite vector of weights for the entire hierarchy. This vector measures the relative priority of all entities at the lowest level that enables the accomplishment of the highest objective of the hierarchy. These relative priority weights can provide guidelines for the allocation of resources among the entities at the lower levels of the hierarchy. When hierarchies are designed to reflect likely environmental scenarios, corporate objectives, current and proposed product/market alternatives, and various marketing strategy options, the AHP can provide a framework and methodology for the determination of several key corporate and marketing decisions.

While we focus on a unique approach, we are not oblivious to the human complexity, if not tragedy, of the conflict. Perhaps to the uninitiated, the Israeli–Palestinian conflict should be readily solvable. If Ireland and England could reach an agreement over the future of Northern Ireland, albeit a rocky agreement, then why is this conflict still unresolved? In the same vein, if South Africans were able to come together and undo institutionalized apartheid and replace a white minority government with a black majority government, then why should Israelis and Palestinians not convene around a table—whether brought together by a third party or not—and resolve, once and for all, the issues that prevent a just settlement for all concerned? While efforts have been made over the years, some meeting with success (e.g., the Oslo Accords, see U.S. Dept. of State, 1993), none has been sufficiently effective to enable the parties to jump over the final hurdle to reach the all-elusive finish line.

There is an endless litany of reasons for this ultimate failure for that is the only way to assess the on-the-ground reality. Truth be told, except for extremists on both sides, or those comfortable with the status quo, akin to a "permanent low-grade fever," the current situation reflects a stalemate whereby neither side is satisfied. Fifty-three years after the 1967 Six Day War, when Israel defeated Jordan, Egypt, and Syria gaining significant land including the Sinai Peninsula and Gaza Strip (from Egypt), the Golan Heights (from Syria), and the West Bank and East Jerusalem (from Jordan), the permanent status of the West Bank-Gaza Strip is as uncertain today as it was on the morning of June 10, 1967, when Palestinians in both areas woke up to a new reality: living under an Israel Defense Forces (IDF) Military Government.

As Israel has never annexed the West Bank or the Gaza Strip, neither is subject to Israeli sovereignty but, rather, both live under a military government. While the Oslo Peace Accords and the establishment of the Palestinian Authority (PA) and subsequent Israeli disengagement from the Gaza Strip changed the relationship between Palestinians and Israel, that impact is ultimately limited, for a Palestinian state exercising sovereignty over land and people has yet to be created. In other words, while the Oslo Accords were a significant step forward as the PA exercises some jurisdiction over the Palestinian population, it is not—and must not be—understood to be akin to an independent state.

In suggesting a model for resolving the conflict, we have, as our goal, a path leading to a two-state solution, the State of Israel and the State of Palestine. However, an important caveat is in order. The caveat, with which we have struggled during the years we have been working on this issue with Palestinians and Israelis, is a question that "hangs in the air" when engaging with Palestinians regarding the contours of a future state. There is, understandably, discomfort surrounding this question because it cuts to the core of whether a Palestinian state would encompass Palestinians living in both the Gaza Strip and the West Bank, or just the West Bank. A few years ago, one of us met with a senior Palestinian official and when this subject was broached, the response was direct, "leave us alone until we have our own house in order." The reference left little doubt: only the Palestinians can resolve this matter. Fair enough. However, in proposing a road map for resolving the conflict, that is not an applicable approach.

We are aware of the bitter internecine conflict between Palestinians living in the Gaza Strip and those living in the West Bank. That has been made consistently clear to us during our work on this project. It has been articulated in different forums, discretely or otherwise, by Palestinians for years. We are not oblivious to the tension, in the past morphing into violent confrontation between the PA and Hamas which effectively rules the Gaza Strip. It is not an exaggeration to state that the PA exercises no control or influence over the lives of Palestinians residing in the Gaza Strip. This issue raises an important dilemma that demands resolution in how we present this book. We do not take this question lightly for we are aware of its tensions and controversies.

After careful consideration and reflecting our years-long engagement with Palestinians, we have decided that although our focus in this project on a two-state solution was centered around the West Bank and Israel, the solution that is proposed here is applicable to Gaza. One of the principles (#2) derived from this work states that the State of Palestine must allow its citizens to have free and safe passage to and from all sites within it. The proposed solution does not depend on which party is in power as long as that party seeks a fair and equitable solution to all parties involved. This is not made lightly but we rely heavily on what Palestinians with whom we have met have repeatedly emphasized. We understand and respect the discomfort, if not anger, this will elicit. Nevertheless, we believe this to be the correct approach. Furthermore, this decision—controversial and discomforting as it may be—reflects what we have learned over the years in engagement with Israelis and Palestinians with whom we met in an effort to develop a framework for resolution of the conflict.

We met in small groups in discrete settings with individuals we identified as deeply knowledgeable and fully versed in the intricate details of the conflict. Those individuals were not official representatives of either the State of Israel or the Palestinian Authority. We guaranteed participants absolute confidentiality regarding their involvement; we felt this was necessary to ensure frank, even heated, discussions that demanded candor and honesty. We exercised discretion if we felt a participant was unwilling to respect the terms of agreement to which each participant was duty bound.

As a result of our efforts, we authored a document that has been made available exclusively to decision makers on both sides. The document which is intended to serve as a road map has not been made available to the wider public. The road map reflects a "win-win" approach—the essence of prioritization—whereby both sides can walk away with a sense of achievement and accomplishment, rather than feeling the other side got the upper hand. This is intended to assuage concerns in the context of domestic consumption; after all, the selling of an agreement is no less important than its details. This is an issue we shall explore at some length in this book.

While the period from 1967 to the outbreak of the First Palestinian Intifada (December 1987–1993) was largely marked by passivity, if not begrudging acceptance of the IDF's presence in the West Bank and Gaza Strip, the subsequent three decades have been marked by significant violence and bloodshed, with a peak in the Second Intifada, 2001–2005 (Vox, 2018). The term passivity (1967–1987) may raise eyebrows in some quarters; some suggest a period of adjustment more accurately reflects the 20-year period; others theorize it took that long for the population to fully internalize the dramatic shift from living under Jordanian rule to living under a military government.

Perhaps for that reason, efforts to resolve the conflict were undertaken only in the aftermath of the Palestinian "uprising"—(1987–1993)—rather than in the previous twenty years. Whether those twenty years (1967–1987) were "wasted" is a matter of historical debate; what is clear is opportunities that may have existed to develop mechanisms for a just and lasting agreement between Israel and the Palestinians were not explored with any degree of seriousness. That is explained, in part, by a (in retrospect) tragic euphoria that characterized Israeli society from June 1967 to October 1973. That six-year period—from the Six-Day War to the Yom Kippur War—gave many Israelis a sense of invincibility, after the stunning victory over the combined armies of Egypt, Jordan, and Syria. It was in that period that Jewish settlements began to be built in the West Bank as the powerful sense—for the Israeli religious right—of a messianic return to the historic Land of the Bible.

It is well-nigh impossible to resolve the conflict without addressing the question of the settlements; to suggest they have been front and center in the conflict is an enormous understatement. That was repeatedly made clear to us in all our meetings. While there is an understanding, spoken and unspoken, among the Palestinians that even were a Palestinian state to be established in the West Bank it is impossible—practically and politically—to remove all the settlements that have been built in the past few decades. To sharpen the point: since 1967, the right–left divide in Israel has focused on one question: the future of the settlements and the end of the Israeli occupation of the West Bank. A caveat is in order: the phrases "end of the settlements" and "Israeli occupation" are rejected by the Israeli right who favor (as we shall discuss) annexation of parts (if not all) of the West Bank and refuse to use the term "occupation" when referring to the relationship between Israel and the West Bank. As we shall come to see, nuances and terminology are of extraordinary importance in our analysis.

In exploring Israeli–Palestinian negotiations, our primary focus is to present to the reader a model that we believe can chart a way forward. That model enabled the crafting of the road map document to which we will refer frequently throughout this book. While we will reference the "road map" document we have created, we will not share it in full in accordance with terms of participation in the discussions we conducted. We are convinced of its relevance and saliency as we have applied it elsewhere. Simply put, we know it works. To understand it will require the reader to engage in a willingness to think outside the box in analyzing negotiations through a mathematical model. Readers uncomfortable with mathematical modeling need not be concerned as the explanations will be "user friendly." The word "model" is used deliberately, signaling to the reader that our approach is predicated on a systemic, systematic approach enabling prioritization of desired goals. That is very different from the traditional negotiating model. In undertaking this project, we were hopeful the parties could examine this historical conflict from a different perspective, using an approach whereby each side "wins," rather than the more traditional, "zero-sum game" mechanism whereby the gains of one side are the losses of the other.

Nevertheless, to strive for cogency and coherence we offer below our definitions. However, it is more complicated than that. As an example: for some, the mere term "Palestinians" is a red herring as they reject, from the outset, the very notion that the term is viable, denying the essence of a Palestinian people. For others, Israel's right to exist is an abomination and they are consistent in their determined efforts to reject that the State of Israel is legitimate.

The same controversy applies to the territory captured by Israel in the aftermath of the 1967 Six-Day War; what for some is "occupied" is for others "liberated" and what for some is the "West Bank" is for others "Judea and Samaria" and "Greater Israel." For those relying on the Hebrew Bible the entire discussion is moot for this is the Land of Israel and no contemporary examination is relevant to what the Divine ordained. For others, the existence of Jewish settlements on land captured in the Six-Day War is THE primary roadblock to resolving the conflict; absent an Israeli decision to withdraw, peace will be forever elusive.

This is akin to the terminological dispute, "one man's terrorist is another man's freedom fighter. The semantic discussion is important; in some cases it is, unfortunately, casus belli. That is one of the tragic realities when considering this most complex conflict. For the purposes of this book, we suggest the following definitions, taking into consideration objections will be raised in some quarters regarding some of the definitions:

- West Bank: the area between pre-1967 Six-Day War Israel and the Jordan River; the "border" between the West Bank and Israel is commonly referred to as the Green Line though there is no official border.
- Gaza Strip: as commonly denoted on agreed upon maps.
- Palestinian Authority: as defined in the Oslo Peace Accords, while there is no Palestinian state as recognized by commonly accepted international law, the PA has state-like functions, albeit is not defined as a State.Jewish settlements: cities in the West Bank built by the Israeli government after 1967, exclusively populated by Jews.
- Areas A, B, and C: areas in the West Bank demarcated by the Oslo Peace Accords.

We will ascribe the pushback to "reasonable minds can reasonably disagree."

In the next chapter, we discuss the origins, evolution, and attempts to resolve the conflict without being too detailed and/or exhaustive. Thus, we only describe the main events that took place in the conflict that led to the current situation when we try to use our approach.

References

Alexander, J. M., & Saaty, T. L. (1977a). The forward and backward processes of conflict analysis. *Behavioral Science, 22*(2), 87–95.

Alexander, J. M., & Saaty, T. L. (1977b). Stability analysis of the forward-backward process: Northern Ireland case study. *Behavioral Science, 22*(6), 375–382.

Saaty, T. L. (1988). The negotiation and resolution of the conflict in South Africa: The analytic hierarchy process. *ORiON, 4*(1), 3–25.

U.S. Dept. of State. (1993). *The Oslo accords and the Arab-Israeli peace process*. Office of the Historian, Foreign Service Institute. https://history.state.gov/milestones/1993-2000/oslo. Accessed June 3, 2021.

Vox. (2018). What were the intifadas? https://www.vox.com/2018/11/20/18080066/israel-palestine-intifadas-first-second. Accessed June 3, 2021.

Chapter 2
The Middle East Conflict: Origins, Evolution, and Attempts to Resolve

Introduction

When future Israeli Prime Minister David Ben-Gurion (born David Grün, he adopted the Hebrew name Ben-Gurion, after the Jewish leading figure Joseph ben Gurion of the Great Jewish Revolt against the Romans) arrived in Palestine in 1906, he ignored the fact that the land was populated by a non-Jewish majority. While the Land of Israel has powerful religious, historical, social, and cultural importance for Jews—religious and non-religious alike—the majority population in 1906 was Moslem. That is a fact. However, that fact does not diminish the 5000-year Biblical connection between the Land of Israel and the Jewish people. That, too, is a fact. These are not competing truths for both are true; these truths—while largely not in dispute—do not prevent an ongoing battle of the narrative. In many ways, that battle is at the root of the conflict; each side claims its historical superiority, each side stakes a claim that it "was here first," and each side believes its claims to be the mantel of historical ascendency.

The ties to the land are deep. For many people those ties define their existential existence, impacting the capability—and willingness—to have a rational discussion regarding how to resolve the conflict. Some, truth be told, have no interest in resolving the conflict; after all, resolution implies compromise, suggesting legitimacy of the other side's claims. There are, obviously, other conflicts that demand the world's attention, whether in the Middle East or elsewhere. The world, after all, is rife with tension points, wars, and battles. However, for a variety of reasons—without minimizing the importance of other conflicts—there is "something" about the Israel-Palestinian conflict that attracts international attention like no other. The conflict stirs passion, even among those whose knowledge is minimal at best; it has become an inherent part of US elections, unlike almost any other international conflict point. The reasons are varied, various, too disparate to count.

The conflict has been the source of endless soundbites, mantras, statements, position papers, white papers, debate, and heated discussion. It is as if "everyone"

T. L. Saaty et al., *Overcoming the Retributive Nature of the Israeli-Palestinian Conflict*, https://doi.org/10.1007/978-3-030-83958-1_2

has a position on the conflict; the list of experts is only as long as the list of "experts." Events, seemingly unrelated to the conflict, are linked to it, oftentimes for no understandable reason. Perhaps that is because of the centrality of Jerusalem to all three monotheistic faiths; perhaps because of the extent of American financial support of Israel; perhaps because of lobbying efforts by various organizations resulting in political pressure, real or imagined; perhaps because of an effort to cast the Israeli–Palestinian conflict as the centerpiece of the Middle East. Whether for these, or other reasons, the conflict has for decades attracted an extraordinary amount of attention.

Nevertheless, notwithstanding the efforts—regardless of their genuine-ness, good faith, and sincerity—the conflict is no closer to resolution than decades ago. What makes the undertaking to resolve so extraordinarily difficult is the lack of core understanding, or agreement, regarding the source of the conflict, much less a mutually desirable endpoint. The lack of consensus regarding the most desired and most achievable result is a reality that negotiators have confronted for years. Whether one is religious or not, it is all but impossible to ignore the role faith plays in the historical underpinning of the conflict.

For Jews, whether a person of faith or not, the connection to the land is rooted in archeology, history, and documented events. Aside from the Biblical narrative recounted in the Torah, archaeological evidence points to the existence of Israel as far back as 1213 BCE. It is irrelevant whether all that is written in the Hebrew Bible is historically "fool-proof"; what is important is the 5000-year yearning of Jews to return to the Land of Israel. The phrase "next year in Jerusalem," which concludes the Passover Seder, resonates with Jews worldwide and represents the historical ties to the Land of Israel. None of this, however, undermines Palestinian claims to the land. Palestinian claims to the land are no less legitimate, and they demand being heard and addressed. Despite extremist views on both sides denying the very existence of a Palestinian people or denying the legitimacy of a State of Israel, both sides in this conflict deserve to have their claims respected.

The amorphism "land without a people, people without a land" has been used to describe the paradigm from the Jewish perspective; its meaning is clear regarding the deep connection between the Jewish people and the Land. It also ignores the fact that Muslims-Arabs-Palestinians were living on that land when Jews began settling it. The Jewish movement to the Land of Israel/Palestine beginning in the late 1880s and continuing through the 1930s was a direct reflection of Zionism as articulated by Theodore Herzl (Israeli Minister of Foreign Affairs, 2004). Herzl, a Viennese Jew, was profoundly impacted by the Dreyfus Trial, believing the anti-Semitism at the trial's root signaled European Jews must leave (Britannica, 2010). That was amplified in the aftermath of the Kishinev Pogroms (The Harvard Gazette, 2009). In addition to Jews moving to/back to the Land of Israel—this is referred to as "Making Aliyah," literally "moving up"—there were 10,000 Jews living in Palestine, the overwhelming religious, eking out, largely, a meager existence. For a broader discussion on this issue, please see (DellaPergola, 2003).

During the years that the Ottoman Empire (1516–1917) (Shaw & Yapp, 2021) ruled Palestine, relations between the minority Jewish community and the majority

Moslem-Arab-Palestinian community ran the gamut from coexistence to violence. However, the acts of violence primarily focused on land disputes, rather than the nationalism that largely defines the nature of today's conflict. That is not to minimize the violence but rather to distinguish between today and during the Ottoman period when the Turks were, largely, disengaged from the local population. In essence, the Turks enabled/tolerated the two population groups living separate existences, even if in the same area, with minimal interference or engagement in their daily lives and affairs. The Jews were focused on maintaining a religious life, based on their orthodoxy and commitment to the Hebrew Bible. This is not to say that there were not improvements in Jewish quality of life at the time. While the eighteenth century was characterized by neglect from Ottoman rulers, the nineteenth century saw European powers begin to vie for power in the "Holy Land." Trade routes, which included the newly created Suez Canal, opened between Europe and Palestine. Because of this, the Jewish population in the area began to increase and by 1880 Jerusalem had a Jewish majority. Further, the Hebrew language was revived helping to set the stage for the founding of the Zionist movement (Israeli Foreign Ministry, 2021).

Conversely, the majority of Arabs were largely secular, working the land, leading a modest life, navigating life under foreign rule (Israeli Foreign Ministry, 2021). There was little, if any, impetus for the notion of nationalism, intended to create an Arab–Muslim state in Palestine. The political culture was more akin to clans, than burgeoning nationalism reflecting a cohesive entity determined to establish an Arab state in Palestine.

Three events accelerated the process: the revitalization of Palestine in the late nineteenth century-early twentieth century: the birth of Zionism, the Balfour Declaration (Rosenberg, 2020), the defeat of the Ottoman Empire—"the sick man of Europe"—in World War I (History.com Editors, 2020), and the subsequent conquering of Palestine by the British army. The picture of General Allenby marching into Palestine on his horse leading his troops heralded the arrival of a new foreign power. The League of Nations' vote on July 22, 1922, which established the British Mandate in Palestine formalized the transfer of power from the Ottoman Empire to the British Empire. It also ensured that those who lived in Palestine would continue to live under the control of a foreign power. Foreign rule was nothing new for those living in Palestine. After all, even the term "Palestine" was first coined by Roman rulers as far back as 132 CE after the Bar-Kochba Revolt as a way of punishing the inhabitants of what was formerly known as Roman Judea.

Centuries before the birth of Islam (History.com Editors, 2019) and well after the Destruction of the First Temple in 569 BCE (Wein & Astor, 2012), the land had seen successive foreign powers occupy it. This included groups such as the Syrians and the Romans. While always holding strong religious sentiment for the Jewish people, eventually Arab-Muslim incursions into the land after the fall of the Western Roman Empire prompted Christian interest in "protecting" the Holy Land. While both Christians and Muslims would at various points control Israel, Crusaders were eventually completely expelled from the land in 1291 by the Mamluks. The fact that the Land, in particular Jerusalem, is the "holiest of holies" for Jews, Christians, and Muslims alike is a central theme of the conflict. Whether it drives the conflict today is a matter of interpretation; what is clear is the important role religion has historically played when seeking to understand the conflict. That is not to suggest it is the dominant issue, for that would be an exaggeration, but it is to draw attention to the historical importance of religion. However, the intractability extends beyond religious conflict; it is too convenient to point an exclusive finger of guilt at faith.

If religion is not the dominant aspect of the conflict, how do we explain that resolution is not in the offing. What is it that makes Palestinians and Israelis unable to end this conflict? The question is not asked rhetorically, but rather to provide the background for understanding issues that have proved unresolvable, or at least a path for resolving them has not been sufficiently compelling. Because our focus is the contemporary conflict, our historical focus is necessarily limited. That is not to gainsay the importance of events dating back to Biblical times—even though much of the conflict is rooted in claims predicated on religious texts and beliefs—but rather to frame the conflict in contemporary terminology. Terminology will help us resolve the conflict today because ultimately the religious aspect of the conflict currently takes a secondary role to the simple lack of political will to resolve the conflict today.

Even that is complicated because of the inexorable link between past and present, a conundrum that drives—if not impacts—the contemporary discussion. Because our effort is to present the reader with an alternative model, based on benefit-cost prioritization, our focus must necessarily be on issues that are on the table today, rather than seeking to address events, regardless of their importance, from yesteryear. In that spirit, and with the readers' understanding, we will focus on six issues. We do so with the understanding that others may reject our seemingly limited approach, or may find that the six events we have chosen are less significant than others and that we have made critical errors in our understanding. We accept that criticism and acknowledge that is endemic to an undertaking of this nature. However, because of our primary focus, we, deliberately, fast-forward over thousands of years of history.

We do so not because history is not important (of course it is) but rather to "set the table" for the discussions to follow. The discussion regarding the six issues will not be presented from one perspective or another as there is no intent to favor one narrative over the other. Rather, the intent is to enable the reader to understand the complexity, nuances, and challenges of the conflict—and efforts to resolve it—by focusing on critical issues that have shaped much of the contemporary discussion.

In that spirit, we suggest examining six events:

1. The Birth of Zionism
2. The Balfour Declaration
3. The Defeat of the Ottoman Empire—The British Mandate
4. The Establishment of the State of Israel
5. The Six-Day War
6. The First and Second Intifadas

At the time when Zionism became a political movement among Jewish inhabitants of Palestine, there were several other nationalist movements such as the Bundists (Mishkinsky, 2008) and Autonomists. These competing ideologies all laid out a plan for eventual Jewish control of the land, but Zionism was the most radical and likely the most influential. The First Zionist Congress was convened on August 29, 1898. The Congress called for the establishment of a national home for Jews in the Land of Israel. By 1907, a national plan is laid out to practice both political and practical Zionism. Political Zionism mainly included international efforts to obtain a charter for Jews in Palestine and to receive international recognition. Practical Zionism, on the other hand, was simply to encourage settlement of the land by Jews. By 1909, Hashomer (Morris, 2020) provided security for Jewish settlements in the land, and the first all Jewish city of Tel Aviv was created in Israel. The beginning of World War I also provided for the possibility of shift in colonial power of the land. In 1917, 400 years of the Ottoman Rule ended with the British conquest of the land. That same year, on November 2, the Balfour Declaration pledged British support for the establishment of a Jewish National Home in Palestine.

The Balfour Declaration marked the first step toward International recognition of the Jewish homeland, and it came less than two decades after the birth of Zionism in Israel. The importance of the Balfour Declaration should not be understated. While it was ultimately a promise from the British government, the British government did not sign the declaration without the support of other prominent players. Prior to publishing the Declaration, British diplomats sought and secured the support of American President Woodrow Wilson—the French having already declared the support a few months earlier. Less than a year after the Declaration was signed, even the Grand Vizier of the Ottoman Empire, Talaat Pasha, declared the support of the failing State for the establishment of a Jewish homeland on the land. By July 24, 1922, the promises of the Balfour Declaration were incorporated into the Mandate of the League of Nations. What started out as a promise of a colonial power quickly turned into an aspect of International Law at the time. All fifty-one member states of the League of Nations supported Jewish settlement of the land. Within 24 years of the establishment of Zionism in Israel, the movement had already secured significant international support for their cause.

Support for a Jewish State began to wane in the 1940s. Both President Franklin D. Roosevelt and Britain opposed the creation of a Jewish State because they feared that it would harm relations with Arabs in the area. However, when President Harry Truman took office, he established a cabinet committee to discuss the future of Palestine with the British. Under the Chairmanship of Dr. Henry F. Grady, negotiations began. In 1947, the United Nations recommended the partition of Palestine into a Jewish State and an Arab State when the British Mandate was scheduled to end in May 1948. Areas of religious significance surrounding Jerusalem, under the UN plan, would be administered by the United Nations rather than by one of the two proposed states. The US State Department, on the other hand, recommended separating Palestine into Jewish and Arab provinces rather than separate states. Despite growing tension between Arabs and Jews in the area and without the endorsement of the State Department, President Truman recognized the State of Israel. Exactly fifty years after the birth of the Zionist movement, a Jewish State became a reality.

The creation of a Jewish State inspired pushback from Arab neighbors. Immediately after the State of Israel was announced as an independent state, Egypt, Jordan, Iraq, Syria, and Lebanon invaded the region in what came to be known as the Arab–Israeli War. A ceasefire agreement was reached in 1949, but that did not end the fighting permanently. For the next two decades, intermittent war broke out. In 1967, King Nasser of Egypt, prompted by Soviet goading, sent 100,000 troops to Sinai, and closed the Straits of Tiran. King Hussein of Syria joined and placed his forces under Egyptian command. On June 5, 1967, Israel attacked Egyptian forces in response to them closing the Straits, and by June 11, Israel gained control of the Sinai Peninsula, the Golan Heights, the West Bank, the Gaza Strip, and East Jerusalem. Although the Palestine Liberation Organization was founded in 1964 with the express purpose to "liberate" Palestine, the First Intifada would not come for another two decades after the Six-Day War.

Twenty years after the Six-Day War, the Palestinians spontaneously rose against the occupation of the West Bank and Gaza Strip in early December 1987. Triggered by a tragic car accident in which an Israeli lorry driver killed several Palestinians, young Palestinians took to the streets, initially in the Gaza Strip and shortly thereafter in the West Bank. The Israeli government, IDF, and intelligence communities were caught totally by surprise; any seething resentment had been missed by all. The same holds true for Yasser Arafat who after the PLO had been forcibly removed from southern Lebanon (in the early 1980s) had moved to Tunis. The "shaking off" (the meaning of the word Intifada) violently expressed deep Palestinian hatred regarding the occupation (History.com Editors, 2010). The weapons of choice were primarily knives, massive demonstrations, stones, and Molotov cocktails. In addition, Palestinians suspected of collaborating with Israel were brutally murdered. In response, Israel adopted a heavy-handed approach, graphically articulated by the then Defense Minister Yitzhak Rabin who ordered the "breaking of hands" of Palestinians. More than 1500 Palestinians were killed (B'tselem, 2000); tens of thousands injured (IMEU, 2012) and over 100,000 arrested (Aljazeera, 2017). Over the course of the six-year period (1987–1993), 200 Israelis were killed and several hundred wounded (JVL, 2019).

The second Intifada (2000–2004) was more violent; rather than the stabbings, rock throwing, massive demonstrations, and Molotov cocktails that defined the First Intifada, Palestinian's suicide bombings became a frequent weapon of choice. The Second Intifada, commonly referred to as the Al-Aqsa Intifada or the second uprising, began in late 2000 because of Israeli occupation policies that continued not only to violate international law but to deprive Palestinians of their basic human rights.

On September 28, 2000, Prime Minister Ariel Sharon appeared at the Al Aqsa mosque compound in Jerusalem's Old City with more than 1000 Israeli police. In a blatant attempt to provoke Palestinians, he repeated a phrase that was broadcast during the 1967 Six-Day War when Israeli Occupation Forces seized East Jerusalem,

"The Temple Mount is in our hands," Sharon shouted. Palestinians reacted almost immediately to the threat to Al Aqsa, the third holiest site in Islam (AMP 2019).

Palestinians grew increasingly discontented with the Oslo peace process. This was because "reality on the ground did not match the expectations created by the peace agreements" (Pressman, 2003, p. 114). As we discuss in Chap. 10, this was mostly caused by a lack of a common "language" so to speak. The framers of the Oslo peace process failed to understand exactly what Palestinians were demanding from Israel. While Palestinians expected greater freedom of movement and improved socioeconomic standing, the reality was that Palestinians received neither from the Israeli government (Pressman, 2003, p. 119). The failure of the Camp David summit in July 2000 increased popular support for confrontation with Israel. On the Palestinian side, younger militants wanted to show Israel "what would happen if they were not sufficiently forthcoming" in negotiations with Palestine (Pressman, 2003, p. 115). As violence and tension escalated, the chances of the Oslo peace process succeeding began to diminish—although it is likely that the chances of Oslo succeeding were already slim, and the Second Intifada simply highlighted that fact. Whichever view you take, the fact of the matter is that because expectations from both Israel's point of view and Palestine's point of view were not met, violence was the result.

References

Aljazeera. (2017). Stories from the first Intifada: They broke my bones. *Aljazeera*, December 10. https://www.aljazeera.com/news/2017/12/10/stories-from-the-first-intifada-they-broke-my-bones. Accessed June 4, 2021.

AMP. (2019). The Second Intifada – Introduction. *American Muslims for Palestine*. https://www.ampalestine.org/palestine-101/history/intifadas/second-intifada-introduction. Accessed June 4, 2021.

Britannica. (2010). *T. Editors of Encyclopaedia. Dreyfus affair*. Encyclopedia Britannica, Invalid Date. https://www.britannica.com/event/Dreyfus-affair. Accessed June 3, 2021.

B'TSELEM. (2000). *Fatalities in the first Intifada*. The Israeli Information Center for Human Right in the Occupied Territories. https://www.btselem.org/statistics/first_intifada_tables. Accessed June 4, 2021.

DellaPergola, S. (2003). Demographic trends in Israel and Palestine: Prospects and policy implications. *The American Jewish Year Book, 103*, 3–68.

History.com Editors. (2019). Islam. *A&E Television Networks*. https://www.history.com/topics/religion/islam. Accessed June 4, 2021.

History.com Editors. (2010). Intifada begins on Gaza Strip. *A&E Television Networks*. https://www.history.com/this-day-in-history/intifada-begins-on-gaza-strip. Accessed June 4, 2021.

History.com Editors. (2020). Ottoman Empire. *A&E Television Networks*. https://www.history.com/topics/middle-east/ottoman-empire#section_10. Accessed June 4, 2021.

IMEU. (2012). *Casualty comparison*. Institute for Middle East Understanding. https://imeu.org/article/casualty-comparison. Last Accessed June 4, 2021.

Israel Minister of Foreign Affairs. (2004). *Herzl and Zionism*. https://mfa.gov.il/MFA/AboutIsrael/History/Zionism/Pages/Herzl and Zionism.aspx

Israeli Foreign Ministry. (2021). https://www.jewishvirtuallibrary.org/ottoman-rule-1517-1917. Accessed June 3, 2021.

JVL. (2019). *Vital statistics: Total casualties, Arab-Israeli conflict (1860 - Present).* Jewish Virtual Library. A project of AICE. https://www.jewishvirtuallibrary.org/total-casualties-arab-israeli-conflict. Accessed June 4, 2021.

Mishkinsky, M. (2008). *Bund.* Jewish Virtual Library. Encyclopaedia Judaica. The Gale Group. https://www.jewishvirtuallibrary.org/bund. Accessed June 4, 2021.

Morris, B. (2020). *The war on history*. Jewish Review of Books. https://www.jewishvirtuallibrary.org/hashomer. Accessed June 4, 2021.

Pressman, J. (2003). The second Intifada: Background and causes of the Israeli-Palestinian conflict. *Journal of Conflict Studies, 23*(2), 114–141. First published Fall 2003. https://journals.lib.unb.ca/index.php/jcs/article/view/220/. Accessed June 4, 2021.

Rosenberg, J. (2020). The history of the Balfour Declaration. *ThoughtCo*, October 29. https://www.thoughtco.com/balfour-declaration-1778163. Accessed June 4, 2021.

Shaw, S. J., & Yapp, M. E. (2021). *Ottoman Empire*. Encyclopedia Britannica, Invalid Date, https://www.britannica.com/place/Ottoman-Empire. Accessed June 3, 2021.

The Harvard Gazette. (2009). *The pogrom that transformed 20th century Jewry* (April 9). https://news.harvard.edu/gazette/story/2009/04/the-pogrom-that-transformed-20th-century-jewry/. Accessed June 3, 2021.

Wein, B., & Astor, Y. (2012). *Destruction of the first temple*. JewishHistory.org. https://www.jewishhistory.org/destruction-of-the-first-temple/. Accessed June 4, 2021.

Chapter 3
The Analytic Hierarchy Process: Beyond "Getting to Yes" in Conflict Resolution

Introduction

A challenge for dealing with controversies as intractable as the Israeli–Palestinian conflict is how to measure the influence intangible factors have on the conflict, which may even have more influence over the outcome than the tangible factors. Because the importance of such factors changes from one problem to another, and because intangible factors do not have known measurement scales, what is needed are relative scales, which in turn yield relative priorities, developed for each problem within the context of its own diversity of factors, and their influences on the actors involved and the concessions that they exchange.

In 1981, the book *Getting to YES* revolutionized the way conflicts were looked at (Fisher & Ury, 1981). Fisher and Ury introduced the concept of *principled negotiation* in which the participants are problem solvers. The approach is based on four principles: (1) separate the people from the problem; (2) focus on interests, not positions; (3) invent options for mutual gain; and (4) insist on using objective criteria. In this approach, the parties do not see each other as adversaries, but as collaborators in search of a fair solution.

However, principled negotiation does not consider the measurement of gains and losses of the parties for different options. Thus, the parties may not be able to perceive how fair the proposed solution is. What is needed is the development of scales that represent the preferences of the parties. It is not enough to assign numbers to preferences without any mathematical assumptions because we want to ensure that the results belong to a measurement scale. This is a difficult problem if the dimensions of the conflict involve intangibles, which, by definition, are considered not to have a scale of measurement. Pairwise comparisons from Saaty's absolute scale (Table 3.1) can be used to build such relative measurement scales. In this book,

Some parts of this chapter have been published in writings of the authors in references (Saaty & Vargas, 1994; Saaty et al., 2015) given at the end of the chapter.

T. L. Saaty et al., *Overcoming the Retributive Nature of the Israeli-Palestinian Conflict*, https://doi.org/10.1007/978-3-030-83958-1_3

Table 3.1 The fundamental scale

Intensity of importance	Definition	Explanation
1	**Equal importance**	**Two activities contribute equally to the objective**
2	Weak	
3	**Moderate importance**	**Experience and judgment slightly favor one activity over another**
4	Moderate plus	
5	**Strong importance**	**Experience and judgment strongly favor one activity over another**
6	Strong plus	
7	**Very strong or demonstrated importance**	**An activity is favored very strongly over another; its dominance demonstrated in practice**
8	Very, very strong	
9	**Extreme importance**	**The evidence favoring one activity over another is of the highest possible order of affirmation**
Reciprocals of above	**If activity *i* has one of the above nonzero numbers assigned to it when compared with activity *j*, then *j* has the reciprocal value when compared with *i***	**A reasonable assumption**
Rationals	**Ratios arising from the scale**	**If consistency were to be forced by obtaining *n* numerical values to span the matrix**

we show that using the approach proposed here a fair solution (developed by those involved in the process) exists. Before we introduce the approach, we need to give some background information as to how decisions with tangibles and intangibles could be made using relative measurement scales. This is what we explain below.

The Analytic Hierarchy Process

In a hierarchy we have levels arranged in descending order of importance. The elements in each level are compared according to dominance or influence with respect to the elements in the level immediately above that level. The arrows descend downward from the goal even if influence, which is a kind of service, is sought for in elements in lower levels that contribute to the well-being and success of elements in higher levels. We can interpret the downward pointing of the arrows as a process of stimulating the influence of the elements in the lower level on those in the level above. Figure 3.1 shows a hierarchy to select an alternative from a set of alternatives, considering criteria important to a decision maker.

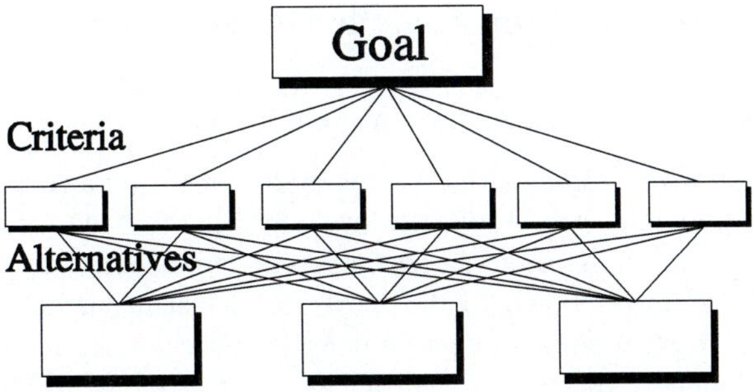

Fig. 3.1 A three-level hierarchy

The analytic hierarchy process (AHP) is a scientific approach used to determine the relative importance of a set of activities or criteria (Saaty, 1977, 1980). The novel aspect and major distinction of this approach is that it structures any complex, multi-person, multi-criteria, and multi-period problem hierarchically. Using a method for scaling the weights of the elements in each level of the hierarchy with respect to an element (e.g., a criterion or property they share) of the next higher level, a matrix of pairwise comparisons of the activities can be constructed, where the entries indicate the strength with which one element dominates another with respect to a given criterion. Structurally, the hierarchy is broken down into a series of paired comparison matrices, and the participants are asked to evaluate the off-diagonal relationship in one-half of each matrix. For example, given a criterion and two alternatives, which alternative is more important according to that criterion and by how much? The answer to this question is a judgment translated into a numerical value using Table 3.1.

The collection of all the pairwise comparison judgments is arranged in a matrix. The entries of that matrix have the reciprocal property, because if A is judged to be 5 times more important than B, then B needs to be 1/5 as important as A. Reciprocals are placed in the transposed positions.

This scaling formulation is translated into a largest eigenvalue problem, which results in a normalized and unique vector of priority weights for each level of the hierarchy (always with respect to the criteria in the level above), which in turn results in a single composite vector of weights for the entire hierarchy. This vector measures the relative priority of all entities at the lowest level that enables the accomplishment of the highest objective of the hierarchy. These relative priority weights can provide guidelines for the allocation of resources among the entities at the lower levels of the hierarchy. When hierarchies are designed to reflect likely environmental scenarios, corporate objectives, current and proposed product/market alternatives, and various marketing strategy options, the AHP can provide a framework and methodology for the determination of several key corporate and marketing decisions (Wind & Saaty, 1980; Zahedi, 1986; Vargas & Whittaker, 1990; Saaty & Vargas, 2001).

Principles of the Analytic Hierarchy Process

The AHP is based on three major principles:

1. *Decomposition*: AHP begins by decomposing a complex problem into a hierarchy (e.g., Fig. 3.1); each level consists of a few manageable elements and each element is, in turn, decomposed into another set of elements. The process continues down to the most specific elements of the problem, typically the specific courses of action considered, which are represented at the lowest level of the hierarchy. Structuring any decision problem hierarchically is an exercise in creative thinking, and it is an efficient way for dealing with complexity and identifying the major components of the problem. There is no single general hierarchical structure. One of the major attributes of the AHP is the flexibility it allows when constructing a hierarchy to fit the idiosyncratic needs of the decision makers. Hence, two decision makers may design two completely different hierarchies. Thus, in group decision making the group needs to agree on the hierarchic structure that represents the decision at hand.
2. *Relative measurement*: A measurement methodology is used to establish priorities among the elements within each stratum of the hierarchy. This is accomplished by asking the participants to evaluate each set of elements in a pairwise fashion with respect to each of the elements in a higher stratum. This measurement methodology provides the framework for deriving numerical priorities for ranking the alternatives of action. Work for data collection and analysis constitutes the heart of the analytic hierarchy process.

   To implement relative measurement, we need to translate qualitative expressions of intensity into numerical values. The scale in Table 3.1 has been used to estimate the intensity of preference in the study presented in this book. Its theoretical foundations can be found in Saaty (1980, 1986).
3. *Synthesis*: After all the pairwise comparisons of the elements in a level with respect to all the elements in the level immediately above are performed, the resulting scales, obtained from the corresponding eigenvectors of the pairwise comparison matrices, are synthesized from the upper levels to the lower levels of the hierarchy using a weighted average principle.

Here are some examples of how relative measurement and the AHP can be applied to a wide variety of problems.

1. Comparing Five Areas

Figure 3.2 shows five geometric areas to which we can apply the paired comparison process to test the validity of the procedure. The object is to compare them in pairs for area by eyeballing them to reproduce the overall relative weights or priorities. The absolute numbers, for each pairwise comparison, are shown in Table 3.2. Inverses are automatically entered in the transpose position. We can approximate the priorities from this matrix by normalizing each column and then taking the average of the corresponding entries in the columns. Table 3.2 gives the actual measurements in relative form on the right. An element on the left is compared with

Fig. 3.2 Five Figures

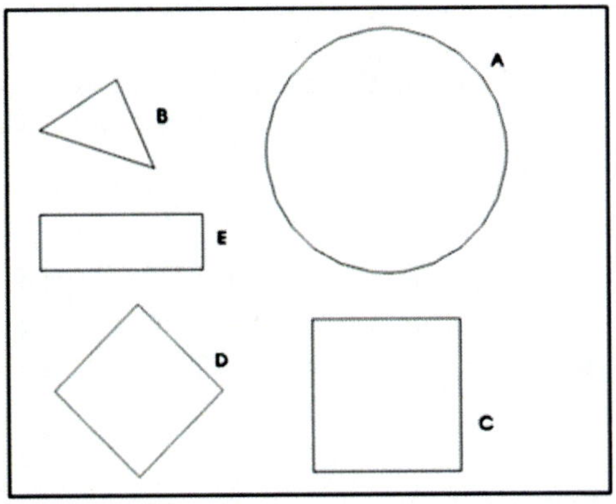

Table 3.2 Judgments, outcomes, and actual relative sizes of the five geometric shapes

Figure	Circle	Triangle	Square	Diamond	Rectangle	Priorities (Eigenvector)	Actual Relative Size
Circle	1	9	2	3	5	.462	.471
Triangle	1/9	1	1/5	1/3	1/2	.049	.050
Square	1/2	5	1	3/2	3	.245	.234
Diamond	1/3	3	2/3	1	3/2	.151	.149
Rectangle	1/5	2	1/3	2/3	1	.093	.096

another at the top as to its dominance. If it is not larger than one, the top element is compared with it and the reciprocal value is used. The next-to-last column in Table 3.2 gives the priorities derived from judgment.

2. Estimating US Consumption of Different Drinks

A more abstract form of comparisons would involve elements with tangible properties that one must think about but cannot be perceived through the senses. See the judgments in Table 3.3 for estimating the relative consumption of drinks. An audience of about 30 people, using consensus to arrive at each judgment, provided judgments to estimate the dominance of the consumption of drinks in the USA (which drink is consumed more in the USA and how much more than another drink?). The derived vector of relative consumption and the actual vector, obtained by normalizing the consumption given in official statistical data sources, are at the bottom of the table.

Note that while in the first example, Table 3.2, the eye perceives different size areas, in the second example, Table 3.3, the mind, through wide experience and education, has a feeling for how much more frequently one drink is consumed than

Table 3.3 Relative consumption of drinks

Which Drink is Consumed More in the U.S.?
An Example of Estimation Using Judgments

Drink Consumption in the U.S.	Coffee	Wine	Tea	Beer	Sodas	Milk	Water
Coffee	1	9	5	2	1	1	1/2
Wine	1/9	1	1/3	1/9	1/9	1/9	1/9
Tea	1/5	2	1	1/3	1/4	1/3	1/9
Beer	1/2	9	3	1	1/2	1	1/3
Sodas	1	9	4	2	1	2	1/2
Milk	1	9	3	1	1/2	1	1/3
Water	2	9	9	3	2	3	1

The derived scale based on the judgments in the matrix is:

Coffee	Wine	Tea	Beer	Sodas	Milk	Water
.177	.019	.042	.116	.190	.129	.327

The actual consumption (from statistical sources) is:

.180	.010	.040	.120	.180	.140	.330

the other is consumed, in a pairwise comparison. Feelings are usually distinguished qualitatively and associated with numerical values. It is fortunate, in this example, that people tend to consume nearly the same amount of liquid, about a glassful, of whatever kind of drink is being consumed. Estimating the quantity of consumption is different than estimating the frequency of consumption.

3. Example of a Hierarchy: Buying a Car

How do we choose the best car from among three alternatives by considering different importance priorities for the four criteria, some intangible and some tangible: prestige, price, miles per gallon, and comfort? We use the hierarchy in Fig. 3.3 to represent this decision.

The pairwise comparisons of the criteria are given in Table 3.4. Criteria must always be compared to derive their priorities. We then compare the alternatives with respect to the criteria in Tables 3.5a, 3.5b, 3.5c and 3.5d. Table 3.6 gives the synthesis of the priorities of the alternatives shown in the next-to-last columns of Tables 3.5a–3.5d, multiplied by the priorities of the criteria given in the last column of Table 3.6. The process of weighting, adding, and normalizing priorities to one is called the distributive mode of synthesis. By contrast, if one divides by the largest priority among the synthesized values, the result is called the ideal mode of synthesis. For more about synthesis modes, see Saaty and Vargas (2001).

The Honda Civic is the most preferred car to buy because it gets the greatest overall priority.

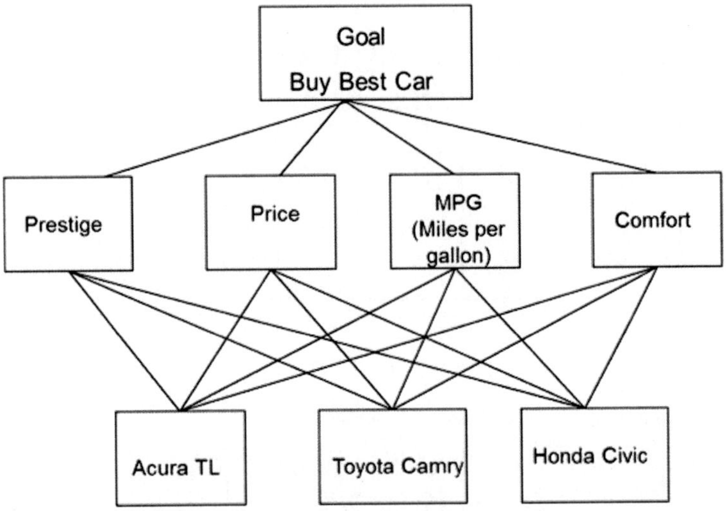

Fig. 3.3 Three-level hierarchy to choose the best car

Table 3.4 Pairwise comparisons of the criteria as to their importance in choosing a best car

Goal	Prestige	Price	MPG	Comfort	Priorities
Prestige	1	1/4	1/3	1/2	0.099
Price	4	1	3	3/2	0.425
MPG	3	1/3	1	1/3	0.169
Comfort	2	2/3	3	1	0.308

Table 3.5a Comparison of cars with respect to prestige

Prestige	Acura TL	Toyota Camry	Honda Civic	Priority Distributive	Priority Ideal
Acura TL	1	8	4	0.707	1
Toyota Camry	1/8	1	1/4	0.07	0.099
Honda Civic	1/4	4	1	0.223	0.315

Table 3.5b Comparison of cars with respect to price

Price	Acura TL	Toyota Camry	Honda Civic	Priority Distributive	Priority Ideal
Acura TL	1	1/4	1/9	0.063	0.085
Toyota Camry	4	1	1/5	0.194	0.261
Honda Civic	9	5	1	0.743	1

Table 3.5c Comparison of cars with respect to MPG

MPG	Acura TL	Toyota Camry	Honda Civic	Priority Distributive	Priority Ideal
Acura TL	1	2/3	1/3	0.182	0.333
Toyota Camry	1 1/2	1	1/2	0.273	0.5
Honda Civic	3	2	1	0.545	1

Table 3.5d Comparison of cars with respect to comfort

Comfort	Acura TL	Toyota Camry	Honda Civic	Priority Distributive	Priority Ideal
Acura TL	1	4	7	0.705	1
Toyota Camry	1/4	1	3	0.211	0.299
Honda Civic	1/7	1/3	1	0.084	0.119

Table 3.6 Synthesis of the priorities of the alternatives

Priorities	Prestige 0.099	Price 0.425	MPG 0.169	Comfort 0.308	Synthesis of overall priorities
Acura TL	0.707	0.063	0.182	0.705	**0.342**
Toyota Camry	0.070	0.194	0.273	0.211	**0.204**
Honda Civic	0.223	0.743	0.545	0.084	**0.454**

Table 3.7 Synthesis of the priorities of the alternatives using ideals to obtain the overall priorities

Priorities	Prestige 0.099	Price 0.425	MPG 0.169	Comfort 0.308	Overall priorities	Normalized
Acura TL	1.000	0.085	0.333	1.000	**0.499**	**0.342**
Toyota Camry	0.099	0.261	0.500	0.299	**0.297**	**0.204**
Honda Civic	0.315	1.000	1.000	0.119	**0.661**	**0.454**

Table 3.8 Priorities of cars with respect to price using actual dollar values

Price in dollars	Average price	Normalized prices used as priorities	Inverted priorities	Final priorities (normalized)	Ideal priorities
Acura TL	32,500	0.425	1/0.425	0.247	**0.554**
Toyota Camry	26,000	0.340	1/0.340	0.308	**0.692**
Honda Civic	18,000	0.235	1/0.235	0.445	**1.000**
Sum	76,500	1	0.00012479	1	

Psychologists have noted that there are two ways to make comparisons of alternatives (Blumenthal 1977). One is to compare them by considering each pair (relative measurement), as we have done above, and the other is to compare each alternative with an ideal one has in mind (absolute measurement). Because, in the case of cars, we only know about the three cars we are considering, we make the best of them under each criterion, the ideal for that criterion. To do that we divide the priorities under each criterion by the largest among them, and that one becomes the ideal. This is shown in the last column of Tables 3.5a–3.5d. Using these values, we have Table 3.7 to obtain the synthesis of the alternatives.

Again, the Honda Civic is the most preferred.

Note that the overall priorities are different, but the ranks and the normalized priorities are the same in Tables 3.6 and 3.7, but they need not be. Frequently people prefer to use the answer in Table 3.7, because if more cars are added, each is compared only with the ideal for that criterion and the rank of the three initial alternatives stays the same.

One would not interpret tangibles to decide for another person and often would use the actual measurements for those tangibles as indicators for their relative worth or importance. Thus, if instead of using judgments for the price, we use the ratio of the actual prices as shown in Table 3.8 (in fact, we use the inverses of these ratios because lower prices should have higher priorities), and then compute the priorities, we would obtain the same answer as simply normalizing the prices. In using direct data, one must be careful to invert the priorities obtained if higher numbers mean less desirable.

With the ratio of the actual prices being used for the vector of priorities, Table 3.9 gives the overall priorities of the alternatives in the ideal mode.

Table 3.9 Ideal synthesis to obtain the priorities of the cars

Priorities	Prestige 0.099	Price 0.425	MPG 0.169	Comfort 0.308	Overall priorities	Normalized to one
Acura TL	1.000	**0.554**	0.333	1.000	0.698	0.379
Toyota Camry	0.099	**0.692**	0.500	0.299	0.480	0.261
Honda Civic	0.315	**1.000**	1.000	0.119	0.661	0.359

In this case, the Acura is slightly more preferred than the Honda, but not very much. As to be expected, the priorities in Table 3.9 are different from those in Table 3.8, obtained from judgments.

The Absolute Ratings Model of the AHP

We note that in making comparisons, the value of any element depends on the value of what it is compared with. It is not like assigning it a number from a scale of measurement with an arbitrary unit. This led to a criticism about rank reversal when new alternatives are added or old ones deleted by those who, in single but not multiple criteria rankings, were only used to assigning elements one at a time numbers from a scale. In multi-criteria decisions, for example, criteria need to always be compared because one cannot meaningfully assign importance to them, even if some people try doing it, and scales are then developed for each criterion separately. *The answer to rank preservation or reversal does not lie in a mathematical theorem that says that rank must always be preserved.* There are numerous examples that show that rank reversals can and should occur in practice (Saaty, 2005).

To preserve rank, the ratings mode was developed by constructing through pairwise comparisons a rating scale for each criterion. These rating scales opened the door for using numerical data in normalized (by dividing each value by the sum of all the values) form and using mathematical functions as desired. Alternatives are then rated independently, one at a time, by selecting the appropriate rating for it on each criterion. By pre-evaluating ranges of data through expert judgment, it makes it possible to automate the process of evaluating data. Thus, one uses comparisons or ratings, depending on the circumstances. When the criteria are changeable, as in selecting the best CEO for a company, one uses comparisons and its corresponding method of synthesis, called the distributive mode. When the criteria are standardized, as in the admission of students to a university, evaluating projects, or military officers, one uses ratings with its ideal mode, even when the ideal may change because of adding new alternatives never previously encountered or conceived. Note: This is the method we use below to derive the priorities of the concessions with respect to benefits, costs, perceived benefits, and perceived costs in the chapters that follow.

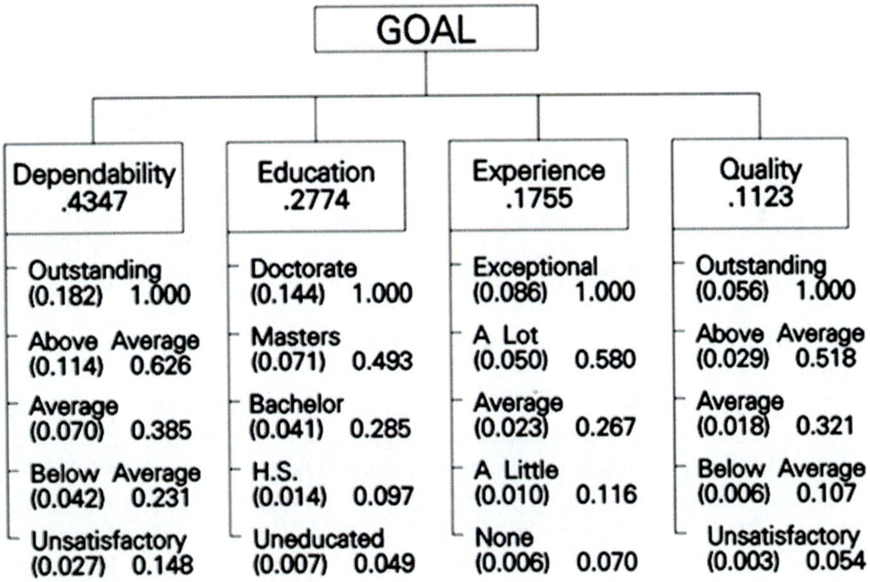

Fig. 3.4 Employee evaluation hierarchy

Table 3.10 Ranking intensities

	Outstanding	Above average	Average	Below average	Unsatisfactory	Priorities
Outstanding	1.0	2.0	3.0	4.0	5.0	0.419
Above average	1/2	1.0	2.0	3.0	4.0	0.263
Average	1/3	1/2	1.0	2.0	3.0	0.160
Below average	1/4	1/3	1/2	1.0	2.0	0.097
Unsatisfactory	1/5	1/4	1/3	1/2	1.0	0.062
	Inconsistency ratio = 0.015					

Suppose we are trying to evaluate employees for raises. The criteria are dependability, education, experience, and quality. Each criterion is subdivided into intensities, standards, or subcriteria as shown in Fig. 3.4. Priorities are set for the criteria by comparing them in pairs, and these priorities are then given in a matrix. The intensities are then pairwise compared according to priority with respect to their parent criterion (as in Table 3.10) and their priorities are divided by the largest intensity for each criterion (second column of priorities in Fig. 3.4). Finally, everyone is rated in Table 3.11 by assigning the intensity rating that applies to him or her under each criterion. The scores of these subcriteria are weighted by the priority of that criterion and summed to derive a total ratio scale score for the individual. This approach can be used whenever it is possible to set priorities for intensities of

Table 3.11 Ranking alternatives

	Dependability 0.4347	Education 0.2774	Experience 0.1775	Quality 0.1123	Total
1. Adams, V	Outstanding	Bachelor	A little	Outstanding	0.646
2. Becker, L	Average	Bachelor	A little	Outstanding	0.379
3. Hayat, F	Average	Masters	A lot	Below average	0.418
4. Kesselman, S	Above average	H.S.	None	Above average	0.369
5. O'Shea, K	Average	Doctorate	A lot	Above average	0.605
6. Peters, T	Average	Doctorate	A lot	Average	0.583
7. Tobias, K	Above average	Bachelor	Average	Above average	0.456

criteria, which is usually possible when sufficient experience with a given operation has been accumulated.

The total priorities in Table 3.11 can now be used to decide the raise everyone should get. Thus, given a pool of money, normalizing the priorities to unity will tell us what percentage of the total available funds should be given to everyone.

The absolute ratings approach is very useful when the number of alternatives is very large and/or the decision maker(s) want to create a set of standards to be reused over a period. This approach allows for revising the priority values of the rating scales as more evidence and experience becomes available. Examples of these situations are admissions to a school, ranking of more livable cities, ranking of schools, Morningstar rating of investment funds, allocation of transplant organs (Cook et al. 1990), and so on.

References

Blumenthal, A. (1977). *The process of cognition*. Prentice-Hall.

Cook, D. R., Staschak, S., & Green, W. T. (1990). Equitable allocation of livers for orthotopic transplantation: An application of the analytic hierarchy process. *European Journal of Operational Research, 48*(1), 49–56.

Fisher, R., & Ury, W. (1981). *Getting to YES: Negotiating agreement without giving in*. Penguin Books.

Saaty, T. L. (1977). A scaling method for priorities in hierarchical structures. *Journal of Mathematical Psychology, 15*(3), 234–281.

Saaty, T. L. (1980). *The analytic hierarchy process*. McGraw Hill International.

Saaty, T. L. (1986). Axiomatic foundation of the analytic hierarchy process. *Management Science, 32*(7), 841–855.

Saaty, T. L. (2005). *Theory and applications of the analytic network process*. RWS Publications.

Saaty, T. L., & Vargas, L. G. (1994). *Decision making in economic, political, social and technological environments with the analytic hierarchy process* (The analytic hierarchy process series) (Vol. VII). RWS Publications.

Saaty, T. L., & Vargas, L. G. (2001). *Models, methods, concepts & applications of the analytic hierarchy process*. Kluwer Academic. 2nd edition 2012.

Saaty, T. L., Vargas, L. G., & Zoffer, H. J. (2015). A structured scientific solution to the Israeli–Palestinian conflict: The analytic hierarchy process approach. *Decision Analytics, 2*(7), 1–53.
Vargas, L. G., & Whittaker, R. W. (1990). Decision making by the analytic hierarchy process: Theory and applications. *European Journal of Operational Research, 48*(1), 1–173.
Wind, Y., & Saaty, T. L. (1980). Marketing applications of the analytic hierarchy process. *Management Science, 26*(7), 641–658.
Zahedi, F. (1986). The analytic hierarchy process: A survey of the method and its applications. *Interfaces, 16*(4), 96–108.

Chapter 4
Retributive Conflicts and the AHP: The Trading Mechanism

Introduction

There are two types of conflict resolution. We call the first kind *constructive*. It is what is conventionally treated in the so-called rational approach to conflict resolution. Each party identifies its demands, and it is assumed that a way can be found to satisfy both parties' demands fairly. Fairly here means that each party forms a ratio of its benefits to those of the opponent and attempts to satisfy its own needs, at least as much as its perceived evaluation of the opponent's benefits, because the utilities or values may be interpreted differently by the two sides. The tug of war by each side can end up in equalizing the ratio to unity. That is why it is inadvisable for either party to give up too early.

In this case, negotiations begin with each party setting down what it expects to get. The negotiations may either result in getting that much or changing the outcome so that both sides receive more or often less **than their** expectations because there is not enough to go around. The parties begin by offering some concessions from a larger set of concessions, which they maintain secretly. An offer is evaluated in terms of the benefits of the counteroffer received and may be withdrawn, if not reciprocated adequately.

The second kind of conflict is called *retributive*, with one or both parties harboring ill will toward each other (Saaty 1988). The idea is particularly relevant in long drawn-out conflicts, which in the end fester and create almost ineradicable resentments. Here a party may be willing to give up much of its demands, if misfortune can be brought to its opponent through some means, including justice as dispensed by the court system. Should the enemy die, they may forgive and forget, or sometimes they may be resentful because they have not extracted their pound of flesh.

Thus, in negotiations, each party not only calculates the incremental benefits it gets, but also the costs to its opponent. The more of either, the greater is the gain. Gain is the product of the benefits to the party and the costs (whose aim may also be

T. L. Saaty et al., *Overcoming the Retributive Nature of the Israeli-Palestinian Conflict*, https://doi.org/10.1007/978-3-030-83958-1_4

long-run benefits) to the opponent. Each side must calculate what it estimates to be the opponent's gain as a product of benefits to the opponent and costs to itself and make sure that the ratio of its gain to the opponent's gain, which it considers as a loss, is greater than unity or not less than what the opponent is perceived to get. Thus, each party is concerned with maximizing its gains via its benefits and the costs to the opponent, and by negotiating to increase this gain and decrease its loss (which is a gain to the opponent). When several concessions are considered simultaneously, sums of the products of benefits and costs must be taken.

The chief purpose of AHP is to provide decision makers with objective, numerical parameters regarding specific core issues. From such a valuation model, decision makers have access to a rationally based model/tool for addressing and resolving specific, complex issues.

The primary benefit of the AHP as a tool for Middle East peace negotiators, whether used internally or together between the parties, is to reduce uncertainties—between and among the parties—on the relative value of core issues as negotiators address the "trade-off/exchange" component of negotiations. The information produced by this tool enhances rationally based decision making, helps reduce emotion in negotiations, and assesses more accurately the relative value that each group attaches to a particular issue.

The trade-off model is predicated upon development and application of a process that reflects both in-depth understanding of values attached by the respective parties (or sub-parties) to an issue and the importance of that issue in relation to other issues, of lesser, similar, or greater value. Of equal importance is determining the value the other side attaches to that issue and the value both sides attach within the context of a trade-off or trade-offs.

The process requires assigning numerical values that measure the respective importance of each issue for the parties involved; it is this assessment/assignment that enables rationally based decision making in the context of potential trade-offs. AHP focuses on articulation and application of self-interest in a paradigm emphasizing trade-offs, whereby both sides seek to "expand the pie"—and avoid zero-sum calculations that emphasize maximization of benefits for one side, to the detriment of the other side.

The Retributive Function

Given the entrenchment of both sides, a negotiator has an opportunity in an appropriate setting to call attention to the gap between the perceived benefits and costs of the concessions made by both sides and to help each party to reach a conclusion through the introduction of "bargaining chips." In the negotiation setting, if A and B are participants, then A considers a particular concession not only with respect to the incremental benefit (cost) to A but also the cost (benefit) to B in providing (receiving) the concession. The greater the perceived cost of each concession to B, the greater the value of that concession is to A.

Hence A's gain from a given concession from B may be described as the product of A's benefits and B's costs (as perceived by A). We have the following ratios for the two parties A and B:

$$\text{(according to A's perceptions)}$$

$$\begin{aligned}\text{A}'\text{s ratio} &= \frac{\text{Gain to A from B}'\text{s Concession}}{\text{A}'\text{s Perception of B}'\text{s Gain from A}'\text{s Concession}} \\ &= \frac{\sum \text{A}'\text{s benefits} \times \text{B}'\text{s perceived costs from B}'\text{s Concession}}{\sum \text{B}'\text{s perceived benefits} \times \text{A}'\text{s costs from A}'\text{s Concession}}\end{aligned}$$

where $\sum$ is the sum over all the benefits obtained by A in the numerator and by B in the denominator. Hence, given A's ratio, A's gain is a product of both the utility benefit received and the cost to B in providing that benefit as described in the numerator of the equation. The total gain to A is diminished by the product of the cost to A in concessions given to B and the perception of the benefit received by B for A's concessions in the denominator. A's benefits and costs are readily measured by A; however, the costs and gains to B are not readily available to A and are therefore estimated as perceived by A. A expects to have a gain ratio greater than one which suggests that the gains to A are greater than the perceived benefits to B. Likewise, B expects to have a gain ratio greater than one. For equality in "trade" to be achieved, the two parties should be nearly equal in value, which suggests that the two parties gain as much as the perceived benefits and costs of concessions to the other. B's utility is given by the function:

$$\text{(according to B's perceptions)}$$

$$\begin{aligned}\text{B}'\text{ ratio} &= \frac{\text{Gain to B from A}'\text{s Concession}}{\text{B}'\text{s Perception of A}'\text{s Gain from B}'\text{s Concession}} \\ &= \frac{\sum \text{B}'\text{s benefits} \times \text{A}'\text{s perceived costs from A}'\text{s Concession}}{\sum \text{A}'\text{s perceived benefits} \times \text{B}'\text{s costs from B}'\text{s Concession}}\end{aligned}$$

The measure of equality between the parties in the trade of concessions may be calculated as the ratio of the two ratios:

$$\text{A's Ratio/B's Ratio} = \text{Retributive Gain (Loss) to A,}$$

where the retributive gain is the amount that A benefits from making B "pay," while a loss is accounted for by the amount that A "lost" in the negotiation process. Under no circumstance would we expect A to agree to concessions when there is a perceived loss when A has dominance over B. In the case where A has dominance over B, the best that B can do is to minimize the disparity in gains.

When perceptions are not used, the ratios are the traditional benefit to cost ratios. We illustrate this with a well-known example used in negotiation—the recruiter-candidate case (Vargas 2017).

The Recruiter–Candidate Case

A recruiter wants to offer a position to a candidate. The terms of the offer are equivalent to a contract. The dictionary definition of "contract" is "a binding agreement between two or more persons or parties" or "a document describing the terms of a contract." This implies that a contract has multiple dimensions, and the parties must agree on each of the dimensions. For example, in the case of a recruiter trying to hire a candidate for a position in a company, the dimensions could be the signing bonus, salary, job assignment, company car, starting date, number of vacation days, percentage of moving expenses covered, the type of insurance coverage offered, and so on. Each dimension has a different impact on the parties. Each dimension can be considered a benefit or a cost. Table 4.1 shows the dimensions of the recruiter-candidate negotiation, and their type.

To develop the contract, the parties need to agree the level at which each of the dimensions must be set. Table 4.2 shows the impact that different values of the dimensions have, i.e., the payoffs, for the recruiter and the candidate. A concession or trade-off in this problem consists of a bundle of values corresponding to each dimension. For example, if both the recruiter and the candidate select the most preferred values for each dimension, we obtain the bundles given in Table 4.3.

The recruiter and the candidate disagree on almost every dimension, except for the job assignment and the company car. How can we find the best selection within each dimension that provides both parties the maximum payoff, while agreeing on all the dimensions?

Table 4.1 Dimensions and their type

Dimensions	Type
SIGNING BONUS (SB)	Benefit
SALARY (S)	Cost
JOB ASSIGNMENT (JA)	Cost
COMPANY CAR (CC)	Benefit
STARTING DATE (SD)	Benefit
VACATION DAYS (VD)	Benefit
MOVING EXPENSES REIMB (MER)	Benefit
INSURANCE COVERAGE (IC)	Benefit

Table 4.2 Payoffs derived from choices

	Choices	RECRUITER	CANDIDATE
SIGNING BONUS (SB)	**10%**	0	4000
	8%	1000	3000
	6%	2000	2000
	4%	3000	1000
	2%	4000	0
SALARY (S)	**$ 60,000.00**	-6000	0
	$ 58,000.00	-4500	-1500
	$ 56,000.00	-3000	-3000
	$ 54,000.00	-1500	-4500
	$ 52,000.00	0	-6000
JOB ASSIGNMENT (JA)	**Division A**	0	0
	Division B	-600	-600
	Division C	-1200	-1200
	Division D	-1800	-1800
	Division E	-2400	-2400
COMPANY CAR (CC)	**LUX EX2**	1200	1200
	MOD 250	900	900
	RAND XTR	600	600
	DE PAS 450	300	300
	PALO LSR	0	0
STARTING DATE (SD)	**1-Jun**	1600	0
	15-Jun	1200	1000
	1-Jul	800	2000
	15-Jul	400	3000
	1-Aug	0	4000
VACATION DAYS (VD)	**30 days**	0	1600
	25 days	1000	1200
	20 days	2000	800
	15 days	3000	400
	10 days	4000	0
MOVING EXPENSES REIMBURSEMENT (MER)	**100%**	0	3200
	90%	200	2400
	80%	400	1600
	70%	600	800
	60%	800	0
INSURANCE COVERAGE (IC)	**Allen Insurance**	0	800
	ABC Insurance	800	600
	Good Health Insurance	1600	400
	Best Insurance Co.	2400	200
	Insure Alba	3200	0

Table 4.3 Most desired trade-offs for the two parties

	SB	S	JA	CC	SD	VD	MER	IC	Total
	2%	$ 52,000.00	Division A	LUX EX2	1-Jun	10 days	60%	Insure Alba	Points
Recruiter	4000	0	0	1200	1600	4000	800	3200	14800
	10%	$ 60,000.00	Division A	LUX EX2	1-Aug	30 days	100%	Allen Insurar	Points
Candidate	4000	0	0	1200	4000	1600	3200	800	14800

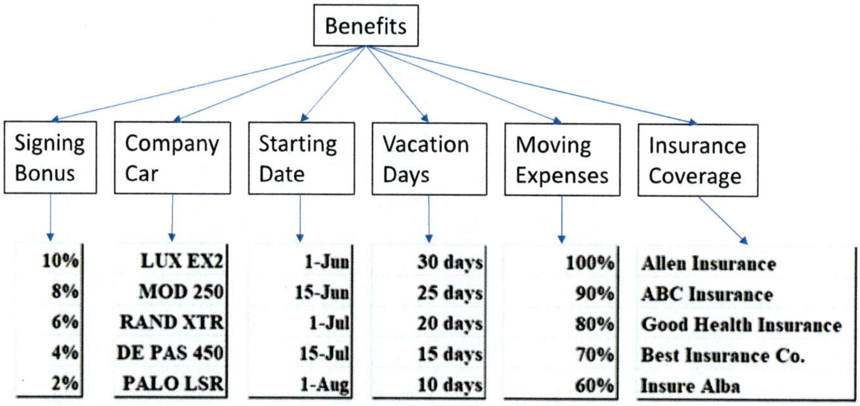

Fig. 4.1 Benefits hierarchy

Fig. 4.2 Costs hierarchy

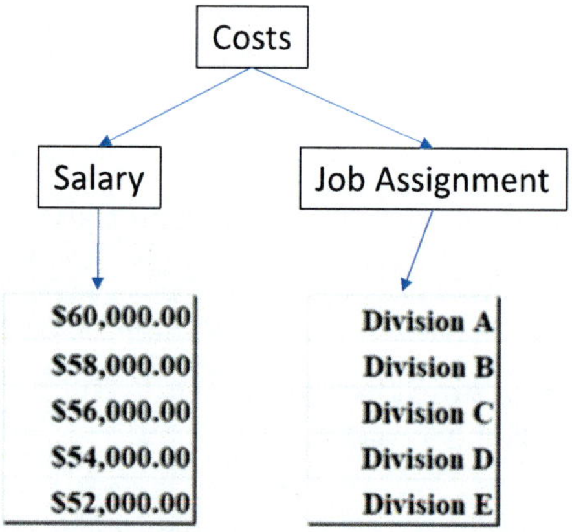

This problem has two hierarchical structures, one for benefits (Fig. 4.1) and one for costs (Fig. 4.2).

Were we to solve the problem with the payoffs given in Table 4.2, then all we need to do is to solve a binary integer optimization model:

Table 4.4 The optimal solution

	SB	S	JA	CC	SD	VD	MER	IC	Total
	6%	$ 56,000.00	Division A	LUX EX2	1-Aug	10 days	100%	Insure Alba	Points
Recruiter	2000	-3000	0	1200	0	4000	0	3200	7400
	6%	$ 56,000.00	Division A	LUX EX2	1-Aug	10 days	100%	Insure Alba	Points
Candidate	2000	-3000	0	1200	4000	0	3200	0	7400

$$\underset{k}{Max}\left\{\underset{i,j}{Min}\left\{\sum_{i=1}^{8}\sum_{j=1}^{5}u_{ijk}x_{ij}\right\}\right\}$$

$$s.t.$$

$$\sum_{j=1}^{5}x_{ij} = 1, \text{for all } i = 1, \ldots, 8,$$

$$\left|\sum_{i=1}^{8}\sum_{j=1}^{5}u_{ij1}x_{ij} - \sum_{i=1}^{8}\sum_{j=1}^{5}u_{ij2}x_{ij}\right| \leq \varepsilon$$

$$x_{ijk} \in \{0, 1\}, \text{for all } i, j, k.$$

Where u_{ijk} represent the payoff to the kth party if she selects the jth level of the ith dimension; x_{ij} is a binary variable that is equal to 1 if the jth level of the ith dimension is selected; otherwise, it is equal to zero. Only one level per dimension can be selected, and the payoffs for both parties need to be within a small percentage of each other, e.g., 1%.

The solution to this problem is given in Table 4.4.

Note that both agree as to the terms of the contract even though the payoffs are not the same for both in all the dimensions, but the total is the same for both.

In real-life contract negotiations, neither the dimensions of the contract nor the intensity scales may be known. To make trade-offs we need to identify the dimensions and the intensity scales. In addition, the dimensions are not equally important. Thus, the benefits and the costs need to be prioritized.

Let us assume that the parties agree on the dimensions in terms of which the contract will be written as given above, and that the priorities are as given in Table 4.5. They show the importance of the dimensions from both the recruiter's and the employee's perspective.

Next, the recruiter and the candidate prioritize the different choices for each dimension. For example, from the recruiter's perspective, how much more does he prefer to give away a 2% versus a 4% signing bonus. The matrix of pairwise comparisons is given in Table 4.6. Because a 10% bonus is the last desirable choice it was assigned a zero in the original scale (see Table 4.2).

The scales for all the dimensions are prioritized for both the recruiter and the candidate. In addition, each dimension has its own priority (Table 4.7). Hence,

Table 4.5 Recruiter/candidate priorities for benefits and costs

	Priorities	
Benefits	Recruiter	Employee
SIGNING BONUS (SB)	0.270	0.270
COMPANY CAR (CC)	0.081	0.081
STARTING DATE (SD)	0.108	0.270
VACATION DAYS (VD)	0.270	0.108
MOVING EXPENSES (MER)	0.054	0.216
INSURANCE COVERAGE (IC)	0.216	0.054

	Priorities	
Costs	Recruiter	Employee
SALARY (S)	0.714	0.714
JOB ASSIGNMENT (JA)	0.286	0.286

Table 4.6 Recruiter's priorities for the levels of signing bonus

Signing Bonus	10%	8%	6%	4%	2%	Priorities
10%	1	0	0	0	0	0
8%	N/A	1	0.5	0.333333	0.25	0.1
6%	N/A	2	1	0.666667	0.5	0.2
4%	N/A	3	1.5	1	0.75	0.3
2%	N/A	4	2	1.333333	1	0.4

multiplying the priority of the dimensions (e.g., signing bonus for the recruiter is 0.270) by the priorities of the corresponding scale yields the global priorities of the scales (e.g., the global priority of a 2% signing bonus is given by the product of 0.270 and 0.4 or 0.108). The global priorities of the benefits and the costs for both the recruiter and the candidate are given in Table 4.7.

To find the solution of this problem, we model it as an integer programming problem. To make the presentation simpler, we represent a solution as an 8-by-5 matrix (x_{ij}) of 0's and 1's. Each row corresponds to a dimension and each column corresponds to an intensity of the scale corresponding to that dimension (see Table 4.8).

As before, a 1 in the table represents that the ith dimension takes the jth intensity value. The benefits and costs are taken from the columns of global priorities in

Table 4.7 Relative and global priorities

Relative Priorities of Dimensions					Relative Priorities				Global Priorities			
Recruiter		Candidate			Recruiter		Candidate		Recruiter		Candidate	
Benefits	Costs	Benefits	Costs		Benefits	Costs	Benefits	Costs	Benefits	Costs	Benefits	Costs
0.2703		0.2703		**SIGNING BONUS**								
				10%	0		0.4		0.000		0.108	
				8%	0.1		0.3		0.027		0.081	
				6%	0.2		0.2		0.054		0.054	
				4%	0.3		0.1		0.081		0.027	
				2%	0.4		0		0.108		0.000	
	0.7143		0.7143	**SALARY**								
				$60,000.00		0.4		0		0.286		0.000
				$58,000.00		0.3		0.1		0.214		0.071
				$56,000.00		0.2		0.2		0.143		0.143
				$54,000.00		0.1		0.3		0.071		0.214
				$52,000.00		0		0.4		0.000		0.286
	0.2857		0.2857	**JOB ASSIGNMENT**								
				Division A		0		0		0.000		0.000
				Division B		0.1		0.1		0.029		0.029
				Division C		0.2		0.2		0.057		0.057
				Division D		0.3		0.3		0.086		0.086
				Division E		0.4		0.4		0.114		0.114
0.0811		0.0811		**COMPANY CAR**								
				LUX EX2	0.4		0.4		0.032		0.032	
				MOD 250	0.3		0.3		0.024		0.024	
				RAND XTR	0.2		0.2		0.016		0.016	
				DE PAS 450	0.1		0.1		0.008		0.008	
				PALO LSR	0		0		0.000		0.000	
0.1081		0.2703		**STARTING DATE**								
				6/1/2014	0.4		0		0.043		0.000	
				6/15/2014	0.3		0.1		0.032		0.027	
				7/1/2014	0.2		0.2		0.022		0.054	
				7/15/2014	0.1		0.3		0.011		0.081	
				8/1/2014	0		0.4		0.000		0.108	
0.2703		0.1081		**VACATION DAYS**								
				30 days	0		0.4		0.000		0.043	
				25 days	0.1		0.3		0.027		0.032	
				20 days	0.2		0.2		0.054		0.022	
				15 days	0.3		0.1		0.081		0.011	
				10 days	0.4		0		0.108		0.000	
0.0541		0.2162		**MOVING EXPENSES REIMBURSEMENT**								
				100%	0		0.4		0.000		0.086	
				90%	0.1		0.3		0.005		0.065	
				80%	0.2		0.2		0.011		0.043	
				70%	0.3		0.1		0.016		0.022	
				60%	0.4		0		0.022		0.000	
0.2162		0.0541		**INSURANCE COVERAGE**								
				Allen Insurance	0		0.4		0.000		0.022	
				ABC Insurance	0.1		0.3		0.022		0.016	
				Good Health Insurance	0.2		0.2		0.043		0.011	
				Best Insurance Co.	0.3		0.1		0.065		0.005	
				Insure Alba	0.4		0		0.086		0.000	

Table 4.7. Note that the trade-off shown in Table 4.8 would not be acceptable to the recruiter because the benefit to cost ratio is less than 1.

The optimal solution or the best trade-off for both parties is given in Table 4.9 and coincides with the solution shown in Table 4.4. This solution is obtained by solving the following optimization problem.

Table 4.8 A solution

A solution	Intensities					Recruiter		Candidate	
	1	2	3	4	5	Benefits	Costs	Benefits	Costs
SB	0	0	1	0	0	0.054	0	0.054	0
S	0	1	0	0	0	0	0.214	0	0.071
JA	0	1	0	0	0	0	0.029	0	0
CC	1	0	0	0	0	0.032	0	0.032	0
SD	0	0	1	0	0	0	0	0.054	0
VD	0	1	0	0	0	0.027	0	0	0
MER	0	0	1	0	0	0	0	0.043	0
IC	0	0	1	0	0	0.043	0	0	0
			B/C Ratio			0.7790		2.2703	

Table 4.9 The best negotiated contract

Optimal solution	Intensities					Recruiter		Candidate	
	1	2	3	4	5	Benefits	Costs	Benefits	Costs
SB	0	0	1	0	0	0.054	0	0.054	0
S	0	0	1	0	0	0	0.143	0	0.143
JA	1		0	0	0	0	0	0	0
CC	1	0	0	0	0	0.032	0	0.032	0
SD	0	0	0	0	1	0	0	0.108	0
VD	0	0	0	0	1	0.108	0	0	0
MER	1	0	0	0	0	0	0	0.086	0
IC	0	0	0	0	1	0.086	0	0	0
			B/C Ratio			1.9676		1.9676	

Let $b_{ij}^R \left(b_{ij}^C\right)$ and $c_{ij}^R \left(c_{ij}^C\right)$ be the benefit and cost corresponding to the jth intensity of the ith dimension for the recruiter (candidate). The benefits/costs ratios of the recruiter and the candidate are given by:

$$r_R(x) = \frac{\text{benefits}}{\text{costs}} = \frac{\sum_i \sum_j x_{ij} b_{ij}^R}{\sum_i \sum_j x_{ij} c_{ij}^R} \text{ and } r_C(x) = \frac{\text{benefits}}{\text{costs}} = \frac{\sum_i \sum_j x_{ij} b_{ij}^C}{\sum_i \sum_j x_{ij} c_{ij}^C},$$

respectively. The objective is to find a solution $x*$ that satisfies:

$$r_R(x*) = r_C(x*) = \underset{x \in X_S}{Max}\{\text{Min}\{r_A(x), r_B(x)\}\},$$

where X_S is the solution space defined as the set of matrices (x_{ij}) that satisfy the conditions $\sum_{j=1}^{5} x_{ij} = 1$, for all i, $x_{ij} = 0, 1$, for all i and j, and the two parties gain the same, i.e., their ratios are equal.

Note that the scales within each dimension need not be linear as in this example. In addition, the best trade-off for both parties was obtained from among $25^8 = 15{,}2587{,}890{,}625$ possible solutions resulting from combining the 8 dimensions and 5×5 possible selections of the candidates within each dimension. However, in real-life negotiations the concessions or trade-offs that each party asks from the other party may not be the same in number, so the actual agreement cannot be obtained by solving a single optimization problem. For example, in the Israeli–Palestinian problem the Israelis asked for 21 concessions from the Palestinians, and the Palestinians asked for 17 concessions from the Israelis. The final agreement will consist of a set of matchings of the 17 concessions from the Israelis and the 21 concessions from the Palestinians. This matching could be one concession (or bundle of concessions) to one concession (or bundle of concessions).

In general, to decide how to match the concessions of one party with the concessions from another party we need to first create all possible concession bundles for both parties. A concession bundle is a set of individual concessions. The parties can then trade concession bundles. The problem is that there are many possible concession bundles even when the parties in conflict have a moderately small number of possible concessions. For example, if one party had 17 concessions and another had 21 concessions, there are 131,071 and 2,097,151 possible concession bundles, respectively. Since we need to match a bundle of one party with all other possible bundles of the other party, to determine which concession bundle is more advantageous we would need to solve a MaxMin problem with $131{,}071 \times 2{,}097{,}151 = 27{,}4875{,}678{,}721$ variables. Thus, the best approach, and the one used in this problem, was one-to-one matching of concessions until no more concessions can be traded.

Discussion: The Gain-to-Loss Ratios of Concessions Made by both Sides Need to be Close to One another

One of the key takeaways that all participants in the exercise appreciated was that they learned more about the other party. One of the primary challenges to the approach turned out to be the same item that created a greater depth in understanding: a lack of common definitions. A lack of common definitions challenged the participants to actively engage in deeper understanding of each other. For future exercises of this sort though, we suggest that one of the first steps to pursue is to define terms and language. For instance, one of the concessions that is offered is to direct more effort to "human rights." How the parties define "human rights," however, differs greatly. Even though philosophically there should be an easily determined common definition for "human rights," the reality is that the parties took different positions on this issue.

The judgment and prioritization process for the concessions was implemented for each party without knowledge of the priorities of the other party.

The object is to make the ratios of the trade-offs between the two parties close. Each party can by itself estimate the gain-to-loss ratio of its opponent and determine if his gain-to-loss ratio is much greater than the other party's gain-to-loss ratio. That also makes the negotiations more difficult. The original model sought a solution that matched the best one-to-one concessions. However, given that the best solution was a standoff, we found that one had to consider trading off bundles of concessions. The role of the mediator is extremely important in this setting. There are two ways that the mediator can help to alter the outcome of ratios. Recall that both the numerator and the denominator of the ratio include perceptions of the other; the numerator is what one party perceives to be the cost of concessions to the adversary, whereas the denominator includes what one party perceives the other party's benefits to be. It is interesting to note that in a retributive conflict one party perceives the costs to the adversary as a benefit to itself and conversely the gain to the adversary as a loss to itself. The mediator has a real opportunity to bridge gaps, given the measured separation between the two parties and their varying perceptions, interpretations, and respect for "international" law.

Our results underline the differences between the Israelis and the Palestinians. In particular, the findings highlight the value of the Israelis' concessions as measured by the Palestinians when compared with the Palestinians' concessions as measured by the Israelis through the large disparities in ratios. Given this disparity, there is a great opportunity for one party to take a leadership role in the resolution process. Moreover, there is an even greater opportunity for a mediator to help bridge the gap in the gain-to-loss ratios. By educating both parties on the true costs and benefits to the adversary, the perceptions are brought more in line with reality and the score disparity minimized. It is possible that external influences or pressures might be necessary to rationalize the disparity in the gain-to-loss ratios to recognize the discrepancies.

Equalizing Concession Trade-Offs

Mistrust and the inclination to act retributively prevent people from making all their concessions at once. To determine the fairest and maximum gain to both parties from concessions being traded off, we computed gain-to-loss ratios for each pair of concessions, one for each party. These gain-to-loss ratios represent the gain to one party from the concession made by the other party divided by that party's loss from the concession it made. The gain to one party's concession is obtained as the benefits accrued from the other party's concession multiplied by the perceived costs to the party making the concession. The loss to one party's concession is obtained as the costs of the concession it made multiplied by the perceived benefits to the other party (see Fig. 4.3). To make the trade-offs, we considered only pairs of concessions with gain-to-loss ratios for both parties greater than one. This means that either side would be reluctant to trade off a concession in return for another from which its gain is less than its loss.

The General Model

In many contract negotiations, the parties not always act in good faith or share information with the other party. In this case, one should also consider the perceptions of the parties about the benefits and costs of the trade-offs. For example, in a merger transaction, the buyer (A) and the seller (B) may not always agree as to the

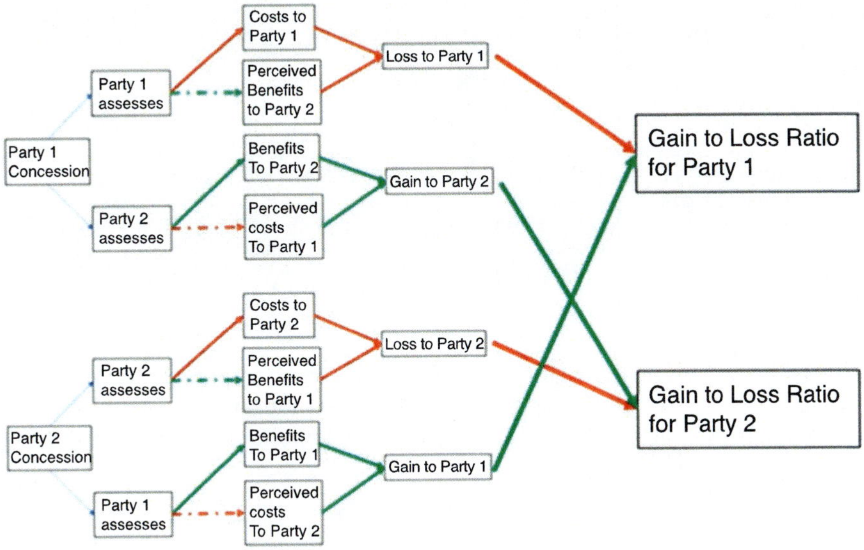

Fig. 4.3 Gain-to-loss ratios

terms of the merger, and hence the transaction fails. The steps to make trade-offs in this more general situation are as follows (Vargas and Zoffer 2019):

1. Identify the dimensions of the problem
2. Identify the trade-offs of each party within the dimensions
3. Identify the benefits accrued by a party from the other party's trade-offs
4. Identify the costs incurred by a party from its own trade-offs
5. Identify the perceived benefits that the other party received from your trade-offs
6. Identify the perceived costs incurred by the other party from their trade-offs
7. Find out what trade-off each party must make to maximize the total minimum gain they obtain, ensuring that what each party gains are as close as possible to the other party gains. This is what makes the final contract equitable and balanced.

The mathematical model that helps identify the proper contract is given below.

Let $X_k(x)$ the scale of the kth dimension. The parties will negotiate on the value of that scale according to their preferences. The realized value of the scale is determined by the benefit, the cost, the perceived benefit, and the perceived cost that this value has for each party.

Let $B_i(x_k)$ be the benefits accrued by party i from the other party trade-offs in dimension k. Let $C_i(x_k)$ be the costs incurred by party i from its own trade-offs in dimension k. Let $PB_i(x_k)$ be the benefits party i perceives the other party receives from its trade-offs in dimension k, and let $PC_i(x_k)$ be the costs the other party perceives that party i incurs from its trade-offs in dimension k. Thus, for a given dimension k, the gain of party i is given by the benefits it accrues from the trade-offs of the other party in that dimension times the costs it perceives the other party incurs in that dimension, i.e., $B_i(x_k)PC_i(x_k)$. Similarly, the loss in each dimension k is given by $C_i(x_k)PB_i(x_k)$. Thus, the gain-to-loss ratio for a party for a given dimension k is given by:

$$\frac{B_i(x_k)PC_i(x_k)}{C_i(x_k)PB_i(x_k)}$$

and the total gain-to-loss ratio for a party is given by:

$$r_i \equiv \frac{\sum\limits_{all\ k} B_i(x_k)PC_i(x_k)}{\sum\limits_{all\ k} C_i(x_k)PB_i(x_k)}.$$

Let $x_k(s)$ be a binary variable, where $x_k(s) = 1$ if the parties agree on selecting the intensity s of the kth dimension as the best decision for both. The problem now consists in finding values of s for each dimension that maximizes the smallest gain-to-loss ratio of both parties, i.e.,

$$\underset{s}{Max}\left\{Min\left\{r_i(s)\equiv\frac{\sum\limits_{all\ k}B_i[x_k(s)]PC_i[x_k(s)]}{\sum\limits_{all\ k}C_i[x_k(s)]PB_i[x_k(s)]},r_j(s)\equiv\frac{\sum\limits_{all\ k}B_j[x_k(s)]PC_j[x_k(s)]}{\sum\limits_{all\ k}C_j[x_k(s)]PB_j[x_k(s)]}\right\}\right\}$$

subject to $\sum\limits_{s}x_k(s)=1$ and $\left|1-\frac{r_i(s)}{r_j(s)}\right|\leq\varepsilon$, where ε is the tolerance that measures how far the two parties are in terms of their total gain-to-loss ratio.

In the next chapter, we structure the Israeli–Palestinian problem using the guidelines given in this chapter. The inputs to hierarchies of trade-offs were given by participants in several meetings. The results shown in the next chapter are the fruit of many hours in brainstorming sessions until everyone involved felt all necessary inputs were considered.

References

Saaty, T. L. (1988). The negotiation and resolution of the conflict in South Africa: The analytic hierarchy process. *ORiON, 4*(1), 3–25.

Vargas, L. (2017). How to write a contract with the AHP. *International Journal of the Analytic Hierarchy Process, 9*(2), 274–284.

Vargas, L., & Zoffer, H. J. (2019). Applying AHP in conflict resolution. *International Journal of the Analytic Hierarchy Process, 11*(1), 143–147.

Chapter 5
Structuring the Hierarchy to Make Trade-Offs: Benefits, Costs, Perceived Benefits, and Perceived Costs

Developing a Comprehensive Approach

One might ask: Why is it that so many distinguished politicians and negotiators have failed to reach consensus after sixty years of trying? Here are some possible reasons:

1. They had no way to measure the importance and value of intangible factors which can dominate the process.
2. They had no overall unifying structure to organize and prioritize issues and concessions.
3. They had no mechanism to trade off concessions by measuring their worth.
4. They had no way to capture each party's perception of the other side's benefits and costs.
5. They had no way to provide confidence for the other party that the opposing party is not gaining more than they are.
6. They had no way to avoid the effect of intense emotions and innuendoes which negatively affect the negotiation process.
7. They had no way to test the sensitivity and stability of the solution to changes in their judgments with respect to the importance of the factors that determined the best outcome.

It is not a coincidence that the analytic hierarchy process addresses each of these reasons in a comprehensive and deliberate way, thus eliminating many of the obstructions for moving forward to identify an equitable final solution.

Some writings in this chapter are based on published work:
(Saaty and Zoffer 2012)—Permission obtained from John Wiley & Sons (lic. #5094901446537).
(Saaty and Zoffer 2013)—First published in Notices Amer. Math. Soc. in Vol. 60, No. 10 (2013): 1300–1322, published by the American Mathematical Society.

T. L. Saaty et al., *Overcoming the Retributive Nature of the Israeli-Palestinian Conflict*, https://doi.org/10.1007/978-3-030-83958-1_5

The Process

The AHP is about breaking a problem down and then aggregating the solutions of all the sub-problems into a conclusion. It facilitates decision making by organizing perceptions, feelings, judgments, and memories into a framework that exhibits the forces that influence a decision. In the simple and most common case, the forces are arranged from the more general and less controllable to the more specific and controllable. The AHP is based on the innate human ability to make sound judgments about small problems and about large problems when a structure like a hierarchy can be built to represent the influences involved. It has been applied in a variety of decisions and planning projects in nearly 40 countries (see ISAHP 2020).

Briefly, we see decision making as a process that involves the following steps:

1. Structure a problem with a model that shows the problem's key elements and their relationships.
2. Elicit judgments that reflect knowledge, feelings, or emotions of the primary parties, as well as all other parties that have influence on the outcome.
3. Represent those judgments with meaningful numbers.
4. Use these numbers to calculate the priorities of the elements of the hierarchy.
5. Synthesize these results to determine an overall outcome.
6. Analyze sensitivity to changes in judgment.

The retributive conflict resolution approach presented here takes into consideration the benefits to A from concessions by B and the costs to A of the return concessions A makes, as well as A's perception of the benefits to B from the concessions A makes, and A's perception of the costs to B of the concessions B makes. A similar consideration is made for B. Findings from this exercise suggest that the development of "bundles" of concessions may minimize the difference in ratios of gains and losses between the two parties that a negotiator can use as a tool to move the resolution process forward.

The expressed objectives of the study described here were:

- To identify the issues, major and minor, and to examine the relative significance or priority of the issues currently inhibiting solution of the Israeli–Palestinian conflict.
- To share knowledge and insights about the current Israeli–Palestinian situation from differing points of view.
- To construct a comprehensive model of the situation.
- To explore the benefits and costs of alternative courses of action.

The traditional approach involving diplomacy and face-to-face negotiations has led to an inconclusive outcome, partially attributable to attitudes colored by strong emotions on both sides. Our approach attempts to address the impact of negative attitudes by focusing the participants on making judgments that measure the intensity of their perceptions about the influences that each of the issues brings to bear upon the outcome.

In this study, we consider each party's list of issues, which, if addressed by the other party by making concessions, would provide sufficient benefit to that side toward meeting their goal. They, in turn, would be willing to make concessions to the other side to balance those concessions with an equivalent trade-off. We refer to these issues as criteria. The process consists of taking a set of concessions from one side and measuring them against these criteria in terms of actual or perceived benefits to the other side. Actual benefits (or costs) are defined as judgments by one party about the relative importance of the concessions they receive (or give). Perceived benefits (or costs) are defined as putting oneself in the shoes of the other side to estimate the benefits (or costs), even though that side may have a totally different opinion about what the concessions received or offered are worth.

Implementing the Process

In the opening day of one of the three-day meetings the panel brainstormed the issues and structured the problem, defined the interested parties, and developed a series of concessions that each party might offer to the other.

The process was not without conflict and negotiation of its own. At times, the panel made judgments without agreement on exact definitions. There was nearly always unanimous agreement on the nature of the conflict, with much debate about the underlying concerns. These concerns differed according to which constituent group was putting them forward. For example, among the Palestinian key constituents are Palestinian refugees, Hamas followers, Fatah followers, Palestinians who still live in Israel, and Diaspora Palestinians. Among the Israeli constituents are the ultra-right orthodox community, Israelis living in settlements in the West Bank, those associated with the Likud movement, those associated with the Labor Party, and those more actively seeking peace as a primary objective, without dwelling on the details of the difficulties to achieve it.

Since the beginning of the conflict, different constituents have proposed many different approaches. These approaches inevitably influenced the panel's perception of the concessions to be made by either side. In fact, one participant suggested that it would be difficult "to think outside the box." He thought that the group was so influenced by previous thinking that they would have difficulty in conceptualizing "creative" alternatives that had not been proposed previously.

The panel defined the goal as an attempt to understand what forces and influences or combinations thereof would tend toward a consensus peace accord for the conflict between Israel and the Palestinians. To accomplish this goal, the panel of nine individuals was assembled to represent a cross section of thinking on both sides. Its members had present or prior experience in academia, government, and business. However, it was recognized that the panel did not represent a complete cross-sample of opinions. The sample of panel participants was not sufficiently large to include all points of view nor was it intended to be so because of limitations of time and resources, nor did it contain participants in actual Israeli–Palestinian negotiations.

This initiative only sought to test the AHP methodology on a problem that had previously evaded resolution. The size of the panel was thought to be sufficient to account for the different populations. However, it was agreed that the work is exploratory in nature and intended to demonstrate how the method can be used over a short period of time to arrive at a process that moves the negotiation process forward.

As mentioned above, at no point in the development and evaluation of the problem was the process easy. In fact, even the "purpose" was not easily agreed upon and at several points in the three days over which the meetings took place, the panel readdressed what the undertaking was intended to accomplish. It looked at the purpose of the project from various perspectives in the hope of finding one that appeared more promising than others that have been tried. The panel brainstormed all the issues they could think of that had to be considered in the framework. They are listed in Table 5.1 below as they were identified by the participants and later organized into categories, with no attempt to eliminate possible duplications. Listing the issues made it easier to identify the concessions, and to structure the problem. Taking time to structure the problem in as comprehensive a fashion as may be feasible is a crucial first step before attempting to prioritize the relative importance of its constituent parts that have causal influence on the concessions and actions to be taken. The structure that emerged in the early discussion depended on the parties, their knowledge, experience, and conditioning. In a strict sense, it was a political rather than a scientific structure. In such a situation, it was not possible to provide a cultural analysis of the parties' narrative and framing of the issues.

The exercise in discussing specific issues sometimes seemed to generate incompatible perceptions of what can and would be achievable in peace negotiations. For example, all the Israelis attending the meeting were adamant that a one state solution is impossible to contemplate, while Palestinians all agreed that a solution that does not grant refugees their internationally recognized rights to return is also impossible to contemplate. But we do know that historically adamant positions have changed when circumstances change. For proper application of the AHP methodology, it is important to include in the structure all factors, including those that some participants feel are so crucial to their preconceived and predetermined positions that any concession on those issues seems inconceivable.

To develop the necessary measurements for prioritization, we need to calculate the gains and losses for each concession from each of the parties. The panel developed a total of eight hierarchies, involving benefits and costs and perceived benefits and costs: four hierarchies for the Israeli group and four hierarchies for the Palestinian group. The exercise in which the 106 issues were identified through the process of brainstorming served as a stimulus to the thinking of the participants to deal with the structuring process. Each of the eight hierarchies involves a goal, for example, Israel's benefits from Palestinian concessions, and a set of criteria that are a subset of the issues relevant to that goal. They are called criteria in terms of which all the possible concessions that were identified were evaluated by scoring them one at a time. The criteria that were developed for these eight models were chosen by each of the Israeli and Palestinian participants, respectively. Because of the volume of

Table 5.1 List of outstanding issues organized by category

GEOGRAPHIC and DEMOGRAPHIC ISSUES	**POLITICAL ISSUES**	**BEHAVIORAL ISSUES**
Access of Palestinians to Available Natural Resources	Accountability and Reasonability of Hamas in the Gaza Strip	Bad Faith Negotiations
Archeological Issues	Agreement on One State Solution	Compromise
Golan Heights	Agreement on Two State Solution	Confidence Building Measures
How to Address the Palestinian Diaspora	AIPAC (American Israel Political Action Committee)	Corruption
How to Re-settle Palestinian Refugees	American Politician	Deception and Manufacturing of History
Immigration (Israelis Making "Aliyah" (return) to Israel	Citizenship Rights of Arab Community in Israel	Equal Treatment of All Parties
Palestinian Access to the Mediterranean Sea	Colonialism	Ethnic Cleansing
Palestinian Problem of Split Land Mass Between Gaza and the West Bank	Condemnation of Violence as a Tool of Negotiation	Harassment
Population	Control	Human Rights
Problems for Israel in Living in an Ocean of Arab Countries	Denunciation of Irrelevant United Nations Resolutions	Human Shields
Right of Palestinians to Return to their Homes in Israel	European Acceptance of Responsibility for the Holocaust and Settlement of Israelis in Israel	Intermarriage
Rights of Palestinians to Israeli-controlled Land	Funding of Terrorism	Learning to Forgive Without Forgetting
Status of Israeli Settlements	Historical Legitimacy of Ownership of Land in the Area	Love
Water	How to Deal with Charges of Apartheid	Mutual Recognition of Rights of Each Party
ECONOMIC and BUSINESS ISSUES	International Relationships	Non Violence
Compensation for Victims of Terrorism	Islamic State	Psychological Barriers
Compensation to Palestinians for Loss of Land	Jewish Refugee Issues	Psychological Damage
Dealing with Property Confiscation Issues	Mutual Compensation	Racism
Economic Choices	Problems Associated With Hamas	Recognition of the Holocaust
How to Re-settle Palestinian Refugees	Residency Rights	Recognition of the Nakba Condition
Restitution	Role of the Druze in Negotiations	Religious Fundamentalism
EDUCATION ISSUES	Sovereignty	Representation of Women in the Negotiations
Education	Status of Israel	Respect
Incitement in the Educational School System	Status of Jerusalem	Subjugation and Humiliation
Indoctrination	Status of Palestinian Authority	Suicide Bombers
Industrial Parks	Status of Ramallah	Trust
Lack of Creativity and Problem Solving	Syrian Accommodation for Settlement of Palestinian Refugees	**MILITARY ISSUES**
Language Training	**SOCIAL ISSUES**	Arms Smuggling
Stolen Culture	Basic Human Needs	Disarmament
SECURITY ISSUES	**RELIGIOUS AND IDEOLOGICAL ISSUES**	House Demolition
Bombing of Israeli Children	Armageddon	Invasion
Gilad Shalit (Release of Prisoners)	Christian Zionism (Evangelists)	Missile Building
Safe Passage	Holy Places	Nuclear Responsibility
Safety and Security	Jewish Zionism	War Crimes
Terrorism	Palestinian Christians	**LEGAL ISSUES**
The Wall	Religious Prophecy	International Law
		Prisoners

issues, we found it necessary in developing the hierarchies to select as criteria a subset of the most crucial issues. The overall goal of each of the corresponding criteria in the four hierarchies involved the apparent equalization of the ratio of the gains to the losses by each side. Concessions by each party are listed in Tables 5.2 and 5.3 below. We list the concessions which the participants identified as possible responses to the issues given in Table 5.1.

Table 5.2 Possible Israelis' concessions

Israelis' Concessions	Description
1	Abandon the Idea of Jewish State
2	Accept Palestinian full control of the borders of the Palestinian State and its outlets
3	Accept the historical responsibility for the Palestinian refugee problem
4	Accept the Palestinian refugee rights to return
5	Accept to abide by the status quo in the holy places in Jerusalem
6	Accept to abolish law of return
7	Accept to respect the integrity of the West Bank and Gaza by allowing free and safe passage between the two areas.
8	Accept to withdraw from East Jerusalem
9	Accept Two-State Solution on the borders of the 4th of June 1967
10	Allow all parties to have equal access to and control of religious sites and holy places
11	Allow the sharing of all natural resources between Palestinians and Israelis
12	Comply with all applicable UN Resolutions
13	Evacuate settlement of Jewish settlers on land claimed by the Palestinians with or without compensation
14	Release all political prisoners including those who are Israeli citizens
15	Shared Jerusalem as a religious and political center with all parties
16	Solve the Palestinian refugee problem in a just and agreed upon manner
17	Stop incitement by the religious and national education and religious leaders in Israel against Muslims and Arabs

Table 5.3 Possible Palestinians' concessions

Palestanians' Concessions	Description
1	Accept mutually agreed upon land swap
2	Accept settlements under Palestinian sovereignty as residents
3	Accept the temporary presence of Israelis military in Jordan Valley
4	Accept Two-State Solution
5	Acceptance a Two-State solution which includes a Non-Contiguous State
6	Acknowledge Israel's Existence as a Jewish State
7	Acknowledge Israel's Existence as an Independent State
8	Agree to Compromise to the Demand of the Right of No Return
9	Agreeing with Palestinian demilitarized state
10	Allow all parties to have equal access to and control of religious sites and holy
11	Allow Israel to use Palestinian airspace
12	Declare Against Iranian Nuclear Development
13	Denounce & Reign in Violence
14	Denounce Iranian pursuit of nuclear arms and support Israelis effort to remove
15	Lobby Arab States to Allow both Israelis and Palestinians to Have the Right to Return to their land of origin
16	Make Compromise on the Status of Jerusalem
17	Palestinians must guarantee that any agreement reached with Israel will be accepted and supported by the majority of the Palestinian people both in Gaza and the West Bank
18	Refrain and work against any anti-Israel sentiments in Palestinian schools
19	Seek Assistance for a Legitimate Settlement of Refugees
20	Sharing of Natural Resources
21	Work Cooperatively and in active engagement w/ Israel

Table 5.4 Rating scale for concession evaluation

Excellent	1.0
Very high	0.9
High	0.8
Medium	0.7
Low	0.5
Very Low	0.4
Negligible	0.3

Goal:	**Israelis' Benefits from Palestinians' Concessions**
Criteria:	Integrity and unity of Israeli society post agreement
	Security
	Strengthening the alliance with the United States
	Make Israel more attractive to Jewish diaspora and Israelis citizens
	End of claims
	Legitimization of the State of Israel
	Stop being occupiers
	Peace, prosperity and stability in region
	Maintain the Jewish majority of Israel alongside with the Arab minority
	Weakening the radical forces in the Middle East headed by Iran
Concessions:	Palestinians' Concessions

Fig. 5.1 Israelis' benefits from Palestinians' concessions

Goal:	**Israelis' Perception of Palestinians' Costs from Palestinians' Concessions**
Criteria:	Giving up on the Idea of a Greater Palestine
	Remainder of part of the Settlement Community
	Loss of 'victim' status
	Loss of land (67 Border) /swap
	Loss of International financial support
	Partial control of East Jerusalem as the capital of Palestine
	Partial solution refuge problem
	Partial control of the Muslim holy places
Concessions:	Palestinians' Concessions

Fig. 5.2 Israelis' perception of Palestinian's costs from Palestinian's concessions

The forgoing concessions comprise the bottom levels of the hierarchies given in Figs. 5.1, 5.2, 5.3, 5.4, 5.5, 5.6, 5.7 and 5.8. The second level of these hierarchies are the criteria used to determine the contribution of the concessions to the benefits, costs, perceived benefits, and perceived costs of both parties. The priorities of these

Goal:	**Israelis' Perception of Palestinians' Benefits from Israelis' Concessions**
Criteria:	Freedom, dignity and feeling of equality
	Independent state
	Evacuation of the settlers in the settlements
	International recognition & permanent boarders
	Maximization of the area (land)
	Economic stability and prosperity
	East Jerusalem as the capital of Palestine
	Solve the refugees problem
	Control of the Muslim holy places
Concessions:	Israelis' Concessions

Fig. 5.3 Israelis' perception of Palestinians' benefits from Israelis' concessions

Goal:	**Israelis' Costs from Israelis' Concessions**
Criteria:	Integrity and unity of Israeli society post agreement
	Security
	Strengthening the alliance with the United States
	Make Israel more attractive to Jewish diaspora and Israelis citizens
	End of claims and end of conflict
	Legitimization of the State of Israel
	Stop being occupiers
	Peace, economy and stability in region
	Maintain the Jewish majority of Israel alongside with the Arab minority
	Weakening the radical forces in the Middle East headed by Iran
Concessions:	Israelis' Concessions

Fig. 5.4 Israelis' costs from Israelis' concessions

criteria are given in Tables 5.5 and 5.6. These priorities are also listed at the top of Tables 5.7, 5.8, 5.9, 5.10, 5.11, 5.12, 5.13 and 5.14.

The panels attempted to accomplish much in a very short period. To facilitate the process and reach some conclusions, we rated each concession under each criterion using the words and corresponding scale values in Table 5.4 as to how strongly it contributed to that criterion that represents the goal it serves.

For example, in Table 5.7 Israeli's concessions were rated using only the highest priority criteria. Two criteria with negligible priorities, one in column four and one in column six, had zero rating priorities for the concessions. These were ignored, ensuring that at least seventy percent of the priorities from the criteria were accounted for in the ratings model. Similarly, we did the same thing in the other tables. Tables 5.7, 5.8, 5.9 and 5.10 present the results for Israeli benefits from

Goal:	**Palestinians' Benefits from Israelis' Concessions**
Criteria:	Permanent borders
	Sovereign Palestinian State
	Share of water and other resources
	Resolution of the refugee problem
	Shared control of Jerusalem and holy places
	International guarantees and assurances to protect Palestine State security and integrity
	Evacuation of the Israeli settlements
	Having full control over air space, maritime, borders and outlets
	Release of political prisoners including those who are Israeli citizens
	Respect the integrity of West Bank and Gaza
	Stop incitement and raging hatred
	East Jerusalem as the capital of the State of Palestine
Concessions:	Israelis' Concessions

Fig. 5.5 Palestinians' benefits from Israelis' concessions

Goal:	**Palestinians' Perception of Israeli's Costs from Israelis' Concessions**
Criteria:	Changing of Zionist narrative
	Property restitution and compensation
	Settlements evacuation
	Rehabilitating evacuated settlers from the Palestinian territories
Concessions:	Israelis' Concessions

Fig. 5.6 Palestinians' perception of Israelis' costs from Israelis' concessions

Palestinian concessions, Israeli perception of Palestinian costs for making these concessions to Israel, Israeli costs of their own concessions, and Israeli perception of Palestinian gains from Israeli concessions, respectively. Similarly, Tables 5.11, 5.12, 5.13 and 5.14 present the results of the Palestinian ratings model.

The relative benefits, costs, perceived benefits, and perceived costs obtained in Tables 5.7, 5.8, 5.9, 5.10, 5.11, 5.12, 5.13 and 5.14 are summarized in Tables 5.15 for the Israelis and Table 5.16 for the Palestinians.

The next step is to compute the gain/loss ratios for pairs of concessions from both parties' perspectives.

For example, let us assume that the Israelis want to trade concession #9 (Accept two-state solution on the borders of the fourth of June 1967) with the Palestinian

Goal:	**Palestinians' Perception of Israelis' Benefits from Palestinians' Concessions**
Criteria:	Gaining legitimacy of the Palestinian and Arab and Muslim world
	Integration in the Middle East with normal relations with its neighbors and Arab World
	End of claims by the Palestinians
	Obtaining security by acceptance and recognition of the Palestinians and Arab and Muslim world
	Sharing the Palestinians with their own natural resources
	Obtaining territorial gains
	Economic relations and new markets including tourism with neighboring Arab and Islamic countries
	Reduction of military expenditures enabling national development
	Regional cooperation against external threats
	Acknowledgement of Israeli control over the Waling Wall and the Jewish Quarter in the Old City of Jerusalem
Concessions:	Palestinians' Concessions

Fig. 5.7 Palestinians' perception of Israelis' benefits from Palestinians' concessions

Goal:	**Palestinians' Costs from Palestinians' Concessions**
Criteria:	Conflict between Palestinian diaspora and the internal leadership
	Giving up the claim over historic Palestine occupied in 1948 and known later as the State of Israel
	Partial loss/depletion of natural resources by sharing them with Israel
	Loss of military capability to defend the State of Palestine
	Territorial loss as a result of unfair land swap
	Accommodation and rehabilitation of Palestinian refugees not allowed to return to Israel
	Restrictions on national sovereignty by accepting demilitarization and multinational monitoring
	Loss of property rights
	Dislocation and fragmentation of Palestinian social fabric
Concessions:	Palestinians' Concessions

Fig. 5.8 Palestinians' costs from Palestinians' concessions

Table 5.5 Israeli and Palestinian costs and perceived benefits

Israeli Costs from its Concessions	Priorities
Integrity and unity of Israeli society post agreement	0.0659
Security	0.1831
Strengthening the alliance with the United States	0.0457
Make Israel more attractive to Jewish diaspora and Israelis citizens	0.0322
End of claims and end of conflict	0.2093
Legitimization of the State of Israel	0.0778
Stop being occupiers	0.0477
Peace, economy and stability in region	0.086
Maintain the Jewish majority of Israel alongside with the Arab minority	0.2249
Weakening the radical forces in the Middle East headed by Iran	0.0274

Israeli Perception of Palestinian Benefits from Israeli Concessions	Priorities
Freedom, dignity and feeling of equality	0.1449
Independent state	0.2145
Evacuation of the settlers in the settlements	0.0661
International recognition & permanent boarders	0.0368
Maximization of the area (land)	0.0816
Economic stability and prosperity	0.0219
East Jerusalem as the capital of Palestine	0.1361
Solve the refugees problem	0.2128
Control of the Muslim holy places	0.0853

Palestinian Costs from its Concessions	Priorities
Conflict between Palestinian diaspora and the internal leadership	0.0948
Giving up the claim over historic Palestine occupied in 1948 and known later as the State of Israel	0.2055
Partial loss/depletion of natural resources by sharing them with Israel	0.1257
Loss of military capability to defend the State of Palestine	0.0575
Territorial loss as a result of unfair land swap	0.2173
Accommodation and rehabilitation of Palestinian refugees not allowed to return to Israel	0.1192
Restrictions on national sovereignty by accepting demilitarization and multinational monitoring	0.1013
Loss of property rights	0.0395
Dislocation and fragmentation of Palestinian social fabric	0.0392

Palestinian Perception of Israeli Benefits from Palestinian Concessions	Priorities
Gaining legitimacy of the Palestinian and Arab and Muslim world	0.1111
Integration in the Middle East with normal relations with its neighbors and Arab World	0.0658
End of claims by the Palestinians	0.2556
Obtaining security by acceptance and recognition of the Palestinians and Arab and Muslim world	0.108
Sharing the Palestinians with their own natural resources	0.0215
Obtaining territorial gains	0.1184
Economic relations and new markets including tourism with neighboring Arab and Islamic countries	0.0999
Reduction of military expenditures enabling national development	0.0239
Regional cooperation against external threats	0.0333
Acknowledgement of Israeli control over the Waling Wall and the Jewish Quarter in the Old City of Jerusalem	0.1626

Table 5.6 Israeli and Palestinian benefits and perceived costs

Israeli Benefits from Palestinian Concessions	Priorities
Integrity and unity of Israeli society post agreement	0.0753
Security	0.1636
Strengthening the alliance with the United States	0.0477
Make Israel more attractive to Jewish diaspora and Israelis citizens	0.0397
End of claims	0.2216
Legitimization of the State of Israel	0.0654
Stop being occupiers	0.0529
Peace, prosperity and stability in region	0.0959
Maintain the Jewish majority of Israel alongside with the Arab minority	0.1899
Weakening the radical forces in the Middle East headed by Iran	0.0479

Israeli Perception of Palestinian Costs from Palestinian Concessions	Priorities
Giving up on the Idea of a Greater Palestine	0.088
Remainder of part of the Settlement Community	0.0964
Loss of 'victim' status	0.0288
Loss of land (67 Border) /swap	0.15
Loss of International financial support	0.0252
Partial control of East Jerusalem as the capital of Palestine	0.1735
Partial solution refuge problem	0.3101
Partial control of the Muslim holy places	0.128

Palestinian Benefits from Israeli Concessions	Priorities
Permanent borders	0.2095
Sovereign Palestinian State	0.2054
Share of water and other resources	0.0181
Resolution of the refugee problem	0.0654
Shared control of Jerusalem and holy places	0.0613
International guarantees and assurances to protect Palestine State security and integrity	0.0403
Evacuation of the Israeli settlements	0.0415
Having full control over air space, maritime, borders and outlets	0.1086
Release of political prisoners including those who are Israeli citizens	0.0186
Respect the integrity of West Bank and Gaza	0.0571
Stop incitement and raging hatred	0.0087
East Jerusalem as the capital of the State of Palestine	0.1654

Palestinian Perception of Israeli Costs from Israeli Concessions	Priorities
Changing of Zionist narrative	0.4541
Property restitution and compensation	0.0689
Settlements evacuation	0.2723
Rehabilitating evacuated settlers from the Palestinian territories	0.2047

Table 5.7 Ratings of Palestinian concessions relative to Israeli benefits from Palestinian concessions

		Giving up on the Idea of a Greater Palestine	Remainder of part of the Settlement Community	Loss of 'Victim' Status	Loss of Land (67 Boarder) / Swap	Loss of International Financial Support	Partial Control of East Jerusalem as the Capital of Palestine	Partial Solution Refuge Problem	Partial Control of the Muslim Holy Places
	Score	.0880	.0964	.0288	.1500	.0252	.1735	.3101	.1280
Accept mutually agreed upon land swap	0.3888	0	0	0	0.7	0	0.354	0.632	0.206
Accept settlements under Palestinian sovereignty as residents	0.2903	0	0	0	0.94	0	0.404	0.224	0.076
Accept the temporary presence of multinational military monitoring system in Jordan Valley	0.0677	0	0	0	0.322	0	0.028	0.028	0.046
Accept Two-State Solution	0.1016	0	0	0	0.174	0	0.124	0.028	0.354
Acceptance of a Two-State solution which includes a Non-Contiguous State	0.1843	0	0	0	0.254	0	0.302	0.144	0.384
Acknowledge Israel's Existence as a Jewish State	0.612	0	0	0	0.482	0	0.91	0.93	0.73
Acknowledge Israel's Existence as an Independent State	0.3792	0	0	0	0.562	0	0.7	0.414	0.352
Agree to Compromise to the Demand of the Right of Return	0.5237	0	0	0	0.79	0	0.094	0.96	0.712
Agreeing with Palestinian demilitarized state for a limited time period	0.0828	0	0	0	0.322	0	0.064	0.064	0.028
Preserve the Status Quo in the Holy places of Jerusalem	0.2053	0	0	0	0.076	0	0.502	0.064	0.68
Allow Israel to use Palestinian airspace	0.0671	0	0	0	0.354	0	0.01	0.028	0.028
Declare Against Iranian Nuclear Development	0.0213	0	0	0	0.028	0	0.028	0.028	0.028
Denounce & Reign in Violence	0.0685	0	0	0	0.094	0	0.194	0.028	0.094
Denounce Iranian pursuit of nuclear arms and support Israelis effort to remove the threat	0.0271	0	0	0	0.046	0	0.046	0.028	0.028
Lobby Arab States to Allow both Israelis and Palestinians to Have the Right to Return to their land of origin	0.2242	0	0	0	0.176	0	0.094	0.554	0.076
Make Compromise on the Status of Jerusalem	0.3807	0	0	0	0.514	0	0.94	0.094	0.87
Palestinians must guarantee that any agreement reached with Israel will be accepted and supported by the majority of the Palestinian people both in Gaza and the West Bank	0.3215	0	0	0	0.352	0	0.602	0.302	0.552
Refrain and work against any anti-Israel sentiments in Palestinian schools	0.1145	0	0	0	0.094	0	0.058	0.24	0.124
Seek Assistance for a Legitimate Settlement of Refugees Anywhere Except Israel	0.5339	0	0	0	0.762	0	0.224	0.98	0.6
Sharing of Natural Resources	0.0333	0	0	0	0.108	0	0.028	0.028	0.028
Work Cooperatively and in active engagement w/ Israel	0.1137	0	0	0	0.126	0	0.176	0.156	0.124

Table 5.8 Ratings of Palestinian concessions relative to Israeli perception of Palestinian costs

	Score	Giving up on the Idea of a Greater Palestine .0880	Remainder of part of the Settlement Community .0964	Loss of 'Victim' Status .0288	Loss of Land (67 Boarder) / Swap .1500	Loss of International Financial Support .0252	Partial Control of East Jerusalem as the Capital of Palestine .1735	Partial Solution Refuge Problem .3101	Partial Control of the Muslim Holy Places .1280
Accept mutually agreed upon land swap	0.3888	0	0	0	0.7	0	0.354	0.632	0.206
Accept settlements under Palestinian sovereignty as residents	0.2903	0	0	0	0.94	0	0.404	0.224	0.076
Accept the temporary presence of multinational military monitoring system in Jordan Valley	0.0677	0	0	0	0.322	0	0.028	0.028	0.046
Accept Two-State Solution	0.1016	0	0	0	0.174	0	0.124	0.028	0.354
Acceptance of a Two-State solution which includes a Non-Contiguous State	0.1843	0	0	0	0.254	0	0.302	0.144	0.384
Acknowledge Israel's Existence as a Jewish State	0.612	0	0	0	0.482	0	0.91	0.93	0.73
Acknowledge Israel's Existence as an Independent State	0.3792	0	0	0	0.562	0	0.7	0.414	0.352
Agree to Compromise to the Demand of the Right of Return	0.5237	0	0	0	0.79	0	0.094	0.96	0.712
Agreeing with Palestinian demilitarized state for a limited time period	0.0828	0	0	0	0.322	0	0.064	0.064	0.028
Preserve the Status Quo in the Holy places of Jerusalem	0.2053	0	0	0	0.076	0	0.502	0.064	0.68
Allow Israel to use Palestinian airspace	0.0671	0	0	0	0.354	0	0.01	0.028	0.028
Declare Against Iranian Nuclear Development	0.0213	0	0	0	0.028	0	0.028	0.028	0.028
Denounce & Reign in Violence	0.0685	0	0	0	0.094	0	0.194	0.028	0.094
Denounce Iranian pursuit of nuclear arms and support Israelis effort to remove the threat	0.0271	0	0	0	0.046	0	0.046	0.028	0.028
Lobby Arab States to Allow both Israelis and Palestinians to Have the Right to Return to their land of origin	0.2242	0	0	0	0.176	0	0.094	0.554	0.076
Make Compromise on the Status of Jerusalem	0.3807	0	0	0	0.514	0	0.94	0.094	0.87
Palestinians must guarantee that any agreement reached with Israel will be accepted and supported by the majority of the Palestinian people both in Gaza and the West Bank	0.3215	0	0	0	0.352	0	0.602	0.302	0.552
Refrain and work against any anti-Israel sentiments in Palestinian schools	0.1145	0	0	0	0.094	0	0.058	0.24	0.124
Seek Assistance for a Legitimate Settlement of Refugees Anywhere Except Israel	0.5339	0	0	0	0.762	0	0.224	0.98	0.6
Sharing of Natural Resources	0.0333	0	0	0	0.108	0	0.028	0.028	0.028
Work Cooperatively and in active engagement w/ Israel	0.1137	0	0	0	0.126	0	0.176	0.156	0.124

Table 5.9 Ratings of Israeli concessions relative to Israeli costs of Israeli concessions

	Score	Integrity and Unity of Israeli Society Post Agreement	Security	Strengthening the Alliance with the United States	Make Israel more Attractive to Jewish Diaspora and Israelis Citizens	End of Claims and End of Conflict	Legitimization of the State of Israel	Stop being Occupiers	Peace, Economy and Stability in Region	Maintain the Jewish Majority of Israel Alongside with the Arab Minority	Weakening the Radical Forces in the Middle East Headed by Iran
		.0659	.1831	.0457	.0322	.2093	.0778	.0477	.0860	.2249	.0274
Abandon the Idea of Jewish State	0.9204	1	1	0.94	1	1	1	0	0.98	1	0
Accept Palestinian full control of the boarders of the Palestinian State and its outlets	0.5932	0.84	0.98	0.452	0.66	0.272	0.76	0	0.37	0.75	0
Accept the historical responsibility for the Palestinian refugee problem	0.8331	0.98	0.85	0.98	0.96	0.85	0.96	0	0.93	0.91	0
Accept the Palestinian refugee rights to return	0.8716	0.98	0.95	0.284	1	0.98	0.98	0	0.95	1	0
Accept to abide by the status quo in the holy places in Jerusalem	0.1805	0.172	0.352	0.174	0.29	0.046	0.094	0	0.192	0.24	0
Accept to abolish law of return	0.8122	1	0.452	0.73	1	1	1	0	1	1	0
Accept to respect the integrity of the West Bank and Gaza by allowing free and safe passage between the two areas.	0.1826	0.39	0.47	0.076	0.154	0.046	0.082	0	0.082	0.175	0
Accept East Jerusalem as the capital of the Palestinian State	0.7638	1	0.7	0.076	0.76	0.96	0.94	0	0.89	0.85	0
Accept Two-State Solution on the borders of the 4th of June 1967	0.0502	0.252	0.094	0.01	0.094	0.028	0.01	0	0.046	0.01	0
Allow all parties to have equal access to and control of religious sites and holy places	0.0926	0.3	0.142	0.046	0.262	0.046	0.028	0	0.082	0.078	0
Allow the sharing of all natural resources between Palestinians and Israelis	0.1031	0.172	0.162	0.028	0.26	0.076	0.046	0	0.082	0.115	0
Comply with all applicable UN Resolutions	0.7912	0.92	0.91	0.692	0.722	0.68	0.89	0	0.91	0.975	0
Evacuate settlers of Jewish settlements on land claimed by the Palestinians with or without compensation	0.3307	0.72	0.39	0.028	0.37	0.452	0.452	0	0.5	0.115	0
Release all political prisoners including those who are Israeli citizens	0.4766	0.7	0.94	0.064	0.63	0.47	0.75	0	0.67	0.093	0
Share Jerusalem as two capitals of two states	0.1503	0.55	0.174	0.064	0.45	0.028	0.046	0	0.094	0.21	0
Solve the Palestinian refugee problem in a just and agreed upon manner	0.1662	0.58	0.254	0.076	0.046	0.094	0.112	0	0.22	0.13	0
Stop incitement by the religious and national education and religious leaders in Israel against Muslims and Arabs	0.0682	0.162	0.156	0.046	0.112	0.028	0.028	0	0.01	0.064	0

Table 5.10 Ratings of Israeli concessions relative to Israeli perceptions of Palestinian benefits

	Score	Freedom, Dignity and Feeling of Equality	Independent State	Evacuation of the Settlers in the Settlements	International Recognition & Permanent Boarders	Maximization of the Area (Land)	Economic Stability and Prosperity	East Jerusalem as the Capital of Palestine	Solve the Refuges Problem	Control of the Muslim Holy Places
		.1449	.2145	.0661	.0368	.0816	.0219	.1361	.2128	.0853
Abandon the Idea of Jewish State	0.7252	0.96	0.84	0	0	0	0	0.88	0.98	0.91
Accept Palestinian full control of the boarders of the Palestin ian State and its outlets	0.5538	0.96	1	0	0	0	0	0.39	0.56	0.32
Accept the historical responsibility for the Palestinian refug ee problem	0.1962	0.37	0.24	0	0	0	0	0.11	0.36	0.03
Accept the Palestinian refugee rights to return	0.5985	0.96	0.83	0	0	0	0	0.35	1	0.24
Accept to abide by the status quo in the holy places in Jerusal em	0.392	0.74	0.30	0	0	0	0	0.94	0.09	0.85
Accept to abolish law of return	0.3104	0.71	0.14	0	0	0	0	0.09	0.72	0.13
Accept to respect the integrity of the West Bank and Gaza by al lowing free and safe passage between the two areas.	0.3734	0.90	0.84	0	0	0	0	0.30	0.08	0.06
Accept East Jerusalem as the capital of the Palestinian State	0.5851	0.93	0.94	0	0	0	0	1	0.14	0.96
Accept Two-State Solution on the borders of the 4th of June 1967	0.595	0.91	0.70	0	0	0	0	0.93	0.78	0.24
Allow all parties to have equal access to and control of religious sites and holy places	0.386	0.89	0.32	0	0	0	0	0.66	0.08	0.95
Allow the sharing of all natural resources between Palestinians and Israelis	0.2069	0.58	0.40	0	0	0	0	0.08	0.08	0.09
Comply with all applicable UN Resolutions	0.6941	0.86	0.91	0	0	0	0	0.81	0.96	0.70
Evacuate settlers of Jewish settlements on land claimed by the Palestinians with or without compensation	0.6465	0.95	0.98	0	0	0	0	0.96	0.63	0.39
Release all political prisoners including those who are Israeli citizens	0.3467	0.94	0.87	0	0	0	0	0.05	0.06	0.05
Share Jerusalem as two capitals of two states	0.4371	0.68	0.53	0	0	0	0	0.75	0.22	0.88
Solve the Palestinian refugee problem in a just and agreed upon manner	0.5315	0.80	0.81	0	0	0	0	0.11	1.00	0.16
Stop incitement by the religious and national education and religious leaders in Israel against Muslims and Arabs	0.0805	0.34	0.06	0	0	0	0	0.03	0.05	0.05

Table 5.11 Ratings of Israeli concessions relative to Palestinian benefits from Israeli concession

		Permanent Borders	Sovereign Palestinian State	Share of Water and Other resources	Resolution of the refugee problem	Shared Control of Jerusalem and Holy Places	International guarantees and assurances to protect Palestine State security and Integrity	Evacuation of the Israeli settlements	Having full control over air space, maritime, borders and outlets	Release of political prisoners including those who are Israeli citizens	Respect the Integrity of West Bank and Gaza	Stop Incitment and raging hatred	East Jerusalem as the capital of the State of Palestine
	Score	.2095	.2054	.0181	.0654	.0613	.0403	.0415	.1086	.0186	.0571	.0087	.1654
Abandon the Idea of Jewish State	0.8333	0.83	0.91	0.09	0.79	0.66	0.84	0.94	0.87	0.65	0.93	0.45	0.86
Accept Palestinian full control of the borders of the Palestinian State and its outlets	0.9288	0.93	0.98	0.81	0.68	0.94	0.89	0.96	0.96	0.71	0.98	0.53	0.98
Accept the historical responsibility for the Palestinian refugee problem	0.8981	0.94	0.87	0.9	0.92	0.89	0.92	0.98	0.81	0.82	0.95	0.84	0.9
Accept the Palestinian refugee rights to return	0.8341	0.71	0.96	0.32	0.87	0.84	0.63	0.93	0.84	0.76	0.87	0.5	0.91
Accept to abide by the status quo in the holy places in Jerusalem	0.7519	0.76	0.69	0.25	0.84	0.78	0.89	0.76	0.63	0.76	0.78	0.6	0.87
Accept to abolish law of return	0.5122	0.53	0.32	0.4	0.58	0.35	0.4	0.55	0.5	0.4	0.7	0.47	0.75
Accept to respect the integrity of the West Bank and Gaza by allowing free and safe passage between the two areas.	0.9237	0.93	0.92	0.8	0.81	0.92	0.9	0.9	0.96	0.89	0.98	0.78	0.96
Accept to withdraw from East Jerusalem	0.9389	1	0.98	0.71	0.83	0.9	0.87	0.96	0.86	0.8	0.96	0.65	0.98
Accept Two-State Solution on the borders of the 4th of June 1967	0.9228	0.98	0.98	0.55	0.84	0.63	0.87	0.98	0.94	0.89	0.98	0.78	0.94
Allow all parties to have equal access to and control of religious sites and holy places	0.7561	0.76	0.78	0.73	0.65	0.84	0.73	0.84	0.76	0.45	0.6	0.68	0.81
Allow the sharing of all natural resources between Palestinians and Israelis	0.6282	0.53	0.6	0.86	0.6	0.63	0.78	0.6	0.73	0.68	0.78	0.39	0.63
Comply with all applicable UN Resolutions	0.9245	0.91	0.89	0.92	0.94	0.87	0.89	0.96	0.95	0.9	1	0.92	0.96
Evacuate settlement of Jewish settlers on land claimed by the Palestinians with or without compensation	0.8741	0.89	0.79	0.81	0.92	0.92	0.81	0.98	0.89	0.79	0.92	0.73	0.91
Release all political prisoners including those who are Israeli citizens	0.7068	0.84	0.65	0.71	0.78	0.55	0.78	0.81	0.55	0.98	0.79	0.84	0.63
Shared Jerusalem as a religious and political center with all parties	0.7954	0.8	0.71	0.73	0.7	0.87	0.74	0.87	0.78	0.89	0.89	0.5	0.89
Solve the Palestinian refugee problem in a just and agreed upon manner	0.8341	0.79	0.82	0.74	0.96	0.9	0.87	0.93	0.84	0.88	0.92	0.5	0.79
Stop incitement by the religious and national education and religious leaders in Israel against Muslims and Arabs	0.3881	0.29	0.42	0.55	0.4	0.44	0.45	0.27	0.35	0.37	0.4	0.93	0.44

Table 5.12 Ratings of Israeli concessions relative to Palestinian perceptions of Israeli costs

		Changing of Zionist narrative	Property restitution and compensation	Settlements evacuation	Rehabilitating evacuated settlers from the Palestinian territories
	Score	.4541	.0689	.2723	.2047
Abandon the Idea of Jewish State	0.8198	0.98	0	0.79	0.78
Accept Palestinian full control of the boarders of the Palestinian State and its outlets	0.8226	0.92	0	0.81	0.9
Accept the Palestinian refugee rights to return	0.8055	0.92	0	0.86	0.75
Accept to abide by the status quo in the holy places in Jerusalem	0.642	0.65	0	0.68	0.79
Accept to abolish law of return	0.6273	0.73	0	0.5	0.78
Accept to respect the integrity of the West Bank and Gaza by allowing free and safe passage between the two areas.	0.7665	0.84	0	0.76	0.87
Accept to withdraw from East Jerusalem	0.8205	0.92	0	0.87	0.81
Accept Two-State Solution	0.7687	0.83	0	0.89	0.73
Allow all parties to have equal access to and control of religious sites and holy places	0.4622	0.4	0	0.79	0.32
Allow the sharing of all natural resources between Palestinians and Israelis	0.4453	0.37	0	0.68	0.45
Comply with all applicable UN Resolutions	0.7683	0.76	0	0.9	0.87
Evacuate settlement of Jewish settlers on land claimed by the Palestinians with or without compensation	0.8466	0.91	0	0.96	0.84
Release all political prisoners including those who are Israeli citizens	0.551	0.55	0	0.55	0.74
Shared Jerusalem as a religious and political center with all parties	0.6209	0.76	0	0.81	0.27
Solve the Palestinian refugee problem in a just and agreed upon manner	0.7767	0.84	0	0.82	0.84
Stop incitement by the religious and national education and religious leaders in Israel against Muslims and Arabs	0.4225	0.42	0	0.34	0.68
Accept the historical responsibility for the Palestinian refugee problem	0.6633	0.76	0	0.71	0.61

Table 5.13 Ratings of Palestinian concessions relative to Palestinian costs from Palestinian concessions

	Score	Conflict between Palestinian diaspora and the internal leadership	Giving up the claim over historic Palestine occupied in 1948 and known later as the State of Israel	Partial loss/depletion of natural resources by sharing them with Israel	Loss of military capability to defend the State of Palestine	Territorial loss as a result of unfair land swap	Accomodation and rehabilitation of Palestinian refugees not allowed to return to Israel	Restrictions on national sovereignty by accepting demilitarization and multinational monitoring	Loss of property rights	Dislocation and fragmentation of Palestinian social fabric
		.0948	.2055	.1257	.0575	.2173	.1192	.1013	.0395	.0392
Accept mutually agreed upon land swap	0.6178	0	0.86	0.87	0	1	0.96	0	0	0
Accept settlers under Palestinian sovereignty as residents	0.5866	0	0.91	0.73	0	0.89	0.96	0	0	0
Accept the temporary presence of multinational military monitoring system in Jordan Valley	0.5353	0	0.81	0.45	0	0.96	0.87	0	0	0
Accept Two-State Solution	0.5629	0	0.86	0.71	0	0.84	0.96	0	0	0
Acceptance of a Two-State solution which includes a Non-Contiguous State	0.5576	0	0.92	0.88	0	0.71	0.87	0	0	0
Acknowledge Israel's Existence as a Jewish State	0.597	0	0.92	0.66	0	0.98	0.94	0	0	0
Acknowledge Israel's Existence as an Independent State	0.5706	0	0.92	0.6	0	0.86	1	0	0	0
Agree to Compromise on the Right of Return	0.6144	0	0.92	0.94	0	0.92	0.9	0	0	0
Agreeing with Palestinian demilitarized state for a limited time period	0.5761	0	0.98	0.79	0	0.79	0.87	0	0	0
Allow all parties to have equal access to and control of religious sites and holy places	0.5082	0	0.87	0.5	0	0.87	0.65	0	0	0
Allow Israel to use Palestinian airspace	0.5919	0	0.93	0.86	0	0.93	0.76	0	0	0
Declare Against Iranian Nuclear Development	0.3649	0	0.81	0.42	0	0.27	0.73	0	0	0
Denounce & Reign in Violence	0.4545	0	0.81	0.76	0	0.48	0.74	0	0	0
Denounce Iranian pursuit of nuclear arms and support Israelis effort to remove the threat	0.3369	0	0.71	0.65	0	0.13	0.68	0	0	0
Lobby Arab States to Allow both Israelis and Palestinians to Have the Right to Return to their land of origin	0.5365	0	0.86	0.83	0	0.66	0.94	0	0	0
Make Compromise on the Status of Jerusalem	0.6608	0	1	0.98	0	0.98	1	0	0	0
Palestinians must guarantee that any agreement reached with Israel will be accepted and supported by the majority of the Palestinian people both in Gaza and the West Bank	0.383	0	0.84	0.5	0	0.35	0.6	0	0	0
Refrain and work against any anti-Israel sentiments in Palestinian schools	0.4858	0	0.85	0.76	0	0.63	0.66	0	0	0
Seek Assistance for a Legitimate Settlement of Refugees except Israel	0.5697	0	1	0.74	0	0.76	0.89	0	0	0
Sharing of Natural Resources	0.5391	0	0.76	0.74	0	0.89	0.81	0	0	0
Work Cooperatively and in active engagement w/ Israel	0	0	0	0	0	0	0	0	0	0

Table 5.14 Ratings of Palestinian concessions relative to Palestinian perceptions of Israeli benefits

	Score	Gaining ligitimacy of the Palestinian and Arab and Muslim World	Integration in the Middle East with normal relations with its neighbors and Arab World	End of claims by the Palestinians	Obtainig security by acceptance and recognition of the Palestinians and Arab and Muslim World	Sharing the Palestinians with their own natural resources	Obtaining territorial gains	Economic relations and new markets including tourism with neighboring Arab and Islamic countries	Reduction of military expenditures enabling national development	Regional cooperation against external threats	Acknowledgement of Israeli control over the Waling Wall and the Jewish Quarter in the Old City of Jerusalem
		.1111	.0658	.2556	.1080	.0215	.1184	.0999	.0239	.0333	.1626
Accept mutually agreed upon land swap	0	0	0	0	0	0	0	0	0	0	0
Accept settlements under Palestinian sovereignty as residents	0	0	0	0	0	0	0	0	0	0	0
Accept the temporary presence of multinational military monitoring system in Jordan Valley	0	0	0	0	0	0	0	0	0	0	0
Accept Two-State Solution	0.5616	0.82	0	0.92	0.84	0	0	0	0	0	0.89
Acceptance a Two-State solution which includes a Non-Contiguous State	0	0	0	0	0	0	0	0	0	0	0
Acknowledge Israel's Existence as a Jewish State	0.5866	0.94	0	0.9	0.86	0	0	0	0	0	0.98
Acknowledge Israel's Existence as an Independent State	0	0	0	0	0	0	0	0	0	0	0
Agree to Compromise to the Demand of the Right of No Return	0.6009	0.94	0	0.96	0.91	0	0	0	0	0	0.94
Agreeing with Palestinian demilitarized state for a limited time period	0	0	0	0	0	0	0	0	0	0	0
Allow all parties to have equal access to and control of religious sites and holy places	0.1463	0	0	0	0	0	0	0	0	0	0.9
Allow Israel to use Palestinian airspace	0	0	0	0	0	0	0	0	0	0	0
Declare Against Iranian Nuclear Development	0	0	0	0	0	0	0	0	0	0	0
Denounce & Reign in Violence	0	0	0	0	0	0	0	0	0	0	0
Denounce Iranian pursuit of nuclear arms and support Israelis effort to remove the threat	0	0	0	0	0	0	0	0	0	0	0
Lobby Arab States to Allow both Israelis and Palestinians to Have the Right to Return to their land of origin	0	0	0	0	0	0	0	0	0	0	0
Make Compromise on the Status of Jerusalem	0.6277	0.98	0	0.98	0.98	0	0	0	0	0	1
Palestinians must guarantee that any agreement reached with Israel will be accepted and supported by the majority of the Palestinian people both in Gaza and the West Bank	0	0	0	0	0	0	0	0	0	0	0
Refrain and work against any anti-Israel sentiments in Palestinian schools	0	0	0	0	0	0	0	0	0	0	0
Seek Assistance for a Legitimate Settlement of Refugees	0.2454	0	0	0.96	0	0	0	0	0	0	0
Sharing of Natural Resources	0	0	0	0	0	0	0	0	0	0	0
Work Cooperatively and in active engagement w/ Israel	0	0	0	0	0	0	0	0	0	0	0

Table 5.15 Israelis' costs and Palestinians' gains

	Israelis					
Concessions	Israelis' Costs (Table 4.8) (2)	Israelis' Perception of Palestinians' Benefits (Table 4.9) (3)	Israelis' Total Loss (2)x(3)x1000	Palestinians' Benefits (Table 4.10) (4)	Palestinians' Perception of Israelis Costs (Table 4.11) (5)	Palestinians' Total Gain (4)x(5)x1000
1	1	1	1000.00	0.8830	0.9683	855.03
2	0.6445	0.7637	492.18	0.9894	0.9717	961.31
3	0.9051	0.2705	244.88	0.9574	0.7835	750.15
4	0.9470	0.8253	781.53	0.8830	0.9515	840.11
5	0.1961	0.5405	106.01	0.7979	0.7583	605.05
6	0.8824	0.4280	377.70	0.5426	0.7410	402.01
7	0.1984	0.5149	102.15	0.9787	0.9054	886.12
8	0.8299	0.8068	669.54	1	0.9692	969.17
9	0.0545	0.8205	44.75	0.9787	0.9080	888.67
10	0.1006	0.5323	53.55	0.8085	0.5459	441.41
11	0.1120	0.2853	31.96	0.6702	0.5260	352.52
12	0.8596	0.9571	822.76	0.9787	0.9075	888.20
13	0.3593	0.8915	320.31	0.9255	1	925.53
14	0.5178	0.4781	247.56	0.7553	0.6508	491.59
15	0.1633	0.6027	98.42	0.8511	0.7334	624.17
16	0.1806	0.7329	132.34	0.8830	0.9174	810.08
17	0.0741	0.1110	8.23	0.4149	0.4991	207.05

concession #6 (Acknowledge Israel's existence as a Jewish State). We denote this trade-off by (I9, P6). From the Israeli's perspective, the gain/loss ratio is given by

$$\frac{\text{Total Israeli Gain from Palestinian concession\#6}}{\text{Total Israeli Cost from Israeli concession\#9}} = \frac{874.13}{44.75} = 19.534 > 1.$$

The numerator can be found in the seventh column of Table 5.16 in the row corresponding to concession #6, and the denominator is in located in the seventh column of Table 5.15 in the row corresponding to concession #9.

From the Palestinian's perspective, the gain/loss ratio is given by

$$\frac{\text{Total Palestinian Gain from Israeli concession\#9}}{\text{Total Palestinian Cost from Palestinian concession\#6}} = \frac{888.67}{844.30} = 1.057 > 1$$

Thus, both concessions could be tradeable, but the Israelis' gain/loss ratio is so much larger than the Palestinians' ratio that this trade-off will probably never take place.

Table 5.16 Palestinians' costs and Israelis' gains

	Palestinians					
Concessions	Palestinians' Costs (Table 4.12) (2)	Palestinians' Perception of Israelis' Benefits (Table 4.13) (3)	Palestinians' Total Loss (2)x(3)x1000	Israelis' Benefits (Table 4.6) (4)	Israelis' Perception of Palestinians Costs (Table 4.7) (5)	Israelis' Total Gain (4)x(5)x1000
1	**0.9349**	**0.2000**	186.99	**0.9233**	**0.6353**	586.55
2	**0.8877**	**0.2000**	177.54	**0.2333**	**0.4743**	110.66
3	**0.8101**	**0.2000**	162.02	**0.7033**	**0.1106**	77.80
4	**0.8518**	**0.8947**	762.14	**0.9944**	**0.1660**	165.08
5	**0.8438**	**0.2000**	168.77	**0.7543**	**0.3011**	227.15
6	**0.9035**	**0.9345**	844.30	**0.8741**	**1**	874.13
7	**0.8635**	**0.2000**	172.70	**0.8055**	**0.6196**	499.09
8	**0.9298**	**0.9573**	890.08	**1**	**0.8557**	855.72
9	**0.8718**	**0.2000**	174.36	**0.5968**	**0.1353**	80.74
10	**0.7691**	**0.2331**	179.25	**0.7031**	**0.3355**	235.85
11	**0.8957**	**0.2000**	179.15	**0.6592**	**0.1096**	72.28
12	**0.5522**	**0.2000**	110.44	**0.3968**	**0.0348**	13.81
13	**0.6878**	**0.2000**	137.56	**0.6153**	**0.1119**	68.87
14	**0.5098**	**0.2000**	101.97	**0.4967**	**0.0443**	22.00
15	**0.8119**	**0.2000**	162.38	**0.2009**	**0.3663**	73.61
16	**1**	**1**	1000.00	**0.9251**	**0.6221**	575.49
17	**0.5796**	**0.2000**	115.92	**0.8541**	**0.5253**	448.69
18	**0.7352**	**0.2000**	147.03	**0.7583**	**0.1871**	141.88
19	**0.8621**	**0.3910**	337.05	**0.9572**	**0.8724**	835.03
20	**0.8158**	**0.2000**	163.17	**0.4069**	**0.0544**	22.14
21	**0.2**	**0.2000**	40.00	**0.7613**	**0.1858**	141.44

There are trade-offs that are feasible to one party but not the other. For example, the trade-off (I6, P6) has a gain/loss ratio of $\frac{874.13}{377.70} = 2.314$ for the Israelis, but a gain/loss ratio $\frac{402.01}{844.30} = 0.476$ for the Palestinians, and hence, it is not an acceptable trade-off to be considered. When a trade-off has a gain/loss ratio that is less than one we enter it in the table of gain/loss ratios as a zero.

Tables 5.17 and 5.18 give the possible trade-offs for the Israelis and the Palestinians, respectively.

In the next chapter, we summarize what was learned up to this point in the project. The idea is to give the reader a view of what was in our minds as we thought what needed to be done to develop an agreement.

Table 5.17 Israelis' gain/loss ratios

Israelis' Ratios	Accept mutually agreed upon land swap	Accept settlements under Palestinian sovereignty as residents	Accept the temporary presence of Israelis military in Jordan Valley	Accept Two-State Solution	Acceptance a Two-State solution which includes a Non-Contiguous State	Acknowledge Israel's Existence as a Jewish State	Acknowledge Israel's Existence as an Independent State	Agree to Compromise to the Demand of the Right of No Return	Agreeing with Palestinian demilitarized state	Allow all parties to have equal access to and control of religious sites and holy places	Allow Israel to use Palestinian airspace	Declare Against Iranian Nuclear Development	Denounce & Reign in Violence	Denounce Iranian pursuit of nuclear arms and support Israelis effort to remove the	Lobby Arab States to Allow both Israelis and Palestinians to Have the Right to Return to their land of origin	Make Compromise on the Status of Jerusalem	Palestinians must guarantee that any agreement reached with Israel will be accepted and supported by the majority of the Palestinian people both in Gaza and the West Bank	Refrain and work against any anti-Israel sentiments in Palestinian schools	Seek Assistance for a Legitimate Settlement of Refugees	Sharing of Natural Resources	Work Cooperatively and in active engagement w/ Israel
Abandon the Idea of Jewish State	0.000	0.000	0.000	0.000	0.000	0.000	0.000	0.000	0.000	0.000	0.000	0.000	0.000	0.000	0.000	0.000	0.000	0.000	0.000	0.000	0.000
Accept Palestinian full control of the borders of the Palestinian State and its outlets	1.192	0.000	0.000	0.000	0.000	1.776	1.014	1.739	0.000	0.000	0.000	0.000	0.000	0.000	0.000	1.169	0.000	0.000	1.697	0.000	0.000
Accept the historical responsibility for the Palestinian refugee problem	2.395	0.000	0.000	0.000	0.000	3.570	2.038	3.494	0.000	0.000	0.000	0.000	0.000	0.000	0.000	2.350	1.832	0.000	3.410	0.000	0.000
Accept the Palestinian refugee rights to return	0.000	0.000	0.000	0.000	0.000	1.118	0.000	1.095	0.000	0.000	0.000	0.000	0.000	0.000	0.000	0.000	0.000	0.000	1.068	0.000	0.000
Accept to abide by the status quo in the holy places in Jerusalem	5.533	1.044	0.000	1.557	2.143	8.246	4.708	8.072	0.000	2.225	0.000	0.000	0.000	0.000	0.000	5.429	4.233	1.338	7.877	0.000	1.334
Accept to abolish law of return	1.553	0.000	0.000	0.000	0.000	2.314	1.321	2.266	0.000	0.000	0.000	0.000	0.000	0.000	0.000	1.524	1.188	0.000	2.211	0.000	0.000
Accept to respect the integrity of the West Bank and Gaza by allowing free and safe passage between the two areas.	5.742	1.083	0.000	1.616	2.224	8.557	4.886	8.377	0.000	2.309	0.000	0.000	0.000	0.000	0.000	5.634	4.392	1.389	8.175	0.000	1.385
Accept to withdraw from East Jerusalem	0.000	0.000	0.000	0.000	0.000	1.306	0.000	1.278	0.000	0.000	0.000	0.000	0.000	0.000	0.000	0.000	0.000	0.000	1.247	0.000	0.000
Accept Two-State Solution on the borders of the 4th of June 1967	13.108	2.473	1.738	3.689	5.076	19.534	11.153	19.123	1.804	5.270	1.615	0.000	1.539	0.000	1.645	12.860	10.027	3.170	18.660	0.000	3.161
Allow all parties to have equal access to and control of religious sites and holy places	10.953	2.066	1.453	3.083	4.242	16.323	9.320	15.980	1.508	4.404	1.350	0.000	1.286	0.000	1.375	10.747	8.379	2.649	15.593	0.000	2.641
Allow the sharing of all natural resources between Palestinians and Israelis	18.354	3.463	2.434	5.166	7.108	27.352	15.617	26.776	2.526	7.380	2.262	0.000	2.155	0.000	2.303	18.008	14.040	4.439	26.129	0.000	4.426
Comply with all applicable UN Resolutions	0.000	0.000	0.000	0.000	0.000	1.062	0.000	1.040	0.000	0.000	0.000	0.000	0.000	0.000	0.000	0.000	0.000	0.000	1.015	0.000	0.000
Evacuate settlement of Jewish settlers on land claimed by the Palestinians with or without compensation	1.831	0.000	0.000	0.000	0.000	2.729	1.558	2.672	0.000	0.000	0.000	0.000	0.000	0.000	0.000	1.797	1.401	0.000	2.607	0.000	0.000
Release all political prisoners including those who are Israeli citizens	2.369	0.000	0.000	0.000	0.000	3.531	2.016	3.457	0.000	0.000	0.000	0.000	0.000	0.000	0.000	2.325	1.812	0.000	3.373	0.000	0.000
Shared Jerusalem as a religious and political center with all parties	5.959	1.124	0.000	1.677	2.308	8.881	5.071	8.694	0.000	2.396	0.000	0.000	0.000	0.000	0.000	5.847	4.559	1.441	8.484	0.000	1.437
Solve the Palestinian refugee problem in a just and agreed upon manner	4.432	0.000	0.000	1.247	1.716	6.605	3.771	6.466	0.000	1.782	0.000	0.000	0.000	0.000	0.000	4.349	3.390	1.072	6.310	0.000	1.069
Stop incitement by the religious and national education and religious leaders in Israel against Muslims and Arabs	71.312	13.453	9.458	20.070	27.616	######	60.678	######	9.816	28.674	8.787	1.679	8.374	2.674	8.949	69.967	54.551	17.249	101.521	2.692	17.196

Table 5.18 Palestinians' gain/loss ratios

Palestinians' Ratios	Accept mutually agreed upon land swap	Accept settlements under Palestinian sovereignty as residents	Accept the temporary presence of Israelis military in Jordan Valley	Accept Two-State Solution	Acceptance a Two-State solution which includes a Non-Contiguous State	Acknowledge Israel's Existence as a Jewish State	Acknowledge Israel's Existence as an Independent State	Agree to Compromise to the Demand of the Right of No Return	Agreeing with Palestinian demilitarized state	Allow all parties to have equal access to and control of religious sites and holy places	Allow Israel to use Palestinian airspace	Declare Against Iranian Nuclear Development	Denounce & Reign in Violence	Denounce Iranian pursuit of nuclear arms and support Israelis effort to remove the threat	Lobby Arab States to Allow both Israelis and Palestinians to Have the Right to Return to their land of origin	Make Compromise on the Status of Jerusalem	Palestinians must guarantee that any agreement reached with Israel will be accepted and supported by the majority of the Palestinian people both in Gaza and the West Bank	Refrain and work against any anti Israel sentiments in Palestinian schools	Seek Assistance for a Legitimate Settlement of Refugees	Sharing of Natural Resources	Work Cooperatively and in active engagement w/ Israel
Abandon the Idea of Jewish State	4.573	4.816	5.277	1.122	5.066	1.013	4.951	0.000	4.904	4.770	4.773	7.742	6.216	8.385	5.266	0.000	7.376	5.815	2.537	5.240	21.376
Accept Palestinian full control of the borders of the Palestinian State and its outlets	5.141	5.415	5.933	1.261	5.696	1.139	5.566	1.080	5.513	5.363	5.366	8.704	6.988	9.428	5.920	0.000	8.293	6.538	2.852	5.892	24.033
Accept the historical responsibility for the Palestinian refugee problem	4.012	4.225	4.630	0.000	4.445	0.000	4.344	0.000	4.302	4.185	4.187	6.792	5.453	7.357	4.620	0.000	6.471	5.102	2.226	4.597	18.754
Accept the Palestinian refugee rights to return	4.493	4.732	5.185	1.102	4.978	0.000	4.865	0.000	4.818	4.687	4.690	7.607	6.107	8.239	5.174	0.000	7.247	5.714	2.493	5.149	21.003
Accept to abide by the status quo in the holy places in Jerusalem	3.236	3.408	3.735	0.000	3.585	0.000	3.503	0.000	3.470	3.375	3.377	5.478	4.398	5.934	3.726	0.000	5.220	4.115	1.795	3.708	15.126
Accept to abolish law of return	2.150	2.264	2.481	0.000	2.382	0.000	2.328	0.000	2.306	2.243	2.244	3.640	2.922	3.943	2.476	0.000	3.468	2.734	1.193	2.464	10.050
Accept to respect the integrity of the West Bank and Gaza by allowing free and safe passage between the two areas.	4.739	4.991	5.469	1.163	5.251	1.050	5.131	0.000	5.082	4.944	4.946	8.023	6.442	8.690	5.457	0.000	7.644	6.027	2.629	5.431	22.153
Accept to withdraw from East Jerusalem	5.183	5.459	5.982	1.272	5.743	1.148	5.612	1.089	5.558	5.407	5.410	8.775	7.045	9.505	5.969	0.000	8.361	6.591	2.875	5.940	24.229
Accept Two-State Solution on the borders of the 4th of June 1967	4.753	5.005	5.485	1.166	5.266	1.053	5.146	0.000	5.097	4.958	4.961	8.046	6.460	8.715	5.473	0.000	7.666	6.044	2.637	5.446	22.217
Allow all parties to have equal access to and control of religious sites and holy places	2.361	2.486	2.724	0.000	2.615	0.000	2.556	0.000	2.532	2.463	2.464	3.997	3.209	4.329	2.718	0.000	3.808	3.002	1.310	2.705	11.035
Allow the sharing of all natural resources between Palestinians and Israelis	1.885	1.986	2.176	0.000	2.089	0.000	2.041	0.000	2.022	1.967	1.968	3.192	2.563	3.457	2.171	0.000	3.041	2.398	1.046	2.161	8.813
Comply with all applicable UN Resolutions	4.750	5.003	5.482	1.165	5.263	1.052	5.143	0.000	5.094	4.955	4.958	8.042	6.457	8.711	5.470	0.000	7.662	6.041	2.635	5.444	22.205
Evacuate settlement of Jewish settlers on land claimed by the Palestinians with or without compensation	4.950	5.213	5.713	1.214	5.484	1.096	5.359	1.040	5.308	5.163	5.166	8.380	6.728	9.077	5.700	0.000	7.984	6.295	2.746	5.672	23.138
Release all political prisoners including those who are Israeli citizens	2.629	2.769	3.034	0.000	2.913	0.000	2.847	0.000	2.819	2.743	2.744	4.451	3.574	4.821	3.027	0.000	4.241	3.343	1.458	3.013	12.290
Shared Jerusalem as a religious and political center with all parties	3.338	3.516	3.853	0.000	3.698	0.000	3.614	0.000	3.580	3.482	3.484	5.652	4.537	6.121	3.844	0.000	5.385	4.245	1.852	3.825	15.604
Solve the Palestinian refugee problem in a just and agreed upon manner	4.332	4.563	5.000	1.063	4.800	0.000	4.691	0.000	4.646	4.519	4.522	7.335	5.889	7.944	4.989	0.000	6.988	5.509	2.403	4.965	20.252
Stop incitement by the religious and national education and religious leaders in Israel against Muslims and Arabs	1.107	1.166	1.278	0.000	1.227	0.000	1.199	0.000	1.187	1.155	1.156	1.875	1.505	2.031	1.275	0.000	1.786	1.408	0.000	1.269	5.176

References

ISAHP. (2020). *International symposium on the analytic hierarchy process*. https://isahp.org/. Accessed June 4, 2021.

Saaty, T. L., & Zoffer, H. J. (2012). A new approach to the Middle East conflict: The analytic hierarchy process. *Journal of Multi-Criteria Decision Analysis, 19*(5–6), 201–225.

Saaty, T. L., & Zoffer, H. J. (2013). Principles for implementing a potential solution to the Middle East conflict. *Notices of the American Mathematical Society, 60*(10), 1300–1322.

Chapter 6
Lessons Learned: The AHP Can Help Achieve Peace

Introduction

In this book, we present an alternative process to address the Israeli–Palestinian conflict. It does so in two ways that are different from past efforts. The first is by formally structuring the conflict, and the second is the way discussions are conducted and conclusions drawn.

The approach will help create a solution to the conflict and provide negotiators with a unique pathway to consider the thorny issues and corresponding concessions underlying the deliberations, together with their implementation. Among the prior contentious issues addressed by this process and encouraged by governments and major participants in the conflicts were the difficult confrontations in South Africa and in Northern Ireland. The outcomes of this process added valuable dimension to the discussions and resolutions of those problems.

The Middle East conflict is a prolonged and interminable struggle between parties deeply committed to unyielding positions related to identity, religion, and territory. Understanding the Israeli–Palestinian conflict necessitates the understanding and recognition that both parties believe there is a theological bond between their people and the land. In addition, all three major religions recognize Jerusalem as symbolic of their belief in a one-god idea.

The severity of this conflict has intensified in our lifetime because international events have catapulted the Middle East into a crucial position in the world's search for peace. Claims are made by these peoples of their right to have a state that ensures their group identity. The problem is greatly compounded by great power rivalries, weapon sales, interference by neighboring countries, economic and social discrepancies, and the threat of nuclear retaliation. Although it is possible that the global framework might accelerate a solution, in fact, it complicates the solution due to the

Some excerpts of the paper (Saaty & Zoffer, 2011) have been used with permission from World Scientific Publishing Company.

T. L. Saaty et al., *Overcoming the Retributive Nature of the Israeli-Palestinian Conflict*, https://doi.org/10.1007/978-3-030-83958-1_6

apparent insolvability of the issues. Hence, a solution continues to elude the global community.

Some of the world's best negotiators, diplomats, and able leaders have grappled with the resolution of this conflict. However, despite their best efforts, the current condition continues to torment all the parties. Since the inception of the analytic hierarchy process (AHP) and its generalization to dependence and feedback, the analytic network process (ANP), authors have conducted numerous case studies (Saaty, 1989; Saaty & Vargas, 2013; Vargas, 1983; Zoffer et al., 2008) that suggest the method as an alternative approach to conflict resolution that will lay bare the structure of the problem and allow reasoned judgment to prevail.

Retributive Conflicts

Nonetheless, when one deals with conflict, especially conflict of a prolonged duration, reason rarely prevails. In fact, with respect to the conflict between the Palestinians and the Israelis, positions have become entrenched, and each party seeks not only to satisfy its own needs but also does not mind increasing the costs of concessions made by the other party. This type of conflict is defined as retributive (Saaty, 2010) because of its prolonged negative emotional content. Retributive responses differ from the usual cooperative conflicts in which the parties work for a win-win outcome, by their partly malevolent intentions, whereby the parties do not care about the losses of the other side.

In most long-lasting conflicts, each party's grievances increase while the concessions they are willing to make decline in number, quality, and perceived value. Both parties lose sight of what they are willing to settle for, generally exaggerate their own needs, and minimize the needs of the other side over time. The concessions worth trading versus the concessions the other party is willing to trade become more indefinite and less concise. Thus, it is precisely the matter of trading that needs to be made more concrete and of higher priority for both sides if a meaningful resolution is to be found.

Without a formal way of trading off the concessions and packages of concessions, both sides are likely to suspect that they are getting the short end of the bargain. After the parties have agreed to a trade, very specific binding language about the terms of the agreement, clear implementation policies, and outside guarantors are needed. The worth of the concessions traded, as perceived by both the giver and receiver, needs to be accurately determined and recorded. All of this requires going beyond verbal descriptions of the concessions to include more broadly their economic, social, geographic, humanitarian, and historical worth. It is critical that all this needs to be translated into priorities derived in terms of the different values and beliefs of the parties. Priorities are universal and include the diversity of measures in terms of which economic, social, and other values are measured. The AHP provides a way to perform such an assessment with the participation of negotiators for the parties. It is a positive approach that makes it possible to reason and express feelings and judgments with numerical intensities to derive priorities.

With the assistance of the panel of Israeli participants and Palestinian participants, AHP has now been applied for the first time with the input of representatives of both sides who were knowledgeable and informed about the issues associated with the Israeli–Palestinian conflict. They obviously did not represent the full spectrum of political ideas and notions. The process makes it clear that moderation in different degrees by both sides is essential to arrive at acceptable agreements on concessions proposed and agreed upon by both sides. The results obtained encourage us to advocate its use in this negotiation process.

We need to begin by emphasizing that the outcome of our effort is the beginning of an elaborate undertaking to produce a viable solution to the Israeli–Palestinian conflict. It is simply a novel framework for dialogue. A differentiation from other approaches is its potential to minimize the influence on the outcome of much of the intense emotions that have usually accompanied such discussions. The framework forces the negotiators to approach the issues using a quantitatively oriented set of judgments to compare and trade off various issues, benefits, costs, and concessions in a way in which each individual item is separated from the influences of other passionately charged items. We acknowledge that in an emotionally charged conflict such as this, there will inevitably remain a residual emotionality and feelings that cannot be ignored and inevitably affect the judgments. This does not affect the viability of the process, because the numerical representation of the judgments allows for such variability up to a limit that can be measured. It essentially allows one to decompose the problem into smaller components that can be dealt with more easily. While judgments may vary according to the perceived power of the parties, the essential nature of the process is not compromised, unless participants are influenced to change their judgments.

Our objective has been to see if the AHP, a new approach to group decision making, could be used productively to move forward the 60-year-old debate about solving the perplexing Middle East problem. It was not our intention to use the process to discover a specific solution to the Israeli–Palestinian conflict. The AHP provided us with a new way to pursue the dialogue in a context which uses a quantitatively oriented approach to attach numerical priorities to the issues in what has been an emotionally charged conflict. Our purpose has been to introduce a process which, were it to be used by the actual negotiators, might offer some new ways of moving forward on the heretofore intractable positions adopted by the parties.

The Contribution of the AHP

One may ask how can a process like this add meaning to the plethora of proposed solutions that have either fallen on deaf ears over 60 years or been destroyed because of the impossibility of implementation? It is important to state the idea that the AHP is a supplement and not a replacement for face-to-face negotiations. Whenever the process has broken down in the past, there has been no next step to take. A number of entities have stepped forward to try to jump-start the stalled negotiation. The USA has been the foremost player in this remediation effort. They have tried to determine what would be a fair outcome, but to date there has been no real way to measure which initiative would constitute a fair and equitable package, because the issues are so varied, complex, interrelated, and affected by extreme emotions.

AHP provides an alternative approach by helping the parties to either think outside the box by themselves or engage in exercises which force this creative behavior. In its simplest terms, AHP would require the actual negotiator to make judgments in a novel way. The outcome of their judgments could provide an outsider like the USA with some confidence that an AHP type solution would yield an outcome that is as fair to each side as is possible with current technology. A third party could then encourage the parties to consider such a solution with increased confidence that the approach allows, for example, the USA to act in a neutral position with some confidence that as fair a solution as possible is being promoted.

It is important to note that the participants in our meetings were knowledgeable, informed, thoughtful Israelis and Palestinians, who might be able to recommend to actual negotiators ideas and ways to solve this long-simmering problem. They were engaged in a simulation—a process to find out if these participants had been, indeed, the actual negotiators, would they have been able to stay with the negotiations and to reach some productive outcome. Whether these participants were representative of their respective constituencies is irrelevant, since the results of their deliberations were never expected to produce a solution to the problem, but merely to test an approach. The outcomes of the deliberations suggested a number of important benefits if the approach were used by real-life negotiators.

We have attempted to find out how the process would work: would it provide a modicum of an objective basis to trade off the concessions and help to drain the emotions, so far as was possible, out of discussions of contentious issues? It was done by rating the issues to prioritize them and then rate the concessions with respect to each issue. We established priorities by assigning quantitative values, which would encourage negotiators to deal with the importance of one issue as compared with another issue. By identifying concessions that each party could potentially make and rating them as to how they addressed each of the identified issues, we reached an outcome whereby certain actions could be seen to be more productive than others. This is achieved either by bundling concessions on one side to address issues raised by the other side or identifying issues that cannot be traded off by amassing concessions from one party, mainly because some of the issues are so fundamental to the negotiations that no number of concessions could balance their importance. While some of these conclusions may be apparent to the concerned observer, the process provides affirmation of the conclusions.

While the casual observer might suggest critically that the conclusions and outcomes of the study were totally dependent on what the positions of the participants on the negotiating team were, we believe that this is indeed an accurate conclusion, but does not in any way invalidate the study. The outcomes depend on the judgments made, and the judgments depend on the opinions of the negotiators. It is self-evident that who does the negotiating will directly affect the outcome. We are less concerned with coming to any solution than we are with demonstrating how the AHP represents an approach that captures reality without the burden of excessive emotion. Ultimately, solutions that emerge from the process will depend on the positions and attitudes of the negotiators. To the extent that the negotiators represent positions which encompass varying proportions of the constituencies they represent, the solution will either be arrived at within a reasonable time, or after extended lengthy discussions, possibly never arriving at a solution. Our recommendations noted below include our response to this phenomenon.

It is important to understand that the process has two major components, the first being the identification of issues, concessions, benefits, and costs to each side and a second which concerns implementation policies. We believe there were eight important conclusions that we could draw.

They are as follows:

1. The exercise validated that our process made it possible to consider the potential concessions each side might make and to consider the trade-offs of such concessions, either individually or in bundles. The participants learned how to trade off such concessions to serve the interests of both parties. They identified 38 concessions, 21 from one side and 17 from the other. We do not have any reason to believe that this included every possible concession that might be made. Since the AHP process requires that everything possible be considered for inclusion in the structure: the issues and their concessions, with benefits and costs, it is recommended that every effort be made to include the full range of issues and concessions. In our exercise, we may well have overlooked one or more of these issues and concessions and thus our structure may be incomplete. That in no way diminishes its effectiveness. However, before beginning to work with combinations of concessions to trade them off, the structure can be trimmed down to include only what are now known to be the major elements.
2. The outcome in many cases reinforced the conventional wisdom of the participants as to what the concrete objectives of each side are and what positions either side is willing to modify with concessions from the other side or is not willing to modify regardless of the other side's concessions. But it was now possible to measure the gains and losses related to various concessions as identified by the party that would be providing the concessions, as well as their judgment as to what the benefits and costs were to the other party in providing their concessions. Obviously, the opinion of one side about the costs and benefits to the other side of specific concessions sometimes varied widely from the other side's opinion as to the costs and benefits to them of the concessions they might possibly make. These differences in perception are revealing, and they often led to differences in gain-to-loss ratios as perceived by each party.
3. The AHP process made it possible for the participants to consider a wide variety of potential trade-offs, either individually or in bundles. By attaching quantitative values to the comparisons, a great deal of the emotionality of the discussion was

defused. It became clear that, at least in the case of these specific participants, certain issues appeared not to be tradable or that the participants did not know how to trade them. For example, the Israeli need to have a Jewish State and the Palestinian need to have a satisfactory solution to the resettlement of refugees appeared to be issues which could not be easily compromised, if at all. One might surmise that solutions to such issues might require the involvement of outside parties and that solutions not totally acceptable to either side might have to be imposed. By comparing costs and benefits of concessions as viewed by either party and establishing hierarchies which permitted comparisons of the issues and concessions, some equivalence of pain or cost and of benefit, either by individual comparisons or in bundles, might suggest a reasonably objective statement of what a "fair" or equally painful or equally beneficial outcome might be. Neither side might feel such a solution would be a "win" for them, an objective each side would prefer to achieve. They might be convinced, perhaps only by outside parties, that a solution that would bring peace could only be achieved if each party recognized through a process such as the AHP or, otherwise, that trading off a similarly beneficial and painful (as objectively measured) set of solutions is the only way to achieve peace. A further advantage would be that outside parties, such as the USA or the European Union or the United Nations, etc., could pressure the parties to settle, using solutions carefully balanced to favor neither side and exacting compromises from both sides that these outside parties could feel reasonably comfortable that their impact was objectively measured.

4. Participants were willing to talk about sensitive issues as part of the concession discussion without feeling threatened by the other party. Though the participants occasionally engaged in heated discussions, in general, an order of civility was engendered. The participants were concerned with looking at issues at a micro-level rather than a macro-level, with comparisons of priorities, establishment of hierarchies, and weighting of judgments considered on an issue-by-issue and concession-by-concession basis. This did not necessarily change the emotionality that each side felt, but by separating the issues and the concessions, participants were encouraged to consider the relative importance of one issue and the effect upon it of one or many concessions. It is obviously an oversimplification to suggest that, by breaking the problem into small pieces and then working to measure judgments mathematically, participants were so engaged in collating relevant tasks that their emotionality largely disappeared. To continue the analogy, participants had cut the puzzle into a jigsaw of tiny pieces where the total picture was not discernible as they decided which piece fit into which another piece. But when the pieces were put back together, the puzzle might look somewhat different.

   When these lines were written, the complete puzzle from this experiment had not yet been put together for a variety of reasons, but as we shall see in the following chapters, when assembled it offers a somewhat different path for proceeding than has been the case thus far.

5. A major outcome of the process thus far is that the parties have identified 106 issues and numerous concessions as being relevant to their deliberations.

We have arbitrarily grouped these issues and concessions into major categories. The richness of the issues in each category as well as the grouping of the concessions has helped to define the issues and concessions more exactly. This approach provided a structure where participants have decomposed the problem rather than seeking immediate solutions. What the parameters of the problem were was one question addressed. What actions the parties could potentially take to address these issues was a second question answered. In each session, we spent only three days for the entire process in this effort, so we cannot suggest that every possible concession and issue was identified. But we do believe that some issues are multifaceted and what was suggested as a separate issue may turn out to be a part, large or small, of another issue. A major outcome was that by examining the issues in contention and the concessions that might address one or many of those issues, the importance of the issues and concessions in terms of gains and losses as perceived by each party was represented by mathematical judgments and quantified.

6. A crucial finding is the need to identify and develop implementation policies for all the concessions. For example, there was much discussion about a possible compromise by the Palestinians on their demand for the right of return of those Palestinians originally living in what is now part of Israel. But without an implementation policy or a set of options, if there is more than one possibility, the mere statement of offering such a concession is ineffective without finding offsetting compromises and policies that would likely be difficult to implement. The process we engaged in has generally identified the issues where implementation policies are necessary. In some of these cases, concessions cannot be provided by the actions of the party alone offering the concession. There need to be other parties involved and willing to play a part, so that the concession is truly on the table and a trade can be achieved. The question of how this concession could be achieved must be answered before the concession becomes viable. We still need to examine each concession and determine by participant involvement just what will be required and by whom to make that concession a real possibility.
7. An important outcome of this effort was to identify what the parties meant using certain terms. For example, we now know that the use of the words "human rights" which came up time and again in the discussions is not easily defined. It means one thing to the Palestinians and something else to the Israelis. How human rights are identified, displayed, defined, executed, and implemented needs to be discussed in some detail. Participants cannot make effective judgments about such terms when they are being mathematically compared with other terms, if the sides have different definitions of the terms. The limitations of time made it impossible to engage in the complex discussions that would have been required to address this matter. Another example is what is exactly meant by the "sharing of Jerusalem." It is again important to emphasize that this problem in no way interfered with the basic question we posed, which was how the Israeli–Palestinian question could be fitted into the AHP structure and would the process be amenable to using the AHP approach. We did not expect a solution to emerge,

but as the process is further employed and the next stage of discussions occurs and perhaps later as the participants in the study are actual negotiators, the outcomes will perhaps yield some promising avenues for negotiation not yet in play.
8. The experiments we conducted convinced us that a reasonably timed conclusion to the conflict would be substantially enhanced if the negotiators represented the viewpoint of some predetermined proportion of their respective constituencies. Recognizing that a suggestion of some non-inclusiveness in the discussion in the interest of expediency is not only controversial but likely to elicit all sorts of opprobrium, there is one other way to achieve the same result. It is complex and may produce similar outcries, but at least it is an alternative. If we could determine, by survey or otherwise, what the proportion in each society was of far right, far left, and center positions, we could use the AHP process (which would weight the judgments based on the proportion of that society the negotiator represented) so that intractable positions are minimized, understanding that someone would need to deal with the anger from those whose judgments were considered less crucial to a solution because they represented a smaller proportion of their respective populations.

A major stumbling block in the negotiations attempted to date results from the determined effort to address all the issues in a single format, in one place, in a comprehensive manner. Results of our experiment suggest that it would be far more feasible to address a few of the issues and concessions at a time.

During these discussions, the Palestinian representatives indicated that they felt strong anger because of their perception that Israel has not taken more responsibility in helping to solve the Palestinian refugee problem. The Israeli representatives, on the other hand, expressed their sense of anger because the Palestinians failed to participate in helping the Israelis to obtain the level of security which is essential to move the process forward from the Israeli position.

In sum, these meetings yielded positive but preliminary results that are clearly inconclusive and incomplete. Nothing that has occurred invalidates the efficacy of the AHP as a novel and comprehensive approach to solve this problem. It needs to be carried to its conclusion including addressing the definition and implementation concerns, using actual negotiators to release the power of the process.

While the foregoing general outcomes represent important progress, the capacity of this process to yield useful conclusions that would move the dialogue forward depends on using the results to identify specific steps that could constitute a new start to the discussions. We also need to examine what remains to be done. Clearly, the approach taken seems to work well to address the problem. But as the effort continued it became clearer as to what needs to be done in the next round of discussions.

We need to identify those terms where definitions are crucial and work out agreed upon statements of exactly what those words or terms meant to permit judgments and comparisons that are more accurate. We also need to identify which areas of concessions need implementation policies developed to make them viable and to examine as many options as possible in considering the implementation.

Summarizing, our participants identified more than 100 issues of small and large import, which were viewed as necessary to address if the Palestinian–Israeli conflict is to be resolved. In the few days available to them, they identified a significant number of concessions both sides could offer, if they were willing to do so, which would address most of these issues. To an extent not all issues were addressed by possible concessions; it was either because the issues were trivial and not worthy of specific concessions or time or imagination did not permit the identification of appropriate concessions to address those issues.

The panel was able to trade off all but two major issues (a secure, independent democratic Jewish State recognized by the Palestinians and a solution to the resettlement of refugees). These two issues would need to be considered in a separate application of AHP to find the difficult concessions necessary to trade off concessions that would meet our restrictions and still address those two issues directly. That process remains to be addressed.

To date the official negotiations have not produced a viable solution. Our research suggests that by organizing the concerns in a more effective way, identifying concessions that would address the issues identified, assuming both sides see an advantage in a peaceful resolution quickly, measuring both tangible and intangible factors, draining the emotions out of the discussions to the extent possible, and decomposing the issues into manageable segments, all of which is possible through the use of the analytic hierarchy process, a chance of resolution is enhanced. What have the parties got to lose?

References

Saaty, T. L. (1989). International center for conflict resolution. *Defense Analysis, 5*(1), 80–82.

Saaty, T. L. (2010). *Principia mathematica decernendi*. RWS Publications.

Saaty, T. L., & Vargas, L. G. (2013). *Economic, political, social & technological applications of the analytic network process (ANP): Benefits, opportunities, costs and risks* (2nd ed.). Springer.

Saaty, T. L., & Zoffer, H. J. (2011). Negotiating the Israeli–Palestinian controversy from a new perspective. *International Journal of Information Technology & Decision Making, 10*(1), 1–60.

Vargas, L. G. (1983). Prospects for the Middle East: is a peaceful settlement attainable? *European Journal of Operational Research, 14*(2), 169–192.

Zoffer, H. J., Bahurmoz, A., Hamid, M. H., Minutolo, M. C., Saaty, T. L., & T.L. (2008). Synthesis of complex criteria decision making: A case towards a consensus agreement for a Middle East conflict resolution. *Group Decision and Negotiation, 17*(5), 363–385.

Chapter 7
The Pittsburgh Principles: Fair and Equitable Trade-Offs

Introduction

In Chap. 4, we developed a model to identify trade-offs that could be used to build an agreement. The next step is finding out which trade-offs are feasible. We need to identify trade-offs that provide the same or almost the same (within a small percentage) gain/loss ratio for both parties. For example, the trade-off (I12, P6) yields the gain/loss ratios 1.062 in Table 5.16 and 1.052 in Table 5.17, for the Israelis and Palestinians, respectively. The values of those trade-offs are within one percent of each other. One could think that if no single sets of concessions can be mapped into trade-offs, bundles of two, three, and more concessions could be used. But in this case, the issues are complex enough to complicate life even more if bundles are created. But the possibility exists.

Using the model explained in Sect. 6 of Chap. 4, and the gain/loss ratios of Chap. 5, we solve the problem in a piecewise manner. First, we find the best matching of one of the Israelis' concessions and one of the Palestinians' concessions with the condition that both parties gain as much as possible, and the gain/loss ratios are within one percent of each other. This yielded the trade-off (I12, P6). These concessions are eliminated from the set of concessions and the problem is solved again. If no trade-offs within one percent of each other are found, we try to find trade-offs within five percent of each other. This yielded, after solving the problem sequentially, four trade-offs, (I12, P6), (I9, P5), (I7, P7), and (I16, P1). Table 7.1 has the single trade-off identified that yielded gain/loss ratios between 1 and 20 percent of each other. Figure 7.1 shows where the selected trade-off matchings (colored in yellow) fall in relation to the line that represents trade-offs with equal values. All other trade-offs are colored in blue.

T. L. Saaty et al., *Overcoming the Retributive Nature of the Israeli-Palestinian Conflict*, https://doi.org/10.1007/978-3-030-83958-1_7

Table 7.1 Israeli–Palestinian one-to-one trade-offs

#	Israeli Concessions	Trade Value	% Separation	#	Palestinian Concessions	Trade Value
12	Comply with all applicable un resolutions	1.062	1%	6	Acknowledge Israel's existence as a Jewish state	1.058
9	Accept two-state solution on the borders of the 4th of June 1967	5.076	5%	5	Acceptance of a two-state solution which includes a non-contiguous state	5.289
7	Accept to respect the integrity of the West Bank and Gaza by allowing free and safe passage between the two areas.	4.885	5%	7	Acknowledge Israel's existence as an independent state	5.159
16	Solve the Palestinian refugee problem in a just and agreed upon manner	4.432	5%	1	Accept mutually agreed upon land swap	4.359
13	Evacuate settlers of Jewish settlements on land claimed by the Palestinians with or without compensation	2.607	10%	19	Seek assistance for a legitimate settlement of refugees	2.763
11	Allow the sharing of all natural resources between Palestinians and Israelis	2.303	10%	15	Lobby Arab states to allow both Israelis and Palestinians to have the right to return to their land of origin	2.168
15	Share Jerusalem as two capitals of two states	4.559	20%	17	Palestinians must guarantee that any agreement reached with Israel will be accepted and supported by the majority of the Palestinian people both in Gaza and the West Bank	5.361
10	Allow all parties to have equal access to and control of religious sites and holy places	2.649	20%	18	Refrain and work against any anti-Israel sentiments in Palestinian schools	2.991
17	Stop incitement by the religious and national education and religious leaders in Israel against Muslims and Arabs	1.679	20%	12	Declare against Iranian nuclear development	1.868
8	Accept east Jerusalem as the capital of the Palestinian state	1.278	20%	8	Agree to compromise to the demand of the right of return	1.089
	Total	30.53			Total	32.105

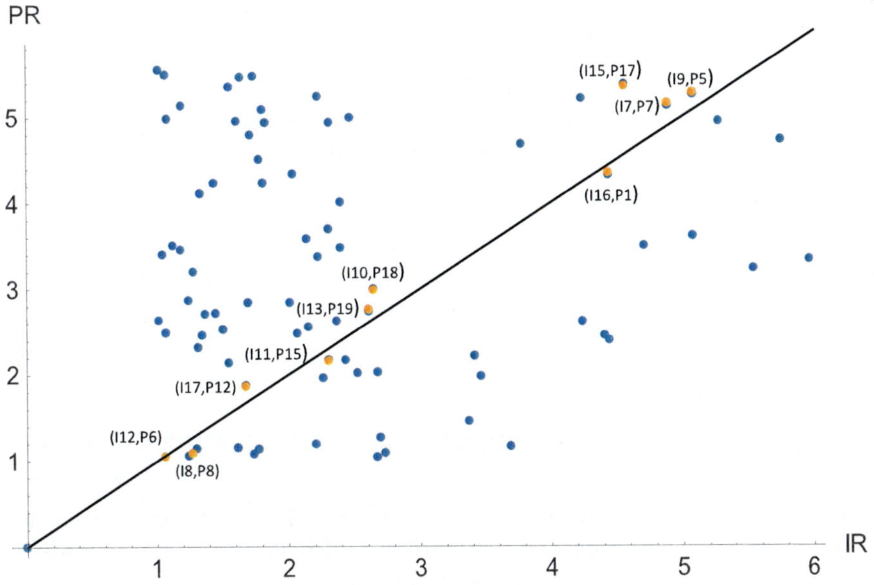

Fig. 7.1 Matching trade-offs in the balanced agreement

Pittsburgh Declaration of Principles

The writing of the Pittsburgh Declaration of Principles did not come out of the trade-offs exactly as the matchings took place. These trade-offs were guidelines used to draft the principles. For example, I9 ("A two-state solution on the borders of the 4th of June 1967, with mutually agreed upon land swaps"), P1 ("Accept mutually agreed land swap"), and P5 ("Acceptance of a two-state solution which includes a non-contiguous state") yielded Principle 1:

1. **A two-state solution on the borders of the fourth of June 1967, with mutually agreed upon land swaps.**

I7 ("Accept to respect the integrity of the West Bank and Gaza by allowing free and safe passage between the two areas") and P17 ("Palestinians must guarantee that any agreement reached with Israel will be accepted and supported by the majority of the Palestinian people both in Gaza and the West Bank") were joined to form Principle 2:

2. **Israel must respect the integrity of the West Bank and Gaza by allowing free and safe passage between the two areas, and the Palestinian State must guarantee that any agreement reached with Israel will be accepted and supported by the majority of the Palestinian people both in Gaza and the West Bank.**

I8 ("Accept East Jerusalem as the capital of the Palestinian State"), I15 ("Share Jerusalem as two capitals of two states"), and P10 ("Preserve the status quo in the Holy places of Jerusalem") yield Principle 3:

3. **East Jerusalem is the capital of the Palestinian State. The parties will maintain the status quo of the Holy places in Jerusalem.**

P6 ("Acknowledge Israel's existence as a Jewish State") was the basis for Principle 4:

4. **Acknowledge Israel's existence as a Jewish State, without jeopardizing the rights of its minority Israeli citizens.**

I13 ("Evacuate settlers of Jewish settlements on land claimed by the Palestinians with or without compensation") produced Principle 5:

5. **Evacuation of Israeli settlers from the Palestinian territories that are not included in the land swap.**

I2 ("Accept Palestinian full control of the borders of the Palestinian State and its outlets") and P3 ("Accept the temporary presence of multinational military monitoring system in Jordan valley") yielded Principle 6:

6. **Palestinian full control of the borders of the Palestinian State and its outlets, and deployment of a temporary agreed upon multinational military monitoring system in the Jordan Valley.**

I16 ("Solve the Palestinian refugee problem in a just and agreed upon manner") and P19 ("Seek assistance for a legitimate settlement of refugees") produced Principle 7:

7. **Solve the Palestinian refugee problem in a just and agreed upon manner.**

P9 ("Agreeing with Palestinian demilitarized state") inspired Principle 8:

8. **Limited arms of the Palestinian State and international guarantees from the international community against aggression from other parties.**

The next two principles are standard language in international accords:

9. **Agreed upon international monitoring mechanism and agreed upon binding international arbitration mechanisms.**
10. **The full implementation of these principles concludes end of the conflict and claims of the two parties.**

Note that the principles were not developed from the paired concessions. All concessions were considered to articulate meaningful principles. For example, Principle 6 was based on I2 and P3 which did not appear as paired in Table 7.1.

To help visualize how the matchings took place we have color coded in Fig. 7.2 the concessions that were used to formulate each of the principles. The principle to which they contributed are given in Roman numerals to the right of the concession.

Israelis' Concessions	Description	
1	Abandon the idea of Jewish state	
2	Accept Palestinian full control of the borders of the Palestinian state and its outlets	VI
3	Accept the historical responsibility for the Palestinian refugee problem	
4	Accept the Palestinian refugee rights to return	
5	Accept to abide by the status quo in the holy places in Jerusalem	
6	Accept to abolish law of return	
7	Accept to respect the integrity of the West Bank and Gaza by allowing free and safe passage between the two areas.	II
8	Accept East Jerusalem as the capital of the Palestinian state	III
9	Accept two-state solution on the borders of the 4th of June 1967	I
10	Allow all parties to have equal access to and control of religious sites and holy places	
11	Allow the sharing of all natural resources between Palestinians and Israelis	
12	Comply with all applicable un resolutions	
13	Evacuate settlers of Jewish settlements on land claimed by the Palestinians with or without compensation	V
14	Release all political prisoners including those who are Israeli citizens	
15	Share Jerusalem as two capitals of two states	III
16	Solve the Palestinian refugee problem in a just and agreed upon manner	VII
17	Stop incitement by the religious and national education and religious leaders in Israel against Muslims and Arabs	

Palestinians' Concessions	Description	
1	Accept mutually agreed upon land swap	I
2	Accept settlers under Palestinian sovereignty as residents	
3	Accept the temporary presence of multinational military monitoring system in Jordan valley	VI
4	Accept two-state solution	
5	Acceptance of a two-state solution which includes a non-contiguous state	I
6	Acknowledge Israel's existence as a Jewish state	IV
7	Acknowledge Israel's existence as an independent state	
8	Agree to compromise to the demand of the right of return	
9	Agreeing with Palestinian demilitarized state	VIII
10	Preserve the status quo in the Holy places of Jerusalem	III
11	Allow Israel to use Palestinian airspace	
12	Declare against Iranian nuclear development	
13	Denounce & reign in violence	
14	Denounce Iranian pursuit of nuclear arms and support Israeli effort to remove the threat	
15	Lobby Arab states to allow both Israelis and Palestinians to have the right to return to their land of origin	
16	Make compromise on the status of Jerusalem	
17	Palestinians must guarantee that any agreement reached with Israel will be accepted and supported by the majority of the Palestinian people both in Gaza and the West Bank	II
18	Refrain and work against any anti-Israel sentiments in Palestinian schools	
19	Seek assistance for a legitimate settlement of refugees	VII
20	Sharing of natural resources	
21	Work cooperatively and in active engagement w/ Israel	

Fig. 7.2 Pairing the concessions that yielded the principles

These principles were the result of long hours of interaction and bargaining. While it would be presumptuous to suggest that these principles would create a solution to the controversy, participants on both sides felt that the statement of the principles provided a great deal that had eluded the face-to-face negotiators. All involved understood that the most difficult task of implementing the general principles remained to be addressed.

All the Critical Issues in the Conflict

The data developed in Chap. 5 provided a veritable trove of practical information not previously available to the participants but based on their own judgments they were now able to understand their own and their protagonists' priorities on a wide variety of issues. It became apparent as to which issue on either side had the highest priority for each side. Directly asking the question as to what was most important and least important would not have yielded an accurate statement of the true priorities. The AHP approach addresses such questions in an oblique manner and creates a reality that is far more accurate than trying to achieve an accurate statement by either party. The pairwise comparison approach yielded results which gives each party the kind of understanding of the true problem that can be rarely achieved in face-to-face negotiations.

Armed with these data, the participants began to consider where agreement might be reached on certain general principles. It became clear that the general principles would be helpful in considering general issues. With full recognition that the devil is in the details, the participants spent considerable time in honing a set of principles that could be agreed upon, word by word, based on knowledge that the AHP approach could provide. After long hours of interaction, the following general principles, dubbed the Pittsburgh Principles, were developed. The general principles agreed upon were as follows:

Pittsburgh Declaration of Principles: August 2011

1. A two-state solution on the borders of the fourth of June 1967, with mutually agreed upon land swaps.
2. Israel must respect the integrity of the West Bank and Gaza by allowing free and safe passage between the two areas, and the Palestinian State must guarantee that any agreement reached with Israel will be accepted and supported by the majority of the Palestinian people both in Gaza and the West Bank.
3. East Jerusalem is the capital of the Palestinian State. The parties will maintain the status quo of the Holy places in Jerusalem.
4. Acknowledge Israel's existence as a Jewish State, without jeopardizing the rights of its minority Israeli citizens.

5. Evacuation of Israeli settlers from the Palestinian territories that are not included in the land swap.
6. Palestinian full control of the borders of the Palestinian State and its outlets, and deployment of a temporary agreed upon multinational military monitoring system in the Jordan Valley.
7. Solve the Palestinian refugee problem in a just and agreed upon manner.
8. Limited arms of the Palestinian State and international guarantees from the international community against aggression from other parties.
9. Agreed upon international monitoring mechanism and agreed upon binding international arbitration mechanisms.
10. The full implementation of these principles concludes end of the conflict and claims of the two parties.

Some issues, for example, I11 and P20, which deal with natural resources, or I17 and P13, which deal with violence and speaking ill of each other, were left out because the participants thought that without solving the major conflicting issues nothing would be solved. The assumption was that if the major issues were addressed all other details should fall into place.

The major issues in the conflict are the recognition of Israel as a Jewish State (Principles 1 and 4), a Palestinian State (Principle 1), the delineation of the borders of the Palestinian State (Principles 2, 3, 5, 6, and 9), the Status of Jerusalem (Principle 3), the refugee problem (Principle 7), sharing of natural resources, and Israel's border security Principle 8). The principles developed address those issues in broad strokes.

In the months that followed, the participants focused exclusively on developing an implementation plan for each of the Pittsburgh Principles. The outcome of these discussions, using AHP methodology, resulted in a detailed agreement reflecting each of the Pittsburgh Principles, except for Principle 7 which reads "Solve the Palestinian refugee problem in a just and agreed upon manner." This principle was addressed in an initial implementation mode but was so complex that we achieved only a few agreed upon details. Several more meetings took place to complete a fully implementable plan for this principle. Nevertheless, what has been agreed upon so far addresses some of the relevant issues. While even a detailed implementation plan will require further discussion between the parties, the participants in our study, who are significant members of the Israeli and Palestinian communities, believe that the level of detail presented below will facilitate agreement on these issues, even if modifications are required.

The next chapter is dedicated to the development of detailed implementation plans for Principles 1 through 8.

Chapter 8
Implementation of the Principles: Getting Down to Earth

Introduction

While even a detailed implementation plan will require further discussion between the parties, the participants in our study, who are significant members of the Israeli and Palestinian communities, believe that the level of detail presented below will facilitate agreement on these issues, even if some modifications are required. To develop each of the principles into a working model, we follow the same process used to arrive at the principles described in Chap. 7:

1. Identify the dimensions of the problem.
2. Identify the trade-offs of each party within the dimensions.
3. Identify the benefits accrued by a party from the other party's trade-offs.
4. Identify the costs incurred by a party from its own trade-offs.
5. Identify the perceived benefits that the other party received from a party's trade-offs.
6. Identify the perceived costs incurred by the other party from their trade-offs.

Principle 1

A two-state solution on the borders of the 4th of June 1967, with mutually agreed upon land swaps.

The first principle proved to be a difficult statement to implement because it essentially sought to determine the borders of the two countries, a very controversial issue. The participants struggled with an implementation statement, but then decided that a small subgroup would meet separately to try and agree upon the principles for land swaps.

T. L. Saaty et al., *Overcoming the Retributive Nature of the Israeli-Palestinian Conflict*, https://doi.org/10.1007/978-3-030-83958-1_8

In a meeting in October 2013, a subcommittee of the participants met at an undisclosed location to draft implementation principles for a land swap. The entire participant group rewrote this material in the format given below.

Land Swap Principles

October 2013

(Revised January 2014)

General Guidelines

- A two-state solution on the borders of the 4th of June 1967, with minimal, mutually agreed upon land swap of the same size and of equal value for both sides.
- Territorial contiguity of both states is a principle of importance for both sides.
- Land swap between the State of Israel and the State of Palestine in a manner beneficial to both sides.
- Systematic and time-limited process for implementing land swap.
- No swap of land for money.
- No empty Palestinian land or land populated by Palestinians, for swap.
- Trade-off issues that go beyond land for land could be discussed and should be mutually agreed upon.
- Maximum number of Israeli citizens and minimum Palestinian land to be annexed with proximity to the 1967 line.
- East Jerusalem is an integral part of the West Bank.
- Jewish neighborhoods built in East Jerusalem after 1967 will be part of the land swap.
- The passage between the Gaza Strip and the West Bank will be part of the land swap.

Jerusalem

Overall arching values relevant to Jerusalem

- One city two capitals.
- The capital of the State of Palestine will be in East Jerusalem.
- Contiguity of neighborhoods for both sides (minimize isolation of communities).
- Mutually agreed arrangement for the Old City.
- Both sides will work toward agreed upon procedures and arrangements to enable the citizens of the two countries to have access to the city of Jerusalem.
- No Israeli population evacuation with the option of staying under Palestinian sovereignty as individual residents respecting and abiding by Palestinian laws.
- Palestinians living in Jewish neighborhoods in Jerusalem will not be evacuated and will live under Israeli sovereignty.
- Develop road links wherever necessary.

West Bank

- Israel is responsible to evacuate the settlers who refuse to comply with the agreement.

- The State of Palestine will take full responsibility for the safety of Israeli citizens who choose to stay under Palestinian sovereignty as residents on an equal footing with its own citizens.
- The State of Israel will take full responsibility for the safety of Palestinian citizens who choose to stay under Israel sovereignty as residents on an equal footing with its own citizens.
- Israel will refrain from any settlement activities in the West Bank or East Jerusalem during the implementation of the agreement.

At the time of the writing of these principles, there were 141 Israeli settlements in the West Bank (see Table 8.1) and an unknown number of outposts. Israel wanted to annex 42 of the settlements in exchange for land in other parts of Israel (See Table 8.2). The other settlements will have to be disposed of appropriately. These settlements contain about 71.81% of the population (as of 2019) in the settlements, and cover an area of approximately 3.17% of the area of the West Bank or 195.8 sq. km. The maps in Figs. 8.1 and 8.2 show the settlements in Table 8.2 (marked in yellow) to be annexed by Israel in this solution.

In exchange for the annexed settlements in Table 8.2 and depicted in Figs. 8.1 and 8.2, the Israeli participants proposed the territories shown in Fig. 8.3.

The surface in sq. km. and the natural resources they provide are given below:

Region		Area (Sq.Km	Natural Resources
Beit Shean Valley		18	Orchards Greenhouses Vegetables Fisheries
Judea Plain			Agriculture Pasture lands
	Northern Lakhish Region	37.3	
	Southern Lakhish Region	16.2	
	Northern Lahav Reserve	3.8	
	Eastern Lahav Reserve	6.1	
Northern Negev			
	Arad Valley	93.5	Forestry Agriculture Nature Reserve
	Yatir Mountains	26.9	Vineyards
Gaza Envelop		67.7	Orchards Greenhouses Vegetables Nature reserve
Halutza Sands		178.1	Aquifer

These territories were evaluated by the Palestinian participants using six criteria:

- Size
- Location
- Infrastructure
- Natural resources
- Territorial continuity
- Potential for development

These criteria are used to determine which territories and how much of them should be part of the land swap. Note that the total surface of these lands is 447.6 sq. km. and only 195.8 sq. km. can be included in the land swap.

To ascertain the importance of the criteria, the Palestinian participants compared them pairwise. The following matrix shows the individual judgments of the participants.

Table 8.1 List of settlements in the West Bank

	Israeli settlements							
	Name	Population 2019	Builtup Area (Dunums)	Character	Est.	Fence[7]	Council	Subarea or bloc
1	Adora	462	159	Secular	1984	E	Har Hebron	West
2	Alei Zahav	3399	255	Secular	1982	W	Shomron	Western S.
3	Alfei Menashe	7952	1085	Secular	1983	W	Shomron	Western S.[8]
4	Alon Shvut	3098	643	Religious	1970	W	Gush Etzion	Etzion
5	Almog	254	111	Secular	1977	V	Megilot	Dead Sea
6	Almon	1420	376	Secular	1982	W	Binyamin	Adumim
7	Argaman	132	165	Secular	1968	V	Bik'at HaYarden	Jordan Valley
8	Ariel	20540	2479	Mixed	1978	W	Shomron	Western S.[9]
9	Asfar (Metzad)	932	178	Orthodox	1983	E	Gush Etzion	Judean Mtns
10	Ateret	900	235	Religious	1981	E	Mateh Binyamin	Western B.
11	Avnat	237	124		1983	V	Megilot	Dead Sea
12	Avnei Hefetz	1,923	493	Religious	1990	E	Shomron	Western S.
13	Barkan	1,895	349	Secular	1981	W	Shomron	Western S.
14	Bat Ayin	1,568	239	Religious	1989	W	Gush Etzion	Etzion
15	Beit Aryeh	5,253	960	Secular	1981	W	Shomron	Western S.[8]
16	Beit El	5,973	944	Religious	1977	E	Mateh Binyamin	[8] Ramallah
17	Beit HaArava	350	280	Secular	1980	V	Megilot	Dead Sea
18	Beit Horon	1,437	181	Mixed	1977	W	Mateh Binyamin	Giv'on
19	Beit Yatir (Mezadot Yehuda)	550	170	Religious	1983	W	Har Hebron	South
20	Beitar Illit	59,270	1773	Orthodox	1985	W	Gush Etzion	Etzion[9]
21	Beka'ot	182	120	Secular	1972	V	Bik'at HaYarden	Jordan Valley
22	Carmei Tzur	1001	160	Religious	1984	E	Gush Etzion	Etzion
23	Carmel	437	177	Religious	1981	E	Har Hebron	South
24	Dolev	1,448	355	Religious	1983	E	Mateh Binyamin	Western B.
25	East Talpiot	13,984	1,195	Secular	1967	W	Jerusalem	East Jerusalem
26	Efrat(a)	10,806	1,090	Religious	1980	W	Gush Etzion	Etzion[8]
27	El'azar	2,459	256	Religious	1975	W	Gush Etzion	Etzion
28	Eli	4,415	776	Mixed	1984	E	Shomron	Eli
29	Elkana	3,838	758	Religious	1977	W	Shomron	Western S.[8]
30	Elon Moreh	1,920	419	Religious	1979	E	Shomron	Nablus
31	Immanuel	3,906	328	Orthodox	1983	W	Shomron	Western S.[8]
32	Einav	891	158	Religious	1981	E	Shomron	Enav
33	Eshkolot	577	133	Secular	1982	W	Har Hebron	South
34	Etz Efraim	2,428	184	Mixed	1985	W	Shomron	Western S.
35	French Hill (Giv'at Shapira)	8,660	2,018	Secular	1969	W	Jerusalem	East Jerusalem
36	Ganim				1983	E	Shomron	Northern S.
37	Geva Binyamin (Adam)	5,682	728	Secular	1984	E	Mateh Binyamin	Ramallah
38	Gilgal, Bik'at HaYarden	203	570	Secular	1970	V	Bik'at HaYarden	Jordan Valley
39	Gilo	29,559	2,859	Secular	1973	W	Jerusalem	East Jerusalem
40	Gitit	504	113	Secular	1973	V	Bik'at HaYarden	Jordan Valley
41	Giv'at Hamivtar	2,944			1970	W	Jerusalem	East Jerusalem
42	Giv'at Ze'ev	18,420	1063	Secular	1983	W	Mateh Binyamin	[8] Giv'on
43	Giv'on Hadasha	1,067	226	Secular	1980	W	Mateh Binyamin	Giv'on
44	Hagai	667	233	Religious	1984	E	Har Hebron	Hebron
45	Hallamish	1,485	450	Religious	1977	E	Mateh Binyamin	Western B.
46	Hamra	173	133	Secular	1971	V	Bik'at HaYarden	Jordan Valley
47	Har Adar (Giv'at HaRadar)	4,988	969	Secular	1986	W	Mateh Binyamin	[8] Giv'on
48	Har Brakha	2,757	258		1983	E	Shomron	Nablus
49	Har Gilo	1,635	127	Secular	1972	W	Gush Etzion	Etzion
50	Har Homa, Givat Hamatos	9,811	2,523/310	Religious	1997	W	Jerusalem	East Jerusalem
51	Hashmonaim	2,771	835	Religious-Orthodox	1985	W	Mateh Binyamin	Modi'in
52	Hebron	850			1980	E	Har Hebron	Hebron[11]
53	Hemdat (Nahal)	296	82	N/A	1980	V	Bik'at HaYarden	Jordan Valley
54	Hermesh	224	134	Secular	1982	E	Shomron	Rehan
55	Hinanit	1,410	280	Mixed	1981	W	Shomron	Rehan
56	Homesh	0		Secular	1980	E	Shomron	Northern S.
57	Itamar	1,269	253	Religious	1984	E	Shomron	Nablus
58	Kadim	0		Secular	1983	E	Shomron	Northern S.
59	Kalia	438	537	Secular	1968	V	Megilot	Dead Sea
60	Karnei Shomron	8,135	1351	Mixed	1978	W	Shomron	Western S.[8]
61	Kedar	1,599	251	Secular	1985	W	Gush Etzion	Adumim
62	Kedumim	4,544	1003	Mixed	1977	W	Shomron	Kedumim[8]
63	Kfar Adumim	4,674	921	Mixed	1979	W	Mateh Binyamin	Adumim
64	Kfar Etzion	1,156	445	Religious	1967	W	Gush Etzion	Etzion
65	Kfar Tapuach	1,312	156	Religious	1978	E	Shomron	Western S.
66	Kiryat Arba	7,326	882	Mixed	1972	E	Har Hebron	Hebron[8]
67	Kiryat Netafim	968	162	Religious	1983	W	Shomron	Western S.
68	Kokhav HaShahar	2,227	586	Religious	1977	V	Mateh Binyamin	Jordan
69	Kokhav Ya'akov (Abir Ya'akov)	8,541	756	Religious	1985	E	Mateh Binyamin	Ramallah
70	Lapid	2,394	386	Secular	1996	W	Hevel Modi'in	Modi'in
71	Ma'ale Adumim	38,155	3589	Mixed	1975	W	Gush Etzion[9]	Adumim
72	Ma'ale Amos	663	155	Orthodox	1981	E	Gush Etzion	Judean Mtns
73	Ma'ale Efraim	1,260	521	Secular	1970	V	Bik'at HaYarden[8]	Jordan Valley
74	Ma'ale Levona	906	251	Religious	1983	E	Mateh Binyamin	Eli
75	Ma'ale Mikhmas	1,529	383	Religious	1981	V	Mateh Binyamin	
76	Ma'ale Shomron	996	216	Mixed	1980	W	Shomron	Western S.
77	Ma'alot Dafna	2,720	380	Secular	1972	W	Jerusalem	East Jerusalem
78	Ma'on	595	173	Religious	1981	E	Har Hebron	South
79	Maskiot	310	32		1986	V	Bik'at HaYarden	Jordan Valley
80	Massu'a	184	160	Secular	1970	V	Bik'at HaYarden	Jordan Valley

(continued)

Table 8.1 (continued)

81	Matityahu	891	195	Religious	1981	W	Mateh Binyamin	Modi'in
82	Mehola	509	190	N/A	1968	V	Bik'at HaYarden	Jordan Valley
83	Mekhora	166	132	Secular	1973	V	Bik'at HaYarden	Jordan Valley
84	Menora	2,657	453	Secular	1998	W	Mateh Binyamin	Modi'in
85	Mevo Dotan	448	122	Secular	1978	E	Shomron	Rehan
86	Mevo Horon	2,669	519	Religious	1970	W	Mateh Binyamin	Modi'in
87	Migdal Oz	575	576	Religious	1977	W	Gush Etzion	Etzion
88	Migdalim	447	130	Secular	1983	E	Shomron	Western S.
89	Mishor Adumim							Adumim
90	Mitzpe Shalem	207	151	Secular	1971	V	Megilot	Dead Sea
91	Mitzpe Yericho	2,560	564	Religious	1978	V	Mateh Binyamin	Jordan
92	Modi'in Illit	76,374	1606	Orthodox	1996	W	Mateh Binyamin	Modi'in[8]
93	Na'ale	2,148	349	Secular	1988	E	Mateh Binyamin	
94	Nahliel	725	114	Orthodox	1984	E	Mateh Binyamin	Western B.
95	Negohot	352	90	Religious	1999	E	Har Hebron	West
96	Nativ HaGdud	212	1042	Secular	1976	V	Bik'at HaYarden	Jordan Valley
97	Neve Daniel	2,322	263	Religious	1982	W	Gush Etzion	Etzion
98	Neve Yaakov	19,703	1,759	Secular	1972	W	Jerusalem	East Jerusalem
99	Nili	1,786	282	Secular	1981	E	Mateh Binyamin	
100	Niran	101	302	Secular	1977	V	Bik'at HaYarden	Jordan Valley
101	Nofim	864	248	Secular	1987	W	Shomron	Western S.
102	Nokdim	2,383	440	Mixed	1982	E	Gush Etzion	Judean Mtns
103	Na'omi	165	280	Secular	1982	V	Bik'at HaYarden	Jordan Valley
104	Ofarim	5,253	351	Secular	1989	W	Mateh Binyamin	
105	Ofra	3,043	1012	Religious	1975	E	Mateh Binyamin	Ramallah
106	Old City Jewish Quarter	3,105	156	Orthodox			Jerusalem	East Jerusalem
107	Oranit	8,955	878	Mixed	1985	W	Shomron	Western S.[8]
108	Otniel	1,044	291	Religious	1983	E	Har Hebron	South
109	Peduel	2,010	171	Religious	1984	W	Shomron	Western S.
110	Ma'ale Hever (Peneh Hever)	635	110	Religious	1982	E	Mateh Binyamin	Ramallah
111	Peza'el	304	319	Secular	1975	V	Bik'at HaYarden	Jordan Valley
112	Pisgat Ze'ev	44,512	5,467	Secular	1985	W	Jerusalem	East Jerusalem
113	Psagot	1,881	234	Religious	1981	E	Har Hebron	Hebron
114	Ramat Eshkol	3,573	682	Secular	1970	W	Jerusalem	East Jerusalem
115	Ramat Shlomo	14,554	741	Orthodox	1995	W	Jerusalem	East Jerusalem
116	Ramot Alon	41,410	2558	Orthodox	1974	W	Jerusalem	East Jerusalem
117	Rehan	330	90	Secular	1977	W	Shomron	Rehan
118	Revava	2632	160	Religious	1991	W	Shomron	Western S.
119	Rimonim	700	314	Secular	1977	V	Mateh Binyamin	Jordan
120	Ro'i	175	134	Secular	1976	V	Bik'at HaYarden	Jordan Valley
121	Rosh Tzurim	933	320	Religious	1969	W	Gush Etzion	Etzion
122	Sanhedria Murhevet	4,094	378		1970	W	Jerusalem	East Jerusalem
123	Sa-Nur	0		Secular	1982	E	Shomron	Northern S.
124	Sal'it	1,331	256	Secular	1977	W	Shomron	Enav
125	Sha'are Tikva	6,039	915	Mixed	1983	W	Shomron	Western S.
126	Shadmot Mehola	666	159	N/A	1979	V	Bik'at HaYarden	Jordan Valley
127	Shaked	962	206	Secular	1981	W	Shomron	Rehan
128	Shani	0		Secular	1989	W	Har Hebron	South
129	Shavei Shomron	977	272	Religious	1977	E	Shomron	Western S.
130	Shilo	4,356	482	Religious	1979	E	Mateh Binyamin	Eli
131	Shim'a	741	212	Secular	1985	E	Har Hebron	South
132	Shvut Rachel	400			1991	E	Mateh Binyamin	Eli
133	Susiya	1,339	352	Religious	1983	E	Har Hebron	South
134	Talmon	4,575	1135	Religious	1989	E	Mateh Binyamin	Western B.
135	Tekoa	4,076	402	Mixed	1977	E	Gush Etzion	Judean Mtns
136	Telem	445	117	Secular	1982	E	Har Hebron	West
137	Tene Omarim	872	272	Secular	1983	E	Har Hebron	South
138	Tomer	276	362	Secular	1978	V	Bik'at HaYarden	Jordan Valley
139	Vered Jericho	341	274	Secular	1980	V	Megilot	Dead Sea
140	Yafit	202	352	Secular	1980	V	Bik'at HaYarden	Jordan Valley
141	Yakir	2,288	342	Religious	1981	W	Shomron	Western S.
142	Yitav	358	170	Secular	1970	V	Bik'at HaYarden	Jordan Valley
143	Yitzhar	1,726	269	Religious	1983	E	Shomron	Nablus
144	Zofin	2,406	219	Mixed	1989	W	Shomron	Kedumim

Table 8.2 List of settlements in the West Bank to be annexed by Israel

Israeli settlements

Name	Population 2019	Builtup Area (Dunums	Character	Est.	Fence[7]	Council	Subarea or bloc
Alfei Menashe	7952	1085	Secular	1983	W	Shomron	Western S.[8]
Alon Shvut	3098	643	Religious	1970	W	Gush Etzion	Etzion
Bat Ayin	1,568	239	Religious	1989	W	Gush Etzion	Etzion
Beit Yatir (Mezadot Yehuda)	550	170	Religious	1983	W	Har Hebron	South
Beitar Illit	59,270	1773	Orthodox	1985	W	Gush Etzion	Etzion[9]
East Talpiot	13,984	1,195	Secular	1967	W	Jerusalem	East Jerusalem
Efrat(a)	10,806	1,090	Religious	1980	W	Gush Etzion	Etzion[8]
El'azar	2,459	256	Religious	1975	W	Gush Etzion	Etzion
Elkana	3,838	758	Religious	1977	W	Shomron	Western S.[8]
Eshkolot	577	133	Secular	1982	W	Har Hebron	South
Etz Efraim	2,428	184	Mixed	1985	W	Shomron	Western S.
French Hill (Giv'at Shapira)	8,660	2,018	Secular	1969	W	Jerusalem	East Jerusalem
Gilo	29,559	2,859	Secular	1973	W	Jerusalem	East Jerusalem
Giv'at Hamivtar	2,944	588		1970	W	Jerusalem	East Jerusalem
Giv'at Ze'ev	18,420	1063	Secular	1983	W	Mateh Binyamin	[8] Giv'on
Giv'on Hadasha	1,067	226	Secular	1980	W	Mateh Binyamin	Giv'on
Har Adar (Giv'at HaRadar)	4,988	969	Secular	1986	W	Mateh Binyamin	[8] Giv'on
Har Homa, Givat Hamatos	9,811	2,833	Religious	1997	W	Jerusalem	East Jerusalem
Hashmonaim	2,771	835	Religious-Orthodox	1985	W	Mateh Binyamin	Modi'in
Hinanit	1,410	280	Mixed	1981	W	Shomron	Rehan
Kfar Etzion	1,156	445	Religious	1967	W	Gush Etzion	Etzion
Lapid	2,394	386	Secular	1996	W	Hevel Modi'in	Modi'in
Ma'ale Adumim	38,155	3589	Mixed	1975	W	Gush Etzion[9]	Adumim
Ma'alot Dafna	2,720	380	Secular	1972	W	Jerusalem	East Jerusalem
Matityahu	891	195	Religious	1981	W	Mateh Binyamin	Modi'in
Menora	2,657	453	Secular	1998	W	Mateh Binyamin	Modi'in
Migdal Oz	575	576	Religious	1977	W	Gush Etzion	Etzion
Modi'in Illit	76,374	1606	Orthodox	1996	W	Mateh Binyamin	Modi'in[8]
Neve Daniel	2,322	263	Religious	1982	W	Gush Etzion	Etzion
Neve Yaakov	19,703	1,759	Secular	1972	W	Jerusalem	East Jerusalem
Oranit	8,955	878	Mixed	1985	W	Shomron	Western S.[8]
Pisgat Ze'ev	44,512	5,467	Secular	1985	W	Jerusalem	East Jerusalem
Ramat Eshkol	3,573	682	Secular	1970	W	Jerusalem	East Jerusalem
Ramat Shlomo	14,554	1126	Orthodox	1995	W	Jerusalem	East Jerusalem
Ramot Alon	41,410	4,979	Orthodox	1974	W	Jerusalem	East Jerusalem
Rehan	330	90	Secular	1977	W	Shomron	Rehan
Rosh Tzurim	933	320	Religious	1969	W	Gush Etzion	Etzion
Sanhedria Murhevet	4,094	378		1970	W	Jerusalem	East Jerusalem
Sal'it	1,331	256	Secular	1977	W	Shomron	Enav
Sha'are Tikva	6,039	915	Mixed	1983	W	Shomron	Western S.
Shaked	962	206	Secular	1981	W	Shomron	Rehan
Zofin	2,406	219	Mixed	1989	W	Shomron	Kedumim
		West Bank Area (Dunums)	5,811,656			5,811,656	West Bank (Dunums)
		Annexed Area	195,800.0	3.17%		365,000	Gaza (Dunums)
		Built up Area	44,365	0.76%		6,176,656	Total
		Population	462,206	71.81%			
		Relocated	181,421	28.19%			

Individual Judgments

Criteria	Size	Location	Infrastructure	Natural Resources	Territorial Contiguity	Potential for Development
Size	1	1/5,1/7,1/7,1/7	1/5,1/7,1/6,1/9	1/5,1/7,1/6,1/8	1/7,1/7,1/8,1/8	1/6,1/7,1/7,1/5
Location		1	7,7,7,5	1,1,6,7	6,1/6,1/7,1/7	7,7,7,8
Infrastructure			1	1/6,1/6,1/7,1/8	1/7,1/7,1/7,1/8	1/5,1/6,1/5,6
Natural Resources				1	1/7,7,7,8	7,7,7,8
Territorial Contiguity					1	7,7,7,7
Potential for Development						1

These judgments were then aggregated using the geometric mean (Aczel & Saaty, 1983). The aggregated judgments and priorities are given in the last column of the table that follows.

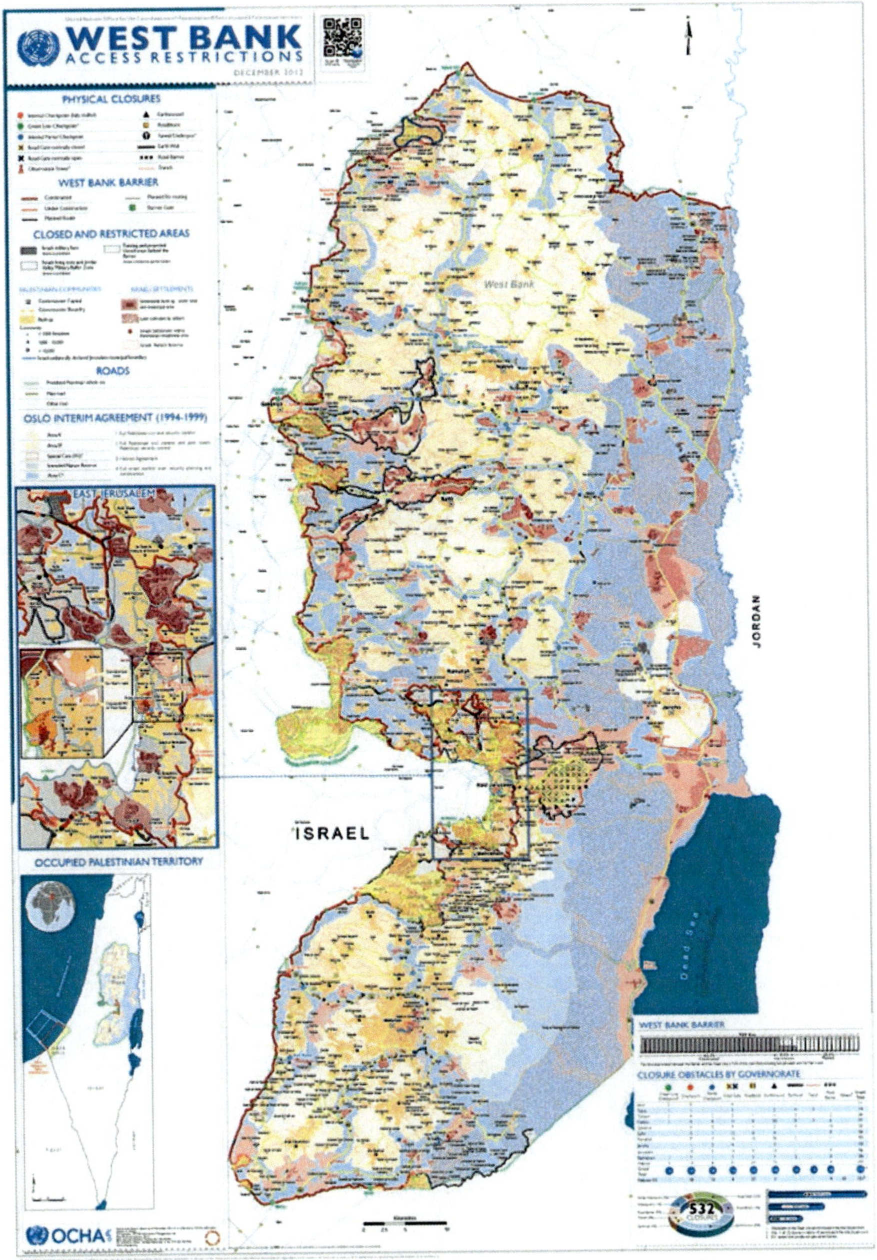

Fig. 8.1 Settlements to be annexed by Israel in the West Bank (Source: United Nations OCHA oPt)

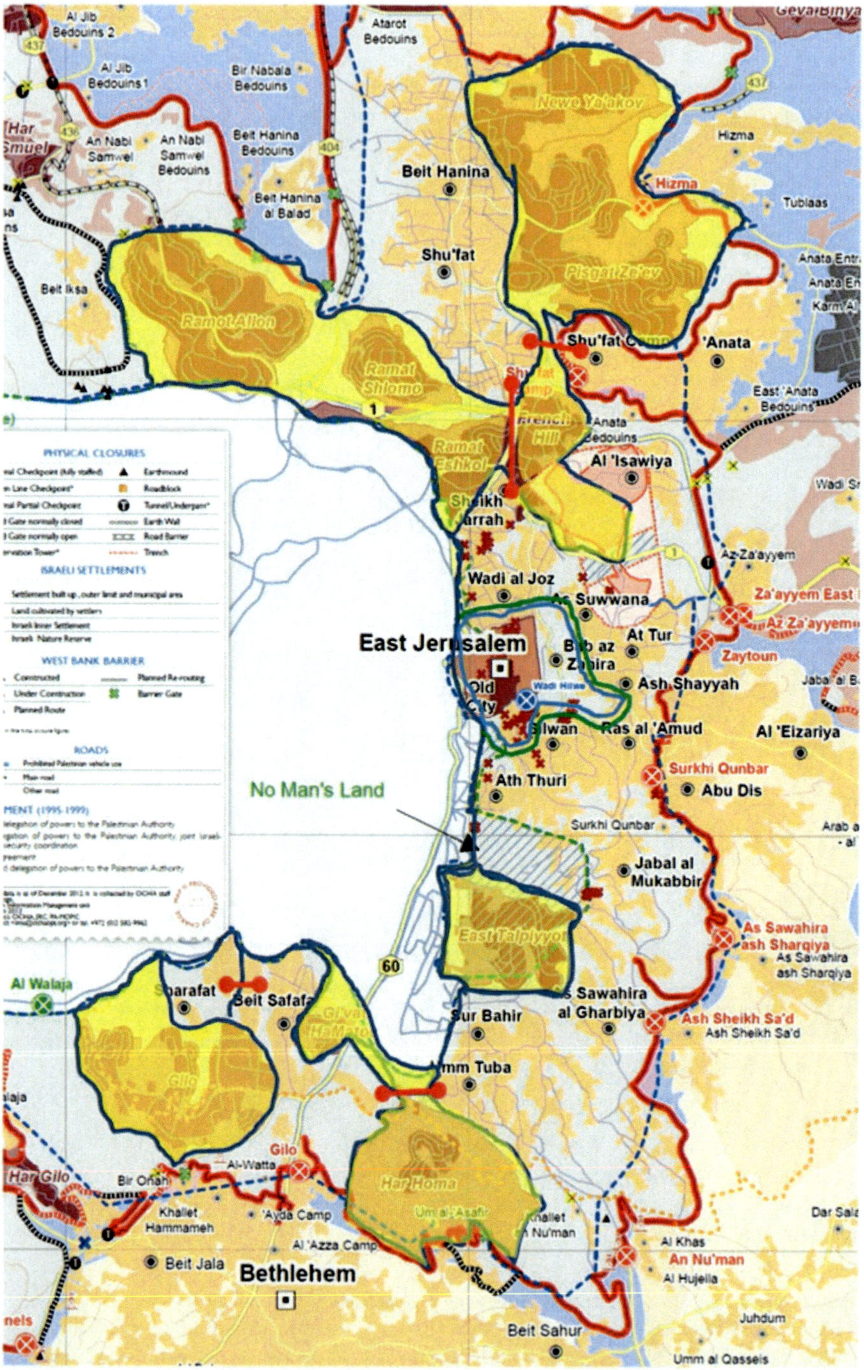

Fig. 8.2 Settlements to be annexed by Israel in East Jerusalem (Source: United Nations OCHA oPt)

Fig. 8.3 Israeli territories proposed for land swap (Reproduced with permission of the author Shaul Arieli)

			Geometric mean				
Criteria	Size	Location	Infrastructure	Natural Resources	Territorial Contiguity	Potential for Development	Priorities
Size	1	0.1554	0.1517	0.1562	0.1336	0.1615	0.02
Location		1	6.4353	2.5457	0.3780	7.2376	0.28
Infrastructure			1	0.1492	0.1382	0.4472	0.05
Natural Resources				1	2.7356	7.2376	0.29
Territorial Contiguity					1	7	0.29
Potential for Development						1	0.06

Note that the most important criteria were location, natural resources, and territorial contiguity reflecting the land swap principles outlined above.

Next each of the territories was evaluated using absolute measurement. The use of absolute measurement avoids having to compare the territories pairwise according to the criteria because some of the lands may not have the same type of natural resources; so they could not be compared. However, using an absolute measurement scale as given below the lands can be rated in an absolute ratio scale according to how much they believe a territory satisfies the criterion in question. Each criterion has its own rating scale, but for simplicity of exposition and without loss of generality, we show the following scale:

Rating	Symbol	Weight
Extreme	E	100.00% (1.00)
Very High	VH	90.00% (0.90)
High	H	75.00% (0.75)
Moderate	M	50.00% (0.50)
Low	L	25.00% (0.25)
Very Low	VL	10.00% (0.10)
Negligible	N	0.00% (0.00)

For example, according to size (area), the participants rated the Beit Shean Valley as follows:

			Beit Shean Valley				
Participants	Extreme	Very High	High	Moderate	Low	Very Low	Negligible
Participant 1				X			
Participant 2			X				
Participant 3				X			
Participant 4			X				

The following table summarizes all the ratings by the four participants that took part in the exercise:

	Size	Location	Infrastructure	Natural Resources	Territorial Contiguity	Potential for Development
Beit Shean Valley	(M, H, M, H)	(H, VH, H, H)	(VH, VH, VH, H)	(VH, H, H, H)	(VH, VH, VH, VH)	(E, VH, E, VH)
Judea Plain	(VH, VH, H, H)	(VH, H, H, H)	(M, M, M, H)	(H, M, M, M)	(VH, H, H, H)	(VH, H, VH, H)
Northen Negev	(H, M, H, M)	(M, M, M, M)	(L, VL, L, L, L)	(L, L, M, M)	(M, M, M, M)	(M, L, M, M)
Gaza Envelop	(VH, VH,VH, H)	(VH, VH, H, H)	(H, H, H, M)	(H, H, H, H)	(VH, H, VH, VH)	(VH, VH, H, VH)
Halutza Sands	(N, N, N, N)	(N, N, N, N)	(N, N, N, N)	(N, N, N, N)	(N, N, N, N)	(L, N, N, N)

Each entry of the table consists of four ratings, one for each participant. These ratings are converted into numerical values and the average computed. Table 8.3 contains the individual scores of each territory and final score obtained by weighting the score under a criterion by the criterion's priority. All numbers are rounded to two digits to simplify the exercise. The final scores were normalized to unity and the total area of the land swap—195.8 sq. km. or 3.17% of the total area of the West Bank—allocated accordingly. Thus, the Beit Shean Valley has the highest priority (0.2964) and it gets allocated the entire area (18 sq. km.); next the Gaza Envelop with a priority of 0.2893 gets allocated all its area (67.7 sq. km.); the Judea Plain received the third highest priority (0.2536) and it is also allocated the entire area (63.4 sq. km.); and finally, the Northern Negev with the lowest priority (0.1607) received the remainder area from the total 195.8 sq. km., i.e., 46.7 sq. km.

Result

The total area to be annexed by Israel is 3.17% of the West Bank or 195.8 km^2. The corresponding land from the sites prioritized above is selected by using the quality points from the final scores as follows: Beit Shean Valley (18 km^2), Gaza Envelop (67.7 km^2), Judea Plain (63.4 km^2), and Northern Negev (46.7 km^2).

Evaluation of the five locations for land swap in terms of their potential to fulfill the five criteria listed

Principle 2

Israel must respect the integrity of the West Bank and Gaza by allowing free and safe passage between the two areas, and the Palestinian State must guarantee that any agreement reached with Israel will be accepted and supported by the majority of the Palestinian people both in Gaza and the West Bank.

The implementation of Principle 2 reflects the feeling of both parties that any peace agreement should be subject to a referendum in each society so that the will of the people of both communities becomes apparent. The consensus of the representatives from both sides was that significant proportions of their respective populations desire peace, if given the opportunity on a plan their leaders approve. Further, the Israeli representatives agreed that there should be free passage between

Table 8.3 Land swap evaluation

				Goal: Evaluation of Land Swap								
Criteria:		Area (Sq.Km.)	Natural Resources	Size (0.02)	Location (0.28)	Infrastructure (0.05)	Natural Resources (0.29)	Territorial Contiguity (0.29)	Potential for Development (0.06)	Final Scores	Relative Priorities	Allocated Area (Sq. Km.)
Alternatives:	Beit Shean Valley	18	Orchards Greenhouses Vegetables Fisheries	0.62	0.79	0.86	0.79	0.9	0.95	0.83	0.2964	18
	Judea Plain		Agriculture Pasture lands	0.82	0.79	0.56	0.56	0.79	0.82	0.71	0.2536	63.4
	Northern Lakhish Region	37.3										
	Southern Lakhish Region	16.2										
	Northern Lahav Reserve	3.8										
	Eastern Lahav Reserve	6.1										
	Northern Negev			0.62	0.5	0.21	0.38	0.5	0.44	0.45	0.1607	46.7
	Arad Valley	93.5	Forestry Agriculture Nature Reserve									
	Yatir Mountains	26.9	Vineyards									
	Gaza Envelop	67.7	Orchards Greenhouses Vegetables Nature reserve	0.86	0.82	0.69	0.75	0.86	0.86	0.81	0.2893	67.7
	Halutza Sands	178.1	Aquifer	0	0	0	0	0	0.06	0	0	0
											Total	195.8

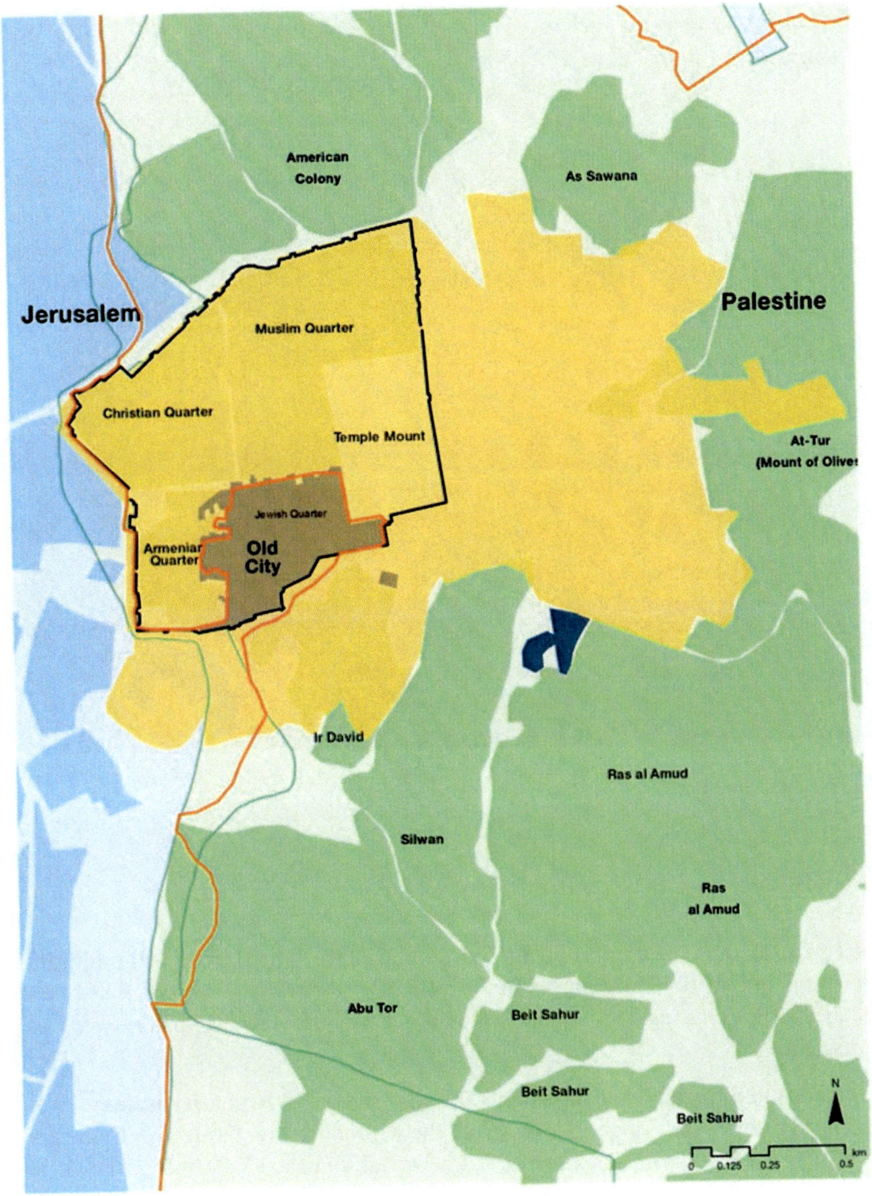

Fig. 8.4 Historic area of Jerusalem

Gaza and the West Bank without any restrictions in moving from one area to the other. This meant that some sort of corridor over Israeli land would be required.

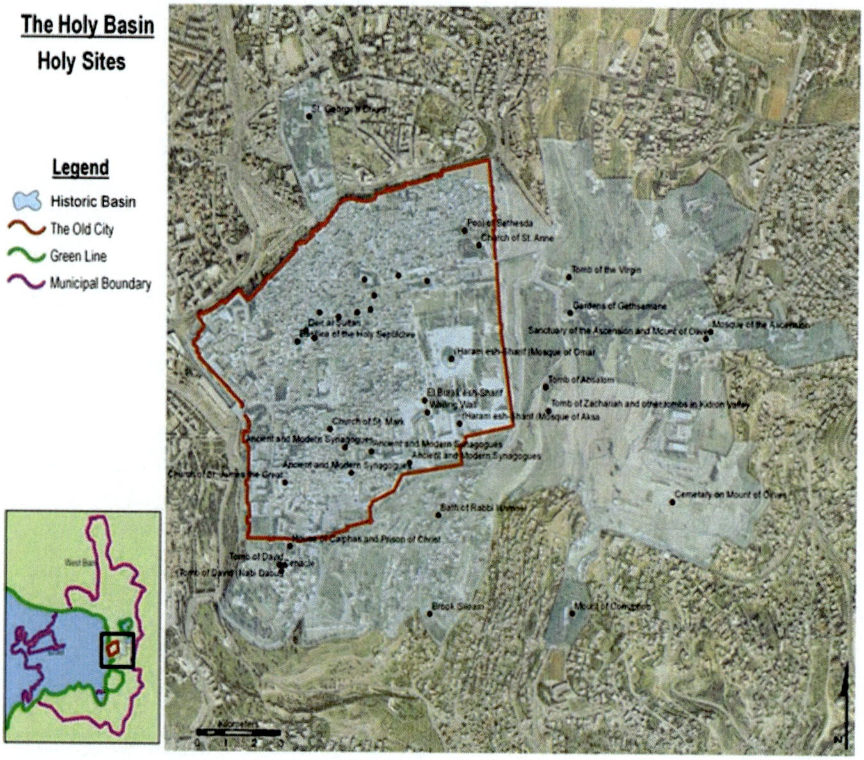

Fig. 8.5 The Holy Basin

Principle 3

East Jerusalem is the capital of the Palestinian State. The parties will maintain the status quo of the Holy places in Jerusalem.

The participants agreed on the following principles for the historic area of Jerusalem.

Principles and Special Arrangements for the Historic Area of Jerusalem

1. The "Historic Area" includes Mt. Zion, the Kidron Valley, the Jewish Cemetery in the Mt. of Olives, the City of King David, and the Old City as shown in Fig. 8.4.
2. This area will function in the model of "Open City." Citizens of either party may not exit this area into the territory of the other party.
3. Upon the implementation of the principles, Palestine will assume sovereignty over the entire area, excluding the Jewish Quarter and Mt. Zion (as in Fig. 8.5).
4. Palestinians will have control over the Haram al-Sharif and Israelis will have control over the Wailing Wall (no one will have sovereignty over these sites).

5. The religious status quo and particularly the existing arrangements pertaining to the exercise of religious practices will remain.
6. The implementation of these principles will be carried out according to the following three stages. A detailed timetable will be agreed upon by the parties:

    (a) Redeployment of the Israeli Defense Forces and Israeli population from the Palestinian areas.
    (b) A multinational force will help assume responsibility in the territory pertaining to the Palestinians.
    (c) The State of Palestine assumes full control over its part of the area.

In addition, to the agreed upon facts noted above, the participants developed a series of actions (concessions—actions a party wants from the other party) for each side:

Israeli's Concessions

I1. Rescind all legal and administrative measures and orders legislated by Israel since 1967.

I2. Preserve and respect the status quo of the Holy places in the city as decreed and accepted by the Ottomans and the international community in 1856.

I3. Demolish the separation wall around the city erected by Israel.

Palestinian's Concessions

P1. Full Palestinian cooperation during transfer of power and beyond it.

P2. Accepting international monitoring on the compliance of the transfer of power process.

Heretofore we will refer to the specific concessions of the parties for the implementation of a principle as "actions."

Next, the actions were prioritized with respect to the benefits, costs, perceived benefits, and perceived costs. Tables 8.4 and 8.5 summarize the priorities assigned and represent the judgments of the participants using the ratings approach of the AHP.

The priorities of the actions with respect to the benefits, costs, perceived benefits, and perceived costs (see Table 8.6) are combined to produce the gain/loss ratios which in turn are used to make trade-offs among the actions. In this principle a pair of actions, considered as a bundle, is traded as shown in Table 8.6.

Note that the Israeli trade-off (I1, P1) yields a gain of 2.735, and it is matched with the Palestinian bundle consisting of the pairs (I1, P1) and (I2, P2) that yield a gain of 2.801, which is within 2.5% of each other, which is an acceptable ratio. As a result of these matched concessions, the actions to be required of each party will be as follows:

Israeli Actions

- Rescind all legal and administrative measures and orders legislated by Israel since 1967.

Table 8.4 Summary of assigned priorities (Israeli perspective) for Principle 3

Israeli benefits from Palestinian concessions	Priorities	P1	P2
Accepting the global recognition of Jerusalem (in its new borders) as the capital of Israel	0.2812	0.6	0.688
Increasing international and regional support for Israel	0.1508	0.75	0.663
Transfer of full governmental and municipal responsibility for the Palestinian residents of Eastern Jerusalem, while sharing social costs	0.0587	0	0
Security	0.0481	0	0
Receiving international legitimization to the Jewish neighborhood in East Jerusalem	0.2189	0.625	0.575
Strengthen Israeli democracy	0.2423	0.438	0.055
		0.5246	0.4324

Israeli costs from Israeli concessions	Priorities	I1	I2	I3
Hurting the feelings of the global Jewish people by conceding on the right of Jews to live everywhere in Jerusalem	0.2255	0.402	0.875	0.12
Increasing potential friction due to the dual management of the city, increasing inefficiencies	0.1582	0.173	0.967	0.12
Hindering the ability to effectively zone and plan super-infrastructure inside and around Jerusalem	0.0954	0.283	0.533	0.287
Loss of security control	0.4271	0.317	0.587	0.67
Loss of demographic control	0.0938	0.37	0.503	0.553
		0.3152	0.6989	0.4115

Israeli perception of Palestinian benefits from Israeli concessions	Priorities	I1	I2	I3
Fulfill our national aspiration and dignity	0.3699	0.503	0.667	0.637
Enforcing the Palestinian national identity	0.2964	0.587	0.367	0.587
Free worship of the three monotheistic religions	0.0562	0	0	0
Social benefit by preserving the social fabric	0.1266	0.387	0.07	0.203
Economic benefit by developing the tourism industry and other aspects of life in the city	0.1509	0.1	0.07	0.583
		0.4241	0.3747	0.5232

Israeli perception of Palestinian costs from Palestinian concessions	Priorities	P1	P2
Political costs by accepting compromise within the land swap approach on parts of the city where Israeli settlements exist	0.5905	0.883	0.367
Limiting the potential urban, economic and social development of the city arising from the existence of Israeli settlements interlocked within the Palestinian capital	0.4095	0.317	0.337
		0.6513	0.3544

Palestinian Actions
P1. Full Palestinian cooperation during transfer of power and beyond it
P2. Accepting international monitoring on the compliance of the transfer of power process

Table 8.5 Summary of assigned priorities (Palestinian perspective) for Principle 3

Palestinian benefits from Israeli concessions	Priorities	I1	I2	I3
Fulfill our national aspiration and dignity	0.2989	1	1	1
Enforcing the Palestinian national identity	0.4114	1	1	1
Free worship of the three monotheistic religions	0.0901	1	0.9	1
Social benefit by preserving the social fabric	0.0679	0.9	0.9	0.9
Economic benefit by developing the tourism industry and other aspects of life in the city	0.1317	1	1	0.9
		0.9932	0.9842	0.98

Palestinian costs from Palestinian concessions	Priorities	P1	P2
Political costs by accepting compromise within the land swap approach on parts of the city where Israeli settlements exist	0.125	0.5	0.5
Limiting the potential urban, economic and social development of the city arising from the existence of Israeli settlements interlocked within the Palestinian capital	0.875	1	0.5
		0.9375	0.5

Palestinian perceptions of Israeli benefits from Palestinian concessions	Priorities	P1	P2
Accepting the global recognition of Jerusalem (in its new borders) as the Capital of Israel	0.5039	0.9	0.9
Increasing international and regional support for Israel	0.065	0.9	0.75
Transfer of full governmental and municipal responsibility for the Palestinian residents of Eastern Jerusalem, while sharing social costs	0.0352	0.9	0.9
Security	0.114	0.9	0.75
Receiving international legitimization to the Jewish neighborhood in East Jerusalem	0.2616	0.9	0.75
Strengthen Israeli democracy	0.0204	0.5	0.5
		0.8919	0.8258

Palestinina perceptions of Israeli costs from Israeli concessions	Priorities	I1	I2	I3
Hurting the feelings of the global Jewish people by conceding on the right of Jews to live everywhere in Jerusalem	0.2561	0.9	0.9	0.5
Increasing potential friction due to the dual management of the city, increasing inefficiencies	0.2519	0.75	0.5	0.5
Hindering the ability to effectively zone and plan super-infrastructure inside and around Jerusalem	0.2046	0.75	0.75	0.75
Loss of security control	0.1642	0.25	0.25	0.5
Loss of demographic control	0.1233	0.01	0.01	0.01
		0.6151	0.5521	0.4908

Israeli Actions
I1. Rescind all legal and administrative measures and orders legislated by Israel since 1967
I2. Preserve and respect the status quo of the holy places in the city as decreed and accepted by the Ottomans and the international community in 1856.
I3. Demolish the separation wall around the city erected by Israel

- Preserve and respect the status quo of the Holy places in the city as decreed and accepted by the Ottomans and the international community in 1856.

Palestinian Actions

- Full Palestinian cooperation during transfer of power and beyond it.
- Acceptance of international monitoring on the compliance of the transfer of power process.

Principle 4

Acknowledge Israel's existence as a Jewish State without jeopardizing the rights of its minority Israeli citizens.

Table 8.6 Israeli and Palestinian benefits and costs, perceived benefits and costs, and gain/loss ratios for Principle 3

Israelis

Concessions	Israelis' Costs	Israelis' _Perception_of _Palestinians' _Benefits	Israelis' Total Loss	Palestinians' Benefits	Palestinians' _Perception_of _Israelis_Costs	Palestinians' Total Gain
1	0.45099442	0.810588685	365570.9737	1	1	1000000
2	1	0.716169725	716169.7248	0.990938381	0.89757763	889444.1231
3	0.588782372	1	588782.3723	0.986709625	0.797919038	787314.3947

Palestinians

Concessions	Palestinians' Costs	Palestinians' _Perception_of _Israelis' _Benefits	Palestinians' Total Loss	Israelis' Benefits	Israelis' _Perception_of _Palestinians' _Costs	Israelis' Total Gain
1	1	1	1000000	1	1	1000000
2	0.533333333	0.925888553	493807.228	0.824247045	0.544142484	448507.8349

Israeli Ratios

	P1	P2
I1	2.735446936	1.226869383
I2	1.396317054	0
I3	1.698420413	0

Palestinian Ratios

	P1	P2
I1	1	2.025081739
I2	0	1.801197052
I3	0	1.594376003

Trade-off

	Concessions	Gain
Israeli	1, 2	2.735
Palestinian	1, 2	2.801

This principle does not deny non-Jewish Israeli citizens the full rights of Israeli citizenship.

Principle 5

Evacuation of Israeli settlers from the Palestinian territories who are not included in the land swap.

Israeli Perspective

Benefits

1. Security benefits
2. Social and economic benefits
3. Increase in the effectiveness of military and police forces

4. Allow Israel to define its borders
5. Increased international support
6. Strengthen the democratic nature of the State of Israel

Costs

1. Economic cost to relocate the settlers
2. Rift in the Israeli society, danger of civil war/Jewish terror
3. Erosion of national ethos
4. Large strain on the Israeli democratic character

Palestinian Actions

P1. Allowing Israel to choose between incremental and rapid removal of settlers/ settlements

P2. A Palestinian commitment to fully collaborate with Israel during the relocation process and maintain a restrained approach toward the actual relocation

P3. Acknowledging the value of infrastructure, residential and commercial buildings, and facilities, after Israel's withdrawal

Palestinian Perspective

Benefits

1. Repossession of land and natural resources
2. Eliminate the harassment by the settlers
3. Ability to develop Palestinian agriculture and urban development
4. Security (feel more secure in the absence of settlers)
5. Psychological and social benefits
6. Ensuring geographic and integral contiguity

Costs

1. Repair the damage caused by the settlers during evacuation
2. Rehabilitation of the land and the facilities

Israeli Actions

I1. Ensure that the infrastructure is preserved

I2. Facilitate the evacuation without causing any damage to the properties or land

I3. Secure the evacuation process in regard to the Palestinian population

The priorities for the benefits, costs, perceived benefits, and perceived costs from both parties along with the ratings of the actions (concessions) for Israelis and Palestinians are given in Tables 8.7 and 8.8, respectively.

Table 8.9 gives the gain/loss ratios for Principles 5 and the required actions for both parties.

As a result of these matched concessions the actions to be required of each party are as follows:

Table 8.7 Israeli benefits, costs, perceived benefits, and perceived costs for Principle 5

Israeli benefits from Palestinian concessions	Priorities	P1	P2	P3
Security benefits	0.0461	0.825	0.788	0.725
Social and Economic benefits	0.109	0.788	0.275	0.115
Increase in the effectiveness of military and police forces	0.0585	0.588	0.825	0.078
Allow Israel to define its borders	0.2023	0.313	0.4	0.078
Increased international support	0.1837	0.213	0.788	0.033
Strengthen the democratic nature of the state of Israel	0.4004	0.563	0.563	0.01
		0.4858	0.5653	0.0762

Israeli costs from Israeli concessions	Priorities	I1	I2	I3
Economic cost to relocate the settlers	0.1282	0.563	0.563	0.275
Rift in the Israeli society, danger of civil war / Jewish terror	0.5261	0.5	0.5	0.75
Erosion of national ethos	0.1208	0.788	0.6	0.4
Puts a large strain on the Israeli democratic character	0.2248	0.275	0.5	0.5
		0.4922	0.5201	0.5906

Israeli perception of Palestinian benefits from Israeli concessions	Priorities	I1	I2	I3
Repossession of land and natural resources	0.3167	0.862	0.725	0.563
Eliminate the harassment by the settlers	0.0775	0.75	0.5	0.888
Ability to develop the Palestinian agriculture and urban development	0.15	0.85	0.725	0.438
Security (feel more secure in the absence of settlers)	0.1171	0.463	0.95	0.863
Psychological and social benefits	0.0909	0.625	0.725	0.825
Ensuring geographic and integral contiguity	0.2478	0.175	0.01	0.055
		0.6131	0.5567	0.5021

Israeli perception of Palestinian costs from Palestinian concessions	Priorities	P1	P2	P3
Repair the damage caused by the settlers during evacuation	0.5074	0.193	0.825	0.115
Rehabilitation of the land and the facilities	0.4926	0.3	0.788	0.4
		0.2455	0.8065	0.2554

Palestinian Actions
P1. Allowing Israeli to choose between incremental and rapid removal of settlers / settlements
P2. A Palestinian commitment to fully collaborate with Israeli during the relocation process and maintaining a restrained approach toward the actual relocation
P3. Acknowledging the value of infrastructure, residential and commercial buildings and facilities, after Israeli withdrawal

Israeli Actions

- I2. Facilitate the evacuation without causing any damage to the properties or land.

Palestinian Actions

- P2. A Palestinian commitment to fully collaborate with Israel during the relocation process and maintain a restrained approach toward the actual relocation.

Principle 6

Palestinian full control of the borders of the Palestinian State and its outlets, and deployment of a temporary agreed upon multinational military monitoring system in the Jordan Valley.

Table 8.8 Palestinian benefits, costs, perceived benefits, and perceived costs for Principle 5

Palestinian Perspective

Palestinian benefits from Israeli concessions	Priorities	I1	I2	I3
Repossession of land and natural resources	0.4034	0.9	0.9	0.9
Eliminate the harassment by the settlers	0.0552	0	0	0
Ability to develop the Palestinian agriculture and urban development	0.0967	0.9	0.9	0.9
Security (feel more secure in the absence of settlers)	0.1647	0.75	0.75	0.9
Psychological and social benefits	0.0196	0	0	0
Ensuring geographic and integral contiguity	0.2604	0.9	0.9	0.75
		0.808	0.808	0.7936

Palestinian costs from Palestinian concessions	Priorities	P1	P2	P3
Repair the damage caused by the settlers during evacuation	0.5	1	0.5	0.9
Rehabilitation of the land and the facilities	0.5	1	0.75	0.75
		1	0.625	0.825

Palestinian perceptions of Israeli benefits from Palestinian concessions	Priorities	P1	P2	P3
Security benefits	0.5537	0.5	0.75	0.9
Social and economic benefits	0.1119	0.75	0.75	0.75
Increase in the effectiveness of military and police forces	0.0553	0	0	0
Allow Israel to define its borders	0.2534	0.5	0.01	0.01
Increased international support	0.0258	0	0	0
		0.4874	0.5017	0.5848

Palestinina perceptions of Israeli costs from Israeli concessions	Priorities	I1	I2	I3
Economic cost to relocate the settlers	0.6505	0.75	0.5	0.75
Rift in the Israeli society, danger of civil war / Jewish terror	0.1557	0.75	0.75	0.75
Erosion of national ethos	0.0468	0.25	0.25	0.25
Large strain on the Israeli democratic process	0.147	0.01	0.01	0.01
		0.6178	0.4552	0.6178

Israeli Actions
I1. Ensure that the infrastructure is preserved
I2. Facilitate the evacuation without causing any damage to the properties or land
I3. Secure the evacuation process in regard to the Palestinian population

Israeli Perspective

Benefits

1. Economic gains from relinquishing control of the borders (typically realized in terms of operational costs)
2. International benefits
   (a) Improved international relationship
   (b) Removal of sanctions
3. Removal of sanctions
4. Tourism
5. Trade
6. Increased security cooperation

Table 8.9 Israeli and Palestinian benefits and costs, perceived benefits and costs, and gain/loss ratios for Principle 5.

Israelis

Concessions	Israelis' Costs	Israelis' _Perception_of _Palestinians' _Benefits	Israelis' Total Loss	Palestinians' Benefits	Palestinians' _Perception_of_Israelis_ Costs	Palestinians' Total Gain
1	0.833389773	1	833389.7731	1	1	1000000
2	0.880629868	0.908008481	799619.3891	1	0.736808028	736808.0285
3	1	0.818952863	818952.8625	0.982178218	1	982178.2178

Palestinians

Concessions	Palestinians' Costs	Palestinians' _Perception_of _Israelis' _Benefits	Palestinians' Total Loss	Israelis' Benefits	Israelis' _Perception_of_Palestini ans'_Costs	Israelis' Total Gain
1	1	0.833447332	833447.3324	0.859366708	0.304401736	261592.7177
2	0.625	0.857900137	536187.5855	1	1	1000000
3	0.825	1	825000	0.134795684	0.316676999	42686.69265

Israeli Ratios	P1	P2	P3
I1	0	1.199918732	0
I2	0	1.250594988	0
I3	0	1.2210715	0

Trade-off

	Action	Gain
Israeli	I2	1.250595
Palestinian	P2	1.374161

Palestinian Ratios	P1	P2	P3
I1	1.199835864	1.865018936	1.212121212
I2	0	1.374160925	0
I3	1.17845265	1.831780974	1.190519052

Costs

1. Security threat
   (a) Palestine itself
   (b) Internal actors such as Hamas
   (c) Non-state actors
   (d) Third-party actors
2. Loss of control
3. Movement
4. Maintenance of borders
5. Cooperation costs
6. Political

Palestinian Actions

P1. Palestinian control over customs
P2. Limited arms—Principle 8
P3. Multinational oversight—Principle 9
P4. Access to airspace for training
P5. Maintain borders with other countries

Palestinian Perspective

Benefits

1. Economic gains internally and from controlling the borders: customs, relationships with neighboring countries
2. International benefits: open and establish international relationships and cooperation with the world
3. Creating a new positive climate for better relations and cooperation between the two parties
4. Free movement of people and goods
5. Development of the tourism industry
6. Trade: controlling import and export on the basis of mutual benefits
7. Political stability
8. Encouraging international investment

Costs

1. Running the border stations
2. Manpower
3. Political costs of engaging in early stages of the new situation with the Israelis

Israeli Actions

I1. Total withdrawal from Palestinian territories.
I2. Hand over fully the control point, border stations.
I3. Provide Palestinians with all the information about the borders and passages.
I4. Ensure no intervention whatsoever in the border control points—respect the independence and integrity of the Palestinian borders.
I5. Any information or requests passed through official channels on Palestinian side.

Tables 8.10 and 8.11 summarize the Israeli and Palestinian benefits, costs, perceived benefits, and perceived costs for Principle 6, respectively. Table 8.12 gives the gain/loss ratios and the required actions for both parties.

As a result of these matched concessions the actions to be required of each party are as follows:

Israeli actions	Gain	Palestinian actions	Gain
I2. Hand over fully the control point, border stations	1.4851	P3. Multinational oversight—Principle 9.	1.5348
I1. Total withdrawal from Palestinian territories I5. Any information or requests passed through official channels on Palestinian side	1.2698	P2. Limited arms—Principle 8 P4. Access to airspace for training	1.2103

Table 8.10 Israeli benefits, costs, perceived benefits, and perceived costs for Principle 6

Israeli benefits from Palestinian concessions	Priorities	P1	P2	P3	P4	P5
Economic gains from relinquishing control	0.1275	0.42	0.6	0.53	0.01	0.32
Improved international relationships	0.302	0.65	0.57	0.6	0.028	0.81
Removal of sanctions	0.0669	0.73	0.29	0.47	0.01	0.73
Tourism	0.1499	0.402	0.242	0.47	0.01	0.63
Trade	0.1591	0.55	0.01	0.112	0.01	0.27
Increased security cooperation	0.1946	0.55	0.98	0.87	0.47	0.55
		0.5535	0.4966	0.5378	0.105	0.5787

Israeli costs from Israeli concessions	Priorities	I1	I2	I3	I4	I5
Security Threat	0.5116	0.84	0.5	0.222	0.6	0.082
Loss of control	0.3104	0.81	0.75	0.22	0.7	0.16
Maintenance of borders	0.0922	0.56	0.45	0.18	0.55	0.1
Cooperation costs	0.0858	0.58	0.86	0.71	0.58	0.53
		0.7826	0.6039	0.2594	0.6247	0.1463

Israeli perception of Palestinian benefits from Israeli concessions	Priorities	I1	I2	I3	I4	I5
Economic gains internally and from controlling the borders: FDI, customs, relationships with neighboring countries	0.1667	0.65	0.4	0.19	0.5	0.24
International benefits: Open and establish international relationships and cooperation with the World	0.1424	0.81	0.55	0.32	0.24	0.16
Creating a new positive climate for better relations and cooperation between the two parties	0.2328	1	0.73	0.65	0.89	0.9
Free movement of people and goods	0.2464	1	0.96	0.45	0.222	0.472
Development of tourism industry	0.0799	0.4	0.81	0.32	0.29	0.224
Political stability	0.1318	0.93	0.6	0.16	0.65	0.046
		0.8574	0.6953	0.3861	0.4883	0.4126

Israeli perception of Palestinian costs from Palestinian concessions	Priorities	P1	P2	P3	P4	P5
Running the border stations	0.5547	0.55	0.55	0.84	0.082	0.89
Political Costs of engaging in early stages of the new situation with the Israelis	0.4453	0.272	0.7	0.45	0.84	0.29
		0.4262	0.6168	0.6663	0.4195	0.6228

Palestinian Actions	
P1.	Palestinian control over customs
P2.	Limited Arms – Principle 8
P3.	Multi-national oversight – Principle 9
P4.	Access to airspace for training
P5.	Maintain borders with other countries

Principle 7

Solve the Palestinian refugee problem in a just and agreed upon manner.

Israeli Perspective

Benefits

1. Preservation of the Jewish and democratic nature of Israel.
2. Compensation for Jews from Arab lands/recognition as refugees (in accordance with Israeli law requiring this issue be raised in the context of I-P negotiations).
3. Starting reconciliation process with the Palestinian people.
4. International recognition of the finality of the refugee problems.

Table 8.11 Palestinian benefits, costs, perceived benefits, and perceived costs for Principle 6

Palestinian benefits from Israeli concessions	Priorities	I1	I2	I3	I4	I5
Economic gains internally and from controlling the borders: customs, relationships with neighboring countries	0.3076	1	1	0.91	0.98	0.87
International benefits: Open and establish international relationships and cooperation with the world	0.0875	1	1	0.9	0.98	0.84
Creating a new positive climate for better relations and cooperation between the two parties	0.0403	0.94	0.98	0.9	0.98	0.86
Free movement of people and goods	0.2912	0.98	0.98	0.37	0.82	0.16
Development of tourism industry	0.0484	0.94	0.84	0.6	0.83	0.4
Trade: Controlling import and export on the basis of mutual benefits	0.0817	1	0.92	0.81	0.79	0.45
Political stability	0.119	1	0.93	0.71	0.91	0.84
Encouraging international investment	0.0243	0.95	0.88	0.76	0.78	0.66
		0.9876	0.9679	0.7009	0.8974	0.5945

Palestinian costs from Palestinian concessions	Priorities	P1	P2	P3	P4	P5
Running the border stations	0.5516	0.87	0.84	0.7	0.95	0.81
Manpower	0.2858	0.76	0.66	0.65	0.95	0.76
Political costs of engaging in early stages of the new situation with the Israelis	0.1627	0.35	0.76	0.73	0.88	0.73
		0.754	0.7755	0.6906	0.9386	0.7827

Palestinian perceptions of Israeli benefits from Palestinian concessions	Priorities	P1	P2	P3	P4	P5
Economic gains from relinquishing control	0.2237	1	0.9	0.25	0.75	0.25
Improved international relationships	0.1759	0.75	0.9	0.9	0.5	0.9
Removal of sanctions	0.0107	0	0	0	0	0
Movement	0.0241	0	0	0	0	0
Tourism	0.0542	0	0	0	0	0
Trade	0.1923	0.1	0.75	0.75	1	0.1
Cooperation	0.0167	0	0	0	0	0
Political	0.3025	0.1	0.9	0.9	1	0.1
		0.4051	0.776	0.6306	0.7505	0.2637

Palestinian perceptions of Israeli costs from Israeli concessions	Priorities	I1	I2	I3	I4	I5
Threat	0.0254	0	0	0	0	0
Loss of control	0.2777	0.25	0.5	0.5	0.25	0.25
Movement	0.0748	0	0	0	0	0
Maintenance of borders	0.4573	1	0.75	0.75	0.01	0.5
Cooperation costs	0.0397	0	0	0	0	0
Political	0.1251	0.01	0.1	0.1	0.25	0.1
		0.5279	0.4943	0.4943	0.1053	0.3106

Israeli Actions
I1. Total withdrawal from Palestinian territories
I2. Hand over fully the control point, border stations
I3. Provide Palestinians with all the information about the borders and passages
I4. Ensure no intervention what so ever in the border control points – respect the independence and integrity of the Palestinian borders
I5. Any information or requests passed through official channels on Palestinian side

Costs

1. Destroying the Jewish democratic nature of the State of Israel.
2. Destruction of towns and villages of Israel and resettlement of millions of Israelis.
3. Creating new imminent friction between Israelis and Palestinians.
4. Political.
5. To remain open to Palestinian claims
6. Israel taking responsibility for the creation of the Palestinian refugee issue will leave Israel solely responsible for solving the refugee issue financially and morally.

Table 8.12 Israeli and Palestinian benefits and costs, perceived benefits and costs, and gain ratios for Principle 6

Israelis

Concessions	Israelis' Costs	Israelis' _Perception_of _Palestinians' _Benefits	Israelis' Total Loss	Palestinians' Benefits	Palestinians' _Perception_of _Israelis_Costs	Palestinians' Total Gain
I1	1	1	1000000	1	1	1000000
I2	0.771658574	0.810940051	625768.8436	0.980052653	0.936351582	917673.8517
I3	0.331459238	0.450314906	149261.0356	0.709700284	0.936351582	664528.983
I4	0.798236647	0.56951248	454605.7322	0.908667477	0.199469597	181251.5349
I5	0.186940966	0.4812223	89960.16162	0.601964358	0.588369009	354177.173

Palestinians

Concessions	Palestinians' Costs	Palestinians' _Perception_of _Israelis' _Benefits	Palestinians' Total Loss	Israelis' Benefits	Israelis' _Perception_of _Palestinians' _Costs	Israelis' Total Gain
P1	0.8033241	0.522036082	419364.166	0.956454121	0.639651808	611797.6084
P2	0.826230556	1	826230.5561	0.858130292	0.92570914	794379.0547
P3	0.735776689	0.812628866	597913.3761	0.929324348	1	929324.3477
P4	1	0.967139175	967139.1753	0.181441161	0.629596278	114234.6798
P5	0.833901556	0.339819588	283376.0827	1	0.934714093	934714.0928

Israeli Ratios	P1	P2	P3	P4	P5
I1	0	0	0	0	0
I2	0	1.26944488	1.485092071	0	1.493705068
I3	4.098843384	5.32207921	6.226168428	0	6.262277953
I4	1.345776274	1.747402196	2.044242476	0	2.056098343
I5	6.800761553	8.83034268	10.33039882	1.269836311	10.3903114

Palestinian Ratios	P1	P2	P3	P4	P5
I1	2.384562347	1.210315925	1.672483072	1.033977348	3.528879327
I2	2.188250514	1.110675277	1.534793982	0	3.238360284
I3	1.584610792	0	1.111413475	0	2.34504259
I4	0	0	0	0	0
I5	0	0	0	0	1.249848504

Trade-off

	Action	Gain
Israeli	I2	1.485092071
Palestinian	P3	1.534793982
Israeli	I5	1.269836311
Palestinian	P4	0
Israeli	I1	0
Palestinian	P2	1.210315925

Palestinian Actions

P1. Recognition of Israel as the nation state of the Jewish people.

P2. Acknowledging the right of Palestinian refugees to return exclusively to the State of Palestine.

P3. Resolution of the Palestinian refugee issue will settle all claims, collective and individual, of the Palestinian refugees.
P4. The State of Israel has the exclusive right to decide who returns or immigrates to the State of Israel.
P5. Claims for compensation of Palestinian refugees will be exclusively resolved by an agreed upon international mechanism with the participation and contribution of Israel.
P6. Israel's contribution as defined by the agreement between the parties will be the total and final compensation to all claims.
P7. Within 5 years of the establishment of the international mechanism, UNRWA will dissolve, and refugee status will be formally annulled.
P8. Palestinians will commit to a reconciliation process, conducted by a joint committee.
P9. Jewish refugees shall be compensated.
P10. This agreement provides for the permanent and complete resolution of the Palestinian refugee issue.

Palestinian Perspective

Benefits

1. Israeli acknowledgment of its responsibility for the Palestinian refugee problem.
2. End of suffering of the Palestinian people.
3. End of conflict.
4. Protecting, maintaining, and enhancing the Palestinian social fabric.
5. Returning Palestinian control over their destiny.
6. Enabling the Palestinian people to have its share of regional development projects.
7. Rehabilitating and integrating the refugees into the Palestinian society and elsewhere.
8. Peace and stability in the region.
9. Contributing to the welfare of the host countries.
10. Create a climate of mutual cooperation and normalization with Israel.

Costs

1. Failure to resolve the refugee problem.
2. Undermining any other option for resolving the refugee problem.
3. Palestinian refugees considered as immigrants to Israel and not as people who have the right of return.
4. Denial of the Palestinian right to participate in the decision making for resolving the refugee problem.
5. Dissolving UNRWA before the final resolution of the refugee problem and ending the status of the refugees as refugees.
6. Exacerbation of the suffering of the refugees as a result of dissolving UNRWA before the final settlement of the claims.
7. Potential for not implementing the agreement.

Israeli Actions

I1. Right to choose to return to their original home.
I2. Right to choose to resettle in the State of Palestine, the host countries, or third countries.
I3. Endorsement of the international community.
I4. Endorsement of the Palestinian refugees' comprehensive and individual justice.
I5. International commission to develop opportunities for the refugees.
I6. International commission to adjudicate property claims.

Tables 8.13 and 8.14 give the Israeli and Palestinian benefits, costs, perceived benefits, and perceived costs for Principle 7, respectively. Table 8.15 has the gain/loss ratios for both parties, and Table 8.16 shows the matched actions. In this case, the concessions are bundled because some concessions for one party may have no gain (e.g., from the Israeli perspective, I1 gas a zero-gain value but provides a large gain if matched with P9 for the Palestinians) if matched with concessions from the other party. Table 8.17 gives the matched actions of the parties as bundles.

To implement these actions, the parties drafted the following principles.

Principles to Solve the Palestinian Refugee Problem

- The Palestinian refugees can choose to resettle in the State of Palestine, other host countries, or third-party countries; those Palestinians who were originally displaced according to UNRWA's registry from the area inside the Green Line and their spouse will be permitted to return to the State of Israel within five years. Palestinian refugees will be eligible for citizenship of the state they choose to resettle in or return to.
- All refugees have the right to compensation for their suffering and loss of property. An agreed upon international commission will handle all claims and implementation.

While the participants spent considerable time in developing the principles noted above to solve the Palestinian refugee problem, it became clear that these principles were guidelines to approach that problem and did not represent a totally implementable program. Still ahead will be a series of meetings to address the following issues which, when resolved, would hopefully yield the details of a workable program. These issues would be addressed in the following order:

1. How can we satisfy the Palestinian narrative about the importance of the right of return? We have already completed some aspects of this question in a previous meeting.
2. How do we get information from the refugees themselves about what their needs and preferences are? And how do we get in touch with refugees in camps and to whom would they have confidence to talk?
3. How and where to resettle the refugees currently in camps, and how can they be appropriately housed and given employment opportunities?
4. How can we compensate Palestinian refugees for the losses they have incurred, including who will be compensated, how much will they receive, and where will the resources come from?

Table 8.13 Israeli benefits, costs, perceived benefits, and perceived costs for Principle 7

Israeli Benefits from Palestinian Concessions	Priorities	P1	P2	P3	P4	P5	P6	P7	P8	P9	P10
Preservation of the Jewish and democratic nature of Israel	0.6723	0.788	1	1	1	0.113	0.575	0.538	0.525	0.363	0.975
Compensation for Jews from Arab lands/recognition as refuge	0.0494	0.088	0.112	0.438	0.025	0.463	0.275	0.213	0.3	1	0.175
Starting reconciliation process with the Palestinian people	0.0853	0.625	0.313	0.763	0.538	0.663	0.563	0.862	1	0.862	0.862
International recognition of the finality of the refugee problems	0.1929	0.5	0.925	0.975	0.763	0.888	0.9	0.975	0.888	0.6	0.925
		0.6836	0.883	0.9471	0.8665	0.3263	0.6218	0.6336	0.6244	0.4825	0.9162

Israeli Costs from Israeli Concesions	Priorities	I1	I2	I3	I4	I5	I6
Destroying the Jewish democratic nature of the State of Israel	0.3833	1	0.112	0	0.8	0.075	0.275
Destruction of towns and villages of Israel and resettlement of millions of Israelis	0.3289	0.975	0.025	0.088	0.913	0.088	0.213
Creating new imminent friction between Israelis and Palestinians	0.0631	0.975	0.075	0.188	0.538	0.112	0.313
Political	0.037	0.925	0.112	0.112	0.925	0.15	0.088
To remain open to Palestinian claims	0.1179	0.338	0.625	0.5	0.888	0.075	0.25
Israel taking responsibility for the creation of the Palestinian refugee issue	0.0698	0.925	0.625	0.215	0.763	0.153	0.34
		0.9041	0.1776	0.1187	0.8328	0.0897	0.2515

Israeli Perceived Palestinian Benefits from Israeli Concessions	Priorities	I1	I2	I3	I4	I5	I6
Israeli acknowledgement of its responsibility for the Palestinian refugee problem	0.1499	0.95	0.463	0.025	0.888	0.112	0.438
End of suffering of the Palestinian people	0.2003	0.925	0.763	0.5	0.625	0.8	0.862
End of conflict	0.066	0.9	0	0	0	0	0
Protecting, maintaining and enhancing the Palestinian social fabric	0.0803	0	0.563	0.663	0.763	0.788	0.4
Retaining Palestinian control over their destiny	0.1627	0.463	0.6	0.663	0.888	0.688	0.5
Enabling the Palestinian people to have its share of regional development projects	0.0476	0	0	0	0	0	0
Rehabilitating and integrating the refugees into the Palestinian society and elsewhere	0.1439	0.275	0.9	0.7	0.8	0.9	0.788
Peace and stability in the region	0.0446	0.663	0.663	0.825	0.7	0.825	0.663
Contributing to the welfare of the host countries	0.0283	0	0	0	0	0	0
Create a climate of mutual cooperation and normalization with Israel	0.0764	0.4	0.8	0.75	0.7	0.825	0.538
		0.562	0.585	0.4597	0.6636	0.5815	0.5357

Israeli Perceived Palestinian Costs from Palestinian Concessions	Priorities	P1	P2	P3	P4	P5	P6	P7	P8	P9	P10
Failure to resolve the refugee problem	0.287	0.8	0.425	0.15	0.862	0.625	0.625	0.725	0.25	0.313	0.763
Undermining any other option for resolving the refugee problem	0.1173	0.862	0.95	0.075	0.1	0.025	0.338	0.4	0.025	0.125	0.5
Palestinian refugees considered as immigrants to Israel and not as people who have the right of return	0.0315	0.825	0.725	0.1	0.088	0.05	0	0.088	0.05	0.025	0.338
Denial of the Palestinian right to participate in the decision making for resolving the refugee problem	0.1092	0.825	0.85	0.563	0.9	0.238	0.275	0.275	0.05	0	0.075
Dissolving UNRWA before the final resolution of the refugee problem and ending the status of the refugees as refugees	0.0634	0.195	0.09	0.1	0.37	0.375	0.115	0.225	0.255	0	0.05
Exacerbation of the suffering of the refugees as a result of dissolving UNRWA before the final settlement of the claims	0.0668	0.065	0.5	0.05	0.338	0.24	0.155	0.625	0.05	0	0.025
Potential for not implementing the agreement	0.3248	0.9	0.862	0.028	0.378	0.277	0.215	0.215	0.125	0.313	0.528
		0.7559	0.6683	0.1351	0.5289	0.3398	0.3365	0.4136	0.1418	0.2066	0.4725

Table 8.14 Palestinian benefits, costs, perceived benefits, and perceived costs for Principle 7

Palestinian Benefits from Israeli Concessions	Priorities	I1	I2	I3	I4	I5	I6
Israeli acknowledgement of its responsibility for the Palestinian refugee problem	0.3099	0.663	0.438	0.338	0.75	0.725	0.925
End of suffering of the Palestinian people	0.1067	0.725	0.788	0.725	0.9	0.862	0.862
End of conflict	0.0396	0	0	0	0	0	0
Protecting, maintaining and enhancing the Palestinian social fabric	0.0909	0.7	0.725	0.688	0.788	0.663	0.862
Retaining Palestinian control over their destiny	0.2104	0.563	0.725	0.788	0.688	0.5	0.725
Enabling the Palestinian people to have its share of regional development projects	0.0312	0	0	0	0	0	0
Rehabilitating and integrating the refugees into the Palestinian society and elsewhere	0.1134	0.438	0.788	0.825	0.763	0.888	0.913
Peace and stability in the region	0.0511	0.725	0.788	0.888	0.825	0.888	0.862
Contributing to the welfare of the host countries	0.0133	0	0	0	0	0	0
Create a climate of mutual cooperation and normalization with Israel	0.0336	0	0	0	0	0	0
		0.5513	0.5675	0.549	0.6733	0.6281	0.7571

Palestinian Costs from Palestinian Concessions	Priorities	P1	P2	P3	P4	P5	P6	P7	P8	P9	P10
Failure to resolve the refugee problem	0.0788	1	1	0	1	0	0.9	0.9	1	1	0
Undermining any other option for resolving the refugee problem	0.3502	0.9	1	0.9	1	0.75	0.9	1	0.9	0	0.9
Palestinian refugees considered as immigrants to Israel and not as people who have the right of return	0.1763	1	1	1	1	0.9	1	1	1	1	0.9
Denial of the Palestinian right to participate in the decision making for resolving the refugee problem	0.3072	1	0.9	0.9	1	0.9	0.75	1	0.9	1	0.9
Dissolving UNRWA before the final resolution of the refugee problem and ending the status of the refugees as refugees	0.0281	1	0.75	0.75	1	0.75	0.75	0.9	0.75	1	0.9
Exacerbation of the suffering of the refugees as a result of dissolving UNRWA before the final settlement of the claims	0.0449	1	1	0.9	1	0.75	0.9	0.9	0.9	1	0.75
Potential for not implementing the agreement	0.0144	1	1	0.9	1	0.9	0.9	1	0.9	1	0.9
		0.965	0.9623	0.843	1	0.7656	0.8673	1	0.92	1	0.82

Palestinian Perceived Israeli Benefits from Palestinian Concessions	Priorities	P1	P2	P3	P4	P5	P6	P7	P8	P9	P10
Preservation of the Jewish and democratic nature of Israel	0.6802	0.1	1	0.75	0.9	0.9	0.9	1	0.9	0	1
Compensation for Jews from Arab lands/recognition as refugee	0.0322	0	0.25	0.25	0.1	0.1	0.1	0	0.9	0	0
Starting reconciliation process with the Palestinian people	0.0925	0.25	0.5	0.5	0.5	0.75	0.75	0.1	0.5	0	0.75
International recognition of the finality of the refugee problem	0.1951	0.25	0.25	0.75	0.75	0.9	0.9	0.5	0.9	0	0.75
		0.1399	0.7832	0.711	0.808	0.8603	0.8603	0.8	0.86	0	0.9

Palestinian Perceived Israeli Costs from Israeli Concessions	Priorities	I1	I2	I3	I4	I5	I6
Destroying the Jewish character of the State of Israel	0.3498	0.75	0.25	0	0	0	0
Destruction of towns and villages of Israel and resettlement of millions of Israelis	0.0324	0.75	0	0	0	0	0
Creating new imminent friction between Israelis and Palestinians	0.0446	0.75	0.1	0	0.1	0	0
Political	0.1433	0.9	0.1	0.1	0.5	0.25	0.75
To remain open to Palestinian claims	0.2069	0.9	0.5	0	0.25	0.75	0.1
Israel taking responsibility for the creation of the Palestinian refugee issue	0.2229	0.9	0	0.5	0.75	0.25	0.1
		0.836	0.2097	0.126	0.295	0.2467	0.1505

When this work is completed, the parties will have in hand a proposal for an approach which is fair to both sides. We develop this program in some detail in Chap. 9.

Principle 8

Limited arms of the Palestinian State and international guarantees from the international community against aggression from other parties.

Israeli Perspective

Benefits

Table 8.15 Israeli and Palestinian benefits and costs, perceived benefits, and costs for Principle 7

Israelis

Concessions	Israelis' Costs	Israelis' _Perception_of_Palestinians' _Benefits	Israelis' Total Loss	Palestinians' Benefits	Palestinians' _Perception_of_Israelis _Costs	Palestinians' Total Gain
I1	1	0.84689572	846895.7203	0.728173293	1	728173.2928
I2	0.196438447	0.881555154	173171.3254	0.74957073	0.250837321	188020.3136
I3	0.131290786	0.692736588	90949.93146	0.725135385	0.150478469	109117.2625
I4	0.921137042	1	921137.0424	0.889314489	0.352870813	313813.1273
I5	0.099214689	0.876280892	86939.93587	0.829612997	0.295095694	244815.2229
I6	0.278177193	0.807263412	224562.2697	1	0.180023923	180023.9234

Palestinians

Concessions	Palestinians' Costs	Palestinians' _Perception_of_Israelis' _Benefits	Palestinians' Total Loss	Israelis' Benefits	Israelis' _Perception_of_ Palestinians' _Costs	Israelis' Total Gain
P1	0.965	0.156155821	150690.3672	0.721782283	1	721782.2828
P2	0.9623	0.87420471	841247.1928	0.932319713	0.884111655	824274.7243
P3	0.8425	0.79339212	668432.8608	1	0.178727345	178727.3449
P4	1	0.901886371	901886.3712	0.91489811	0.699695727	640150.2982
P5	0.7656	0.960263422	735177.6761	0.344525393	0.449530361	154874.6245
P6	0.8673	0.960263422	832836.4661	0.656530461	0.445164704	292264.1887
P7	0.9848	0.878446255	865093.8721	0.668989547	0.547162323	366045.8747
P8	0.9213	0.963277151	887467.2396	0.659275684	0.187590951	123674.1526
P9	0.6498	0.130371693	84715.52629	0.5094499	0.273316576	139241.1024
P10	0.8223	1	822300	0.967374089	0.625082683	604688.7911

1. Reduction in threat from conventional military risk from Palestinians.
2. No other country can support/aid Palestinians with military assistance.
3. Social psyche—without the threat of military presence the social psyche will be relieved (sense of security).
4. Using Palestinian airspace for military training.
5. Allows for finalization of the conflict.

Costs

1. Lack of control
2. Threat
3. Political
4. Restructuring of how to "deal" with the new status

Palestinian Actions

P1. List of forbidden weapons:

a. Strategic weapons
b. Tanks
c. Missiles/rocket
d. Aircraft

Table 8.16 Israeli and Palestinian gain/loss ratios for Principle 7

Israelis' Ratios — Palestinian's Concessions

		P1	P2	P3	P4	P5	P6	P7	P8	P9	P10
	I1	0	0	0	0	0	0	0	0	0	0
Israelis'	I2	4.168024	4.75988	1.032084	3.69663	0	1.687717	2.113779	0	0	3.491853
Concessions	I3	7.93604	9.06295	1.965118	7.038491	1.702856	3.213462	4.024697	1.359805	1.530964	6.64859
	I4	0	0	0	0	0	0	0	0	0	0
	I5	8.30208	9.480968	2.055757	7.363133	1.781398	3.361679	4.210331	1.422524	1.601578	6.955248
	I6	3.214174	3.670584	0	2.850658	0	1.301484	1.630042	0	0	2.692744

Palestinian's Ratios — Palestinian's Concessions

		P1	P2	P3	P4	P5	P6	P7	P8	P9	P10
	I1	4.832248	0	1.089374	0	0	0	0	0	8.595512	0
Israelis'	I2	1.247726	0	0	0	0	0	0	0	2.219432	0
Concessions	I3	0	0	0	0	0	0	0	0	1.288043	0
	I4	2.082503	0	0	0	0	0	0	0	3.704317	0
	I5	1.624624	0	0	0	0	0	0	0	2.889851	0
	I6	1.194661	0	0	0	0	0	0	0	2.12504	0

Trade-off	Action	Gain	Total
Israeli	I1	0	10.2672
Palestinian	P9	8.595512	10.22014
Israeli	I3	1.965118	
Palestinian	P3	0	
Israeli	I5	8.30208	
Palestinian	P1	1.624624	

Table 8.17 Matched concessions as bundles for Principle 7

Israeli actions	Gain	Palestinian actions	Gain
I1. Right to choose to return to their original home	0	P9. Jewish refugees shall be compensated	8.595
I3. Endorsement of the international community	1.965	P3. Resolution of the Palestinian refugee issue will settle all claims, collective and individual, of the Palestinian refugees	0
I5. International commission to develop opportunities for the refugees	8.302	P1. Recognition of Israel as the Nation State of the Jewish people	1.625
Total	10.27		10.22

P2. Monitoring by private groups
P3. Multinational monitoring (Principle 9)

Palestinian Perspective

Benefits

1. Allocation of resources for economic development rather than military expenditures.

2. Declare and ensure the neutrality of the State of Palestine.
3. Ensure the security of the State of Palestine through international guarantees.

Costs

1. Threat
2. Loss of control
3. Redeployment and restructuring how to "deal" with the new status

Israeli Actions

I1. Israeli commitment not to violate the Palestinian sovereignty by invading air space.

I2. Israel should abide by the international commitment to support Principle 8.

I3. Israeli commitment not to violate the Palestinian sovereignty by invading borders.

Tables 8.18 and 8.19 give the Israeli and Palestinian benefits, costs, perceived benefits, and perceived costs for Principle 8. Table 8.20 gives the gain/loss ratios for Principle 8.

As a result of these matched concessions, the actions to be required of each party will be as follows:

Israeli Actions

- Israeli commitment not to violate the borders of the State of Palestine.

Palestinian Actions

- Multinational oversight—Principle 9.

Principle 9

Agreed upon international monitoring mechanism and agreed upon binding international arbitration mechanisms.

What is needed for the implementation of this principle is:

- **Monitor and verify** the implementation of the agreement
- **Timetable for the implementation** of the agreement
- **International arbitration mechanism** to deal with any problems arising during implementation of agreements based on differences in interpretations.

Summary

In sum, we now have a detailed set of actions from both parties to implement the principles. Table 8.21 contains a summary of the specific actions required from both parties to implement the principles outlined.

Table 8.18 Israeli benefits, costs, perceived benefits, and perceived costs for Principle 8

Israeli benefits from Palestinian concessions	Priorities	P1	P2	P3
Reduction in threat from conventional military risk from Palestinians	0.3278	1	0.975	0.862
No other country can support / aid Palestinians with military	0.1883	0.563	0.525	1
Sense of security	0.1726	0.975	1	0.862
Using Palestinian airspace for military training	0.3113	0.938	0.033	0.07
		0.8939	0.6012	0.6417

Israeli costs from Israeli concessions	Priorities	I1	I2	I3
Threat	0.4448	1	0.01	0.725
Loss of control	0.4757	0.888	0.375	0.825
Redeployment and restructuring how to 'deal' with the new status	0.0795	0.813	0	0
		0.9316	0.1828	0.715

Israeli perception of Palestinian benefits from Israeli concessions	Priorities	I1	I2	I3
Allocation of resources for economic development rather than military expenditures	0.5978	0.195	0.01	0.663
Declare and ensure the neutrality of the State of Palestine	0.1127	0.725	0.925	0.888
Ensure the security of the State of Palestine through international guarantees	0.2895	0.318	0.725	0.862
		0.2902	0.3201	0.7458

Israeli perception of Palestinian costs from Palestinian concessions	Priorities	P1	P2	P3
Risk associated with limited national defense	0.11	0.725	0.563	0.1
Political cost associated with the limitations of arms	0.2364	0.725	0.5	0.5
Financial burden incurred by the international community and to be shared by the State of Palestine	0.1688	0.033	0.502	0.313
National pride undermined by limited arms policy	0.4849	0.75	0.1	0.725
		0.6203	0.3133	0.5335

Palestinian Actions
P1. List of forbidden weapons
a. Strategic Weapons
b. Tanks
c. Missiles / Rocket
d. Aircraft
P2. Monitoring. a. Private groups
P3. Multinational monitoring (Principle 9)

Table 8.19 Palestinian benefits, costs, perceived benefits, and perceived costs for Principle 8

Palestinian benefits from Israeli concessions	Priorities	I1	I2	I3
Allocation of resources for economic development rather than military expenditures	0.2176	0.9	0.9	0.9
Declare and ensure the neutrality of the State of Palestine	0.0503	1	1	0.9
Ensure the security of the State of Palestine through international guarantees	0.7322	1	1	0.9
		0.9782	0.9782	0.9

Palestinian costs from Palestinian concessions	Priorities	P1	P2	P3
Risk associated with limited national defense	0.6668	0.9	0.5	0.5
Political cost associated with the limitations of arms	0.2181	0.75	0.75	0.75
Financial burden incurred by the international community and to be shared by the State of Palestine	0.0376	0.25	0.25	0.25
National pride undermined by limited arms policy	0.0775	0.75	0.75	0.75
		0.8312	0.5645	0.5645

Palestinian perception of Israeli benefits from Palestinian concessions	Priorities	P1	P2	P3
Reduction in threat from conventional military risk from Palestinians	0.2389	0.75	0.75	0.9
No other country can support / aid Palestinians with military	0.0478	0	0	0
Social psyche – without the threat of military presence the social psyche will be relieved	0.1082	1	0.75	0.9
Using Palestinian airspace for military training	0.0222	0	0	0
Allows for finalization of the conflict	0.5828	0.9	0.75	0.9
		0.8119	0.6975	0.837

Palestinian perception of Israeli costs from Israeli concessions	Priorities	I1	I2	I3
Threat	0.0377	0.25	0.01	0.01
Loss of control	0.0998	0.01	0.01	0.01
Restructuring how to 'deal' with the new status	0.5986	0.1	0.01	0.1
Political	0.2639	0.5	0.5	0.25
		0.2023	0.1393	0.1272

Israeli Actions
1. Israeli commitment not to violate the Palestinian sovereignty by invading air space
2. Israel should abide by the international commitment to support principle 8
3. Israeli commitment not to violate the Palestinian sovereignty by invading borders

Table 8.20 Israeli and Palestinian benefits and costs, perceived benefits and costs, and gain/loss ratios for Principle 8

Israelis

Concessions	Israelis' Costs	Israelis' _Perception_of _Palestinians' _Benefits	Israelis' Total Loss	Palestinians' Benefits	Palestinians' _Perception_of _Israelis_Costs	Palestinians' Total Gain
1	1	0.389112363	389112.3626	1	1	1000000
2	0.196221554	0.42920354	84218.9857	1	0.688581315	688581.3149
3	0.76749678	1	767496.7797	0.920057248	0.628769155	578503.6181

Palestinians

Concessions	Palestinians' Costs	Palestinians' _Perception_of _Israelis' _Benefits	Palestinians' Total Loss	Israelis' Benefits	Israelis' _Perception_of _Palestinians' _Costs	Israelis' Total Gain
1	1	0.970011947	970011.9474	1	1	1000000
2	0.679138595	0.833333333	565948.829	0.672558452	0.505078188	339694.6041
3	0.679138595	1	679138.5948	0.717865533	0.860067709	617412.9645

Israeli Ratios	P1	P2	P3
I1	2.569951757	0	1.586721533
I2	11.87380721	4.033468241	7.331042512
I3	1.302937063	0	0

Palestinian Ratios	P1	P2	P3
I1	1.030915137	1.766944198	1.472453499
I2	0	1.216684759	1.013903966
I3	0	1.022183612	0

Trade-off

	Action	Gain
Israeli	I1	1.586721533
Palestinian	P3	1.472453499

Table 8.21 Summary of principles and implementation actions

Principle	Narrative	Israeli's Actions	Palestinian's Actions
1	**A Two-State Solution on the borders of the 4th of June 1967, with mutually agreed upon land swaps.**		
2	**Israel must respect the integrity of the West Bank and Gaza by allowing free and safe passage between the two areas, and the Palestinian State must guarantee that any agreement reached with Israel will be accepted and supported by the majority of the Palestinian people both in Gaza and the West Bank.**		
3	**East Jerusalem is the capital of the Palestinian State. The parties will maintain the status quo of the holy places in Jerusalem.**	☒ Rescind all legal and administrative measures and orders legislated by Israel since 1967. ☒ Preserve and respect the status quo of the holy places in the city as decreed and accepted by the Ottomans and the international community in 1856.	☒ Full Palestinian cooperation during transfer of power and beyond it. ☒ Acceptance of international monitoring on the compliance of the transfer of power process.
4	**Acknowledge Israel's Existence as a Jewish State without jeopardizing the rights of its minority Israeli citizens.**		
5	**Evacuation of Israeli settlers from the Palestinian territories who are not included in the land swap.**	☒ Facilitate the evacuation without causing any damage to the properties or land.	☒ A Palestinian commitment to fully collaborate with Israel during the relocation process and maintain a restrained approach toward the actual relocation.
6	**Palestinian full control of the borders of the Palestinian State and its outlets, and deployment of a temporary agreed upon multinational military monitoring system in the Jordan Valley.**	☒ Hand over fully the control point, border stations. ☒ Total withdrawal from Palestinian territories. ☒ Any information or requests passed through official channels on Palestinian side.	☒ Multi-national oversight – Principle 9. ☒ Limited Arms - Principle 8. ☒ Access to airspace for training.
7	**Solve the Palestinian refugee problem in a just and agreed upon manner.**	☒ Right to choose to return to their original home. ☒ Endorsement of the international community. ☒ International commission to develop opportunities for the refugees.	☒ Jewish refugees shall be compensated. ☒ Resolution of the Palestinian refugee issue will settle all claims, collective and individual, of the Palestinian refugees. ☒ Recognition of Israel as the Nation State of the Jewish people.
8	**Limited Arms of the Palestinian state and international guarantees from the international community against aggression from other parties.**	☒ Israeli commitment not to violate the borders of the State of Palestine.	☒ Multi-national oversight – Principle 9.
9	**Agreed upon international monitoring mechanism and agreed upon binding international arbitration mechanisms.**	☒ **Monitor and verify** the implementation of the agreement, ☒ **Timetable for the implementation** of the agreement, ☒ **International arbitration mechanism** to deal with any problems arising during implementation of agreements based on differences in interpretations.	

Reference

Aczel, J., & Saaty, T. L. (1983). Procedures for synthesizing ratio judgments. *Journal of Mathematical Psychology, 27*(1), 93–102.

Chapter 9
The Palestinian Refugee Problem: Compensation and Reparation Program

Introduction

In 1947, the United Nations (UN) adopted a Partition Plan for Palestine leading to the creation of independent Arab and Jewish states, and an internationalized Jerusalem. The Declaration of the Establishment of the State of Israel was proclaimed on May 14, 1948, by David Ben-Gurion, the then Executive Head of the World Zionist Organization, Chairman of the Jewish Agency for Palestine, and soon to be the first Prime Minister of Israel. The declaration of independence of the State of Israel started the 1948 Arab–Israeli War. However, Palestinians have departed their homes starting in 1947 with the UN Partition Plan. From 1947 to 1949, more than 700,000 Palestinians departed their homes. This departure took place in four stages ending in 1949 (Shlaim, 2001).

We are not interested in studying how and why those departures took place. Our sole objective is to study the refugee problem in the context of Principle 7 of the Pittsburgh Declaration of Principles—August 2011.

To accomplish this objective, the same group of Israeli and Palestinian representatives who develop the principles met to study the problem using the same technology employed to develop the principles—the analytic hierarchy process.

Program Prioritization

The goal of the meetings was to find a solution for the Palestinian refugees within the broader context of the Peace Agreement developed in the previous meetings. The participants developed a hierarchy (Fig. 9.1) which included the following levels:

T. L. Saaty et al., *Overcoming the Retributive Nature of the Israeli-Palestinian Conflict*, https://doi.org/10.1007/978-3-030-83958-1_9

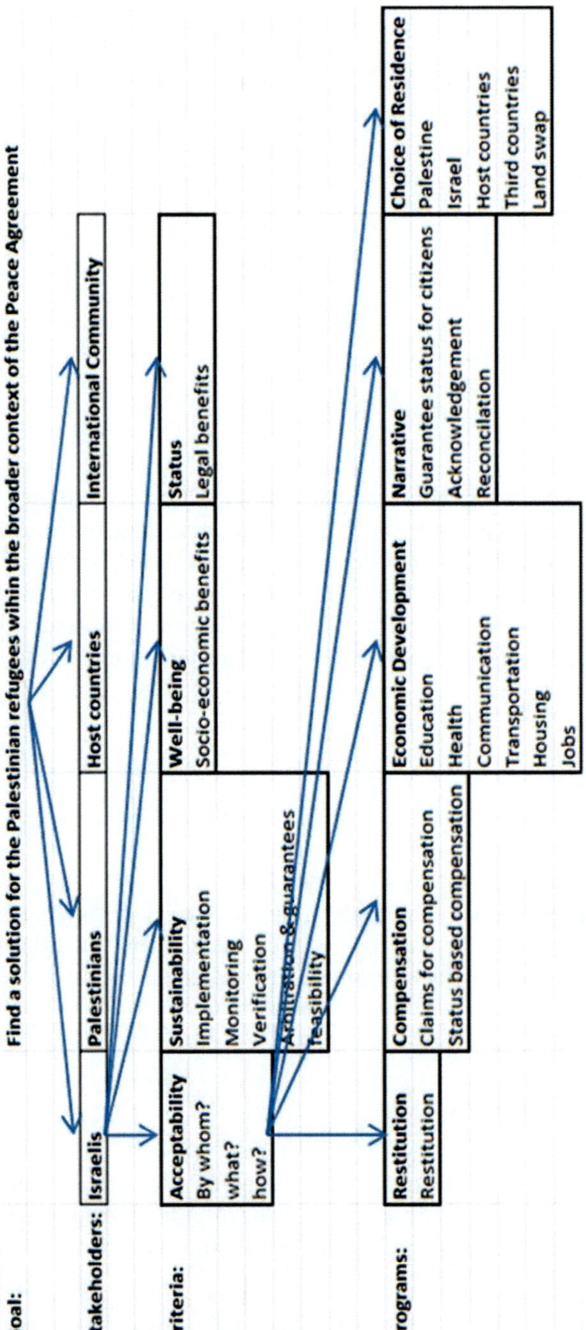

Fig. 9.1 Palestinian refugee hierarchy

(1) Stakeholders

(a) Israel
(b) Palestinians
(c) Host countries
(d) International community

(2) Criteria

(a) Acceptability—By whom? What? How?
(b) Sustainability—Implementation, monitoring, verification, arbitration and guarantees, feasibility
(c) Well-being—Socioeconomic benefits
(d) Status—Legal benefits to evaluate the programs developed in the next level.

(3) Programs

(a) Property restitution—Return to the owner the right of ownership, e.g., deed of a track of land.
(b) Property compensation—claims-based vs status based.
(c) Economic development—Education, health, communication, transportation, housing, jobs.
(d) Narrative—Guarantee status for citizens, acknowledgment of wrongdoing, reconciliation
(e) Choice of residence—Palestine, Israel, host countries, third countries, and land swap.

To evaluate the programs, the participants first evaluated the criteria for each stakeholder. The question asked was: Given a stakeholder, and two criteria, which criterion is more important for that stakeholder and how much? For example, for the stakeholder Israel, what is more important, acceptability or sustainability, and by how much? They answered sustainability was more important, but only slightly more important, i.e., between equal and moderate, which corresponds to the numeric value two in Table 3.1 in Chap. 3. All the judgments (attained by consensus) for these comparisons are given in Table 9.1. The resulting priorities are given in the last column of the table.

Next, the programs are evaluated according to each criterion. The participants needed to answer questions such as:

Given a criterion and two programs, which program is more relevant and how much to find a solution to the Palestinian refugee issue? Table 9.2 contains the Israeli's and the Palestinian's perspectives.

Because the stakeholders in the Palestinian refugee problem could not be compared to determine their power to solve the problem, and it is not politically wise to do so even if we could, we needed to find a way to ascertain which stakeholder had

Table 9.1 Criteria comparison

Israelis	Acc	Sust	M-W	Status	Priorities
Acc	1	0.5	5	5	0.3492
Sust	2	1	3	5	0.4437
M-W	0.2	0.333333	1	0.2	0.0682
Status	0.2	0.2	5	1	0.1388
			CR		0.242

Palestinians	Acc	Sust	M-W	Status	Priorities
Acc	1	3	0.2	7	0.3032
Sust	0.333333	1	5	5	0.2832
M-W	5	0.2	1	0.142857	0.2092
Status	0.142857	0.2	7	1	0.2043
				CR	1.881

more influence to make the programs succeed. Influence was loosely defined as a conglomerate of properties such as internal/external political power, money, confidence building, experience solving similar problems, guarantees, and incentive/motivation to solve the issue. The question that needed to be answered was:

Given a program and two stakeholders, who has more influence to make the program succeed?

Comparing the influence of the stakeholders to make the programs succeed created a loop that connected the bottom of the hierarchy, given in Fig. 9.1, with the level of stakeholders. Figure 9.2 puts in perspective what Tables 9.1, 9.2, and 9.3 represent in the evaluation process.

This network can be represented in matrix form known as the supermatrix (Saaty, 1980) given in Eq. 9.1. The nonzero entries of the matrix W, i.e., W_{21}, W_{32}, and W_{13}, correspond to the priorities given in Table 9.1, 9.2, and 9.3, respectively. The supermatrix is given in Table 9.4.

$$W = \begin{array}{l} \text{Stakeholders } (S) \\ \text{Criteria } \quad (C) \\ \text{Programs } \ (P) \end{array} \overset{\begin{array}{ccc} S & C & P \end{array}}{\begin{pmatrix} 0 & 0 & W_{13} \\ W_{21} & 0 & 0 \\ 0 & W_{32} & 0 \end{pmatrix}} \tag{9.1}$$

To obtain the synthesized priorities of the elements of the network—the limiting priorities—we use the extension of the analytic hierarchy process to networks, the analytic network process (ANP) (see, for example, Saaty & Vargas, 2013). The matrix in Eq. 9.1 is a column stochastic matrix (i.e., the columns add to one) of cyclicity 4 which means that the powers of W, $(W^4)^k$, $k = 1, 2, \ldots$, yield a matrix with nonzero values in the same entries as the matrix W. For this type of matrices, the

Table 9.2 Comparison of programs with respect to the criteria

Israelis' Perspective

Acceptability	Restitution	Compensation	Economic Development	Narrative	Choice of Residence	Priorities
Restitution	1	0.111	0.111	0.5	0.5	0.0528
Compensation	9	1	0.50	3	1	0.2579
Economic Development	9	2	1	5	1	0.3671
Narrative	2	0.333333333	0.2	1	0.2	0.0722
Choice of residence	2	1	1	5	1	0.2501

Sustainability	Restitution	Compensation	Economic Development	Narrative	Choice of residence	Priorities
Restitution	1	0.111	0.111	0.25	1	0.0624
Compensation	9	1	0.25	4	1	0.2258
Economic Development	9	4	1	6	0.5	0.3806
Narrative	4	0.25	0.166666667	1	0.25	0.0796
Choice of residence	1	1	2	4	1	0.2517

Well-Being	Restitution	Compensation	Economic Development	Narrative	Choice of residence	Priorities
Restitution	1	0.1111	0.1111	0.5	0.11	0.0266
Compensation	9	1	0.3333	5	1	0.2265
Economic Development	9	3	1	5	0.5	0.2920
Narrative	2	5	0.2	1	0.25	0.1908
Choice of residence	9	1	2	4	1	0.2641

Status	Restitution	Compensation	Economic Development	Narrative	Choice of Residence	Priorities
Restitution	1	1	1.000	0.5	0.111111111	0.0682
Compensation	1	1	1.00	0.5	0.142857143	0.0724
Economic Development	1	1	1	0.5	0.142857143	0.0724
Narrative	2	2	2	1	0.111111111	0.1220
Choice of residence	9	7	7	9	1	0.6650

(continued)

Table 9.2 (continued)

Palestinians' Perspective

Acceptability	Restitution	Compensation	Economic Development	Narrative	Choice of Residence	Priorities
Restitution	1	1.000	0.333	3	0.33333333	0.1394
Compensation	1	1	3.00	5	3	0.3633
Economic Development	3	0.333333333	1	5	0.33333333	0.1848
Narrative	0.333333333	0.2	0.2	1	0.33333333	0.0510
Choice of residence	3	0.333333333	3	3	1	0.2614

Sustainability	Restitution	Compensatio n	Economic Development	Narrative	Choice of Residence	Priorities
Restitution	1	1	0.20	3	0.3333333	0.1200
Compensation	1	1	5.00	1	1	0.2644
Economic Development	5	0.2	1	3	0.2	0.1760
Narrative	0.333333333	1	0.333333333	1	0.1666667	0.0777
Choice of residenc	3	1	5	6	1	0.3619

Well-Being	Restitution	Compensation	Economic Development	Narrative	Choice of Residence	Priorities
Restitution	1	1	5	3	6	0.3625
Compensation	1	1	3	3	3	0.2648
Economic Development	0.2	0.333333333	1	0.25	3	0.1101
Narrative	0.333333333	0.333333333	4	1	0.2	0.1212
Choice of residence	0.166666667	0.333333333	0.333333333	5	1	0.1415

Status	Restitution	Compensation	Economic Development	Narrative	Choice of Residence	Priorities
Restitution	1	1.000	5.000	3	1	0.2804
Compensation	1	1	5.00	4	1	0.3006
Economic Development	0.2	0.2	1	0.333333333	0.333333333	0.0574
Narrative	0.333333333	0.25	3	1	0.333333333	0.1035
Choice of resider	1	1	3	3	1	0.2580

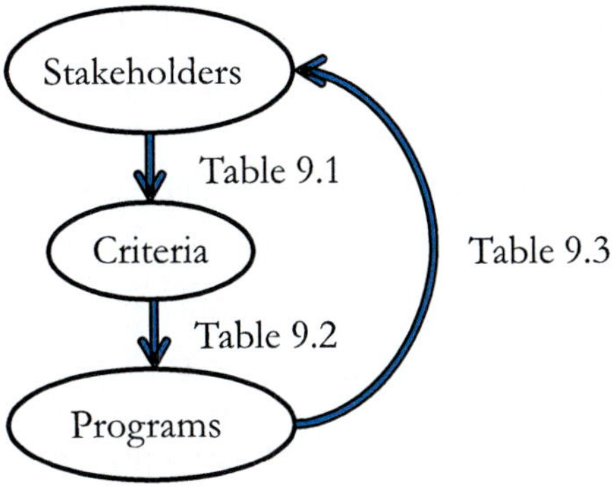

Fig. 9.2 Network of influences

limiting priorities are obtained by raising the matrix to larger powers. In this case, the limiting priorities are given by $\lim_{k \to \infty} \left(W^4\right)^k$. This matrix has blocks in the same position as the matrix *W*, but all their columns have the same values within each block. The limiting priorities are given in Table 9.5. A summary of those priorities is given in Table 9.6 below.

From these limiting priorities, we observe that:

(1) Both Israelis and Palestinians think that the international community has more power to solve the problem.
(2) The Israelis and Palestinians disagree as to who has more influence to solve the issue. The Israelis think that the host countries have more influence, while the Palestinians think that Israel has more influence.
(3) Both the Israelis and the Palestinians agree that sustainability is the main criterion to use in the implementation of the programs.
(4) The Israelis and Palestinians disagree as to the focus of the programs. The Israelis want to pay more attention to economic development, while the Palestinians think that the choice of residence is the most important. Choice of residence is also important for Israel but not as much as economic development.
(5) The Israelis and Palestinians agree that compensation needs to be considered.

Program Implementation

Each of the programs prioritized in the previous section are now developed into specific actions or focus. To prioritize the actions/focus of the programs, the participants identified five criteria for implementation:

- **Speed**: Emphasis on implementing the program as fast as possible.
- **Comprehensive**: Emphasis on implementing the program in all its details.
- **Funds' commitment**: Emphasis on making sure funds are available.
- **Clarity of rules**: Emphasis on making sure the rules are easily understood.
- **Transparency**: Emphasis on making sure all the steps are known.

Table 9.3 Stakeholders' influence with respect to the programs

Israelis' Perspective

Restitution	Israel	Palestinians	Host countries	Int'l community	Priorities
Israel	1	9	9	9	0.750
Palestinians	0.111111	1	1	1	0.083
Host countries	0.111111	1	1	1	0.083
Int'l communit\	0.111111	1	1	1	0.083
				CR	0.00

Compensation	Israel	Palestinians	Host countries	Int'l community	Priorities
Israel	1	3	2	0.142857143	0.1576
Palestinians	0.333333	1	1	0.125	0.0725
Host countries	0.5	1	1	0.2	0.0911
Int'l communit\	7	8	5	1	0.6788
				CR	0.049

Economic Development	Israel	Palestinians	Host countries	Int'l community	Priorities
Israel	1	2	0.333333333	0.125	0.09308548
Palestinians	0.5	1	1	0.142857143	0.08726725
Host countries	3	1	1	0.166666667	0.14511578
Int'l community	8	7	6	1	0.67453148
				CR	0.096

Acknowledgement of responsibility for creation of the refugee problem:

Narrative	Israel	Palestinians	Host countries	Int'l community	Priorities
Israel	1	1	1	1	0.2389
Palestinians	1	1	0.5	2	0.2530
Host countries	1	2	1	1	0.2994
Int'l community	1	0.5	1	1	0.2087
				CR	0.060

Acknowledgement of responsibility for solution of the refugee problem:

Narrative	Israel	Palestinians	Host countries	Int'l community	Priorities
Israel	1	3	1	1	0.3065
Palestinians	0.333333	1	0.5	0.5	0.1254
Host countries	1	2	1	0.5	0.2349
Int'l community	1	2	2	1	0.3333
				CR	0.026

Choice of residence	Israel	Palestinians	Host countries	Int'l community	Priorities
Israel	1	1	0.142857143	0.2	0.0680
Palestinians	1	1	0.142857143	0.333333333	0.0756
Host countries	7	7	1	4	0.6236
Int'l community	5	3	0.25	1	0.2328
				CR	0.033

(continued)

Table 9.3 (continued)

Palestinian Perspective

Restitution	Israel	Palestinians	Host countries	Int'l community	Priorities
Israel	1	7	7	4	0.6261
Palestinians	0.142857	1	0.333333333	0.333333333	0.0607
Host countries	0.142857	3	1	0.333333333	0.1067
Int'l communit\	0.25	3	3	1	0.2065
				CR	0.061

Compensation	Israel	Palestinians	Host countries	Int'l community	Priorities
Israel	1	4	2	1	0.3308
Palestinians	0.25	1	3	0.142857143	0.1286
Host countries	0.5	0.33333333	1	0.333333333	0.1014
Int'l communit\	1	7	3	1	0.4392
				CR	0.159

Economic Development	Israel	Palestinians	Host countries	Int'l community	Priorities
Israel	1	1	3	0.142857143	0.1318
Palestinians	1	1	3	0.142857143	0.1318
Host countries	0.333333	0.33333333	1	0.2	0.0678
Int'l community	7	7	5	1	0.6685
				CR	0.086

Acknowledgement of responsibility for creation of the refugee problem:

Narrative	Israel	Palestinians	Host countries	Int'l community	Priorities
Israel	1	9	7	5	0.5883
Palestinians	0.111111	1	0.111111111	0.111111111	0.0271
Host countries	0.142857	9	1	0.111111111	0.0903
Int'l community	0.2	9	9	1	0.2943
				CR	0.318

Acknowledgement of responsibility for solution of the refugee problem:

Narrative	Israel	Palestinians	Host countries	Int'l community	Priorities
Israel	1	7	7	3	0.6229
Palestinians	0.142857	1	1	0.5	0.0924
Host countries	0.142857	1	1	0.5	0.0924
Int'l community	0.333333	2	2	1	0.1922
				CR	0.001

Choice of residence	Israel	Palestinians	Host countries	Int'l community	Priorities
Israel	1	7	0.25	0.166666667	0.2047
Palestinians	0.142857	1	3	0.166666667	0.1437
Host countries	4	0.33333333	1	1	0.2322
Int'l community	6	6	1	1	0.4194
				CR	0.815

Table 9.4 Supermatrix corresponding to the network of influences

	Israelis' Perspective	Stakeholders				Criteria				Programs				
		Israel	Palestinians	Host countries	Int'l community	Acceptability	Sustainability	Well-being	Status	Restitution	Compensation	Economic Development	Narrative	Choice of residence
Stakeholders	Israel	0	0	0	0	0	0	0	0	0.7500	0.1576	0.0931	0.2896	0.0680
	Palestinians	0	0	0	0	0	0	0	0	0.0833	0.0725	0.0873	0.1573	0.0756
	Host countries	0	0	0	0	0	0	0	0	0.0833	0.0911	0.1451	0.2510	0.6236
	Int'l community	0	0	0	0	0	0	0	0	0.0833	0.6788	0.6745	0.3021	0.2328
Criteria	Acceptability	0.3492	0.3032	0	0	0	0	0	0	0	0	0	0	0
	Sustainability	0.4437	0.2832	1	1	0	0	0	0	0	0	0	0	0
	Well-being	0.0682	0.2092	0	0	0	0	0	0	0	0	0	0	0
	Status	0.1388	0.2043	0	0	0	0	0	0	0	0	0	0	0
Programs	Restitution	0	0	0	0	0.0528	0.0624	0.0266	0.0682	0	0	0	0	0
	Compensation	0	0	0	0	0.2579	0.2258	0.2265	0.0724	0	0	0	0	0
	Economic Developmen	0	0	0	0	0.3671	0.3806	0.2920	0.0724	0	0	0	0	0
	Narrative	0	0	0	0	0.0722	0.0796	0.1908	0.1220	0	0	0	0	0
	Choice of residence	0	0	0	0	0.2501	0.2517	0.2641	0.6650	0	0	0	0	0

	Palestinians' Perspective	Stakeholders				Criteria				Programs				
		Israel	Palestinians	Host countries	Int'l community	Acceptability	Sustainability	Well-being	Status	Restitution	Compensation	Economic Development	Narrative	Choice of Residence
Stakeholders	Israel	0	0	0	0	0	0	0	0	0.6261	0.3308	0.1318	0.6143	0.2047
	Palestinians	0	0	0	0	0	0	0	0	0.0607	0.1286	0.1318	0.0761	0.1437
	Host countries	0	0	0	0	0	0	0	0	0.1067	0.1014	0.0678	0.0919	0.2322
	Int'l community	0	0	0	0	0	0	0	0	0.2065	0.4392	0.6685	0.2178	0.4194
Criteria	Acceptability	0.3492	0.3032	0	0	0	0	0	0	0	0	0	0	0
	Sustainability	0.4437	0.2832	1	1	0	0	0	0	0	0	0	0	0
	Well-being	0.0682	0.2092	0	0	0	0	0	0	0	0	0	0	0
	Status	0.1388	0.2043	0	0	0	0	0	0	0	0	0	0	0
Programs	Restitution	0	0	0	0	0.1394	0.1200	0.3625	0.2804	0	0	0	0	0
	Compensation	0	0	0	0	0.3633	0.2644	0.2648	0.3006	0	0	0	0	0
	Economic Development	0	0	0	0	0.1848	0.1760	0.1101	0.0574	0	0	0	0	0
	Narrative	0	0	0	0	0.0510	0.0777	0.1212	0.1035	0	0	0	0	0
	Choice of residence	0	0	0	0	0.2614	0.3619	0.1415	0.2580	0	0	0	0	0

Table 9.5 Supermatrix of limiting priorities

	Israelis' Perspective	Stakeholders				Criteria				Programs				
		Israel	Palestinians	Host countries	Int'l community	Acceptability	Sustainability	Well-being	Status	Restitution	Compensation	Economic Development	Narrative	Choice of residence
Stakeholders	Israel	0	0	0	0	0	0	0	0	0.1571	0.1571	0.1571	0.1571	0.1571
	Palestinians	0	0	0	0	0	0	0	0	0.0865	0.0865	0.0865	0.0865	0.0865
	Host countries	0	0	0	0	0	0	0	0	0.2666	0.2666	0.2666	0.2666	0.2666
	Int'l community	0	0	0	0	0	0	0	0	0.4898	0.4898	0.4898	0.4898	0.4898
Criteria	Acceptability	0.0811	0.0811	0.0811	0.0811	0	0	0	0	0	0	0	0	0
	Sustainability	0.8506	0.8506	0.8506	0.8506	0	0	0	0	0	0	0	0	0
	Well-being	0.0288	0.0288	0.0288	0.0288	0	0	0	0	0	0	0	0	0
	Status	0.0395	0.0395	0.0395	0.0395	0	0	0	0	0	0	0	0	0
Programs	Restitution	0	0	0	0	0.0608	0.0608	0.0608	0.0608	0	0	0	0	0
	Compensation	0	0	0	0	0.2223	0.2223	0.2223	0.2223	0	0	0	0	0
	Economic Developmen	0	0	0	0	0.3648	0.3648	0.3648	0.3648	0	0	0	0	0
	Narrative	0	0	0	0	0.0839	0.0839	0.0839	0.0839	0	0	0	0	0
	Choice of residence	0	0	0	0	0.2682	0.2682	0.2682	0.2682	0	0	0	0	0

	Palestinians' Perspective	Stakeholders				Criteria				Programs				
		Israel	Palestinians	Host countries	Int'l community	Acceptability	Sustainability	Well-being	Status	Restitution	Compensation	Economic Development	Narrative	Choice of Residence
Stakeholders	Israel	0	0	0	0	0	0	0	0	0.3211	0.3211	0.3211	0.3211	0.3211
	Palestinians	0	0	0	0	0	0	0	0	0.1202	0.1202	0.1202	0.1202	0.1202
	Host countries	0	0	0	0	0	0	0	0	0.1390	0.1390	0.1390	0.1390	0.1390
	Int'l community	0	0	0	0	0	0	0	0	0.4197	0.4197	0.4197	0.4197	0.4197
Criteria	Acceptability	0.1486	0.1486	0.1486	0.1486	0	0	0	0	0	0	0	0	0
	Sustainability	0.7352	0.7352	0.7352	0.7352	0	0	0	0	0	0	0	0	0
	Well-being	0.0470	0.0470	0.0470	0.0470	0	0	0	0	0	0	0	0	0
	Status	0.0691	0.0691	0.0691	0.0691	0	0	0	0	0	0	0	0	0
Programs	Restitution	0	0	0	0	0.1454	0.1454	0.1454	0.1454	0	0	0	0	0
	Compensation	0	0	0	0	0.2816	0.2816	0.2816	0.2816	0	0	0	0	0
	Economic Development	0	0	0	0	0.1660	0.1660	0.1660	0.1660	0	0	0	0	0
	Narrative	0	0	0	0	0.0776	0.0776	0.0776	0.0776	0	0	0	0	0
	Choice of residence	0	0	0	0	0.3294	0.3294	0.3294	0.3294	0	0	0	0	0

Table 9.6 Limiting priorities*

Limiting Priorities	Israelis	Palestinians	
Israel	0.1571	0.3211	(2)
Palestinians	0.0865	0.1202	
Host countries	0.2666	0.1390	(2)
Int'l community	0.4898	0.4197	(1)
Acceptability	0.0811	0.1486	
Sustainability	0.8506	0.7352	(3)
Well-being	0.0288	0.0470	
Status	0.0395	0.0691	
Restitution	0.0608	0.1454	
Compensation	0.2223	0.2816	(5)
Economic Development	0.3648	0.1660	(4)
Narrative	0.0839	0.0776	
Choice of residence	0.2682	0.3294	(4)

*The numbers in parenthesis next to the column of priorities are discussed below.

*The numbers in parenthesis next to the column of priorities are discussed below

Under these five criteria, there were the four impact criteria of acceptability, sustainability, well-being, and status. The programs developed and evaluated by the participants were compensation, development, narrative, and choice of residence. The implementation of these programs needs the creation of an organization, perhaps under the auspices of the United Nations. According to one of the experts, there could be two possible structures as given in Figs. 9.3 and 9.4. The difference between the two models is in structure and focus. The comprehensive mandate model (Fig. 9.3) will deal with restitution, compensation, and choice of residence, while the lean mandate model (Fig. 9.4) will only deal with restitution and compensation.

Compensation

This program was developed thinking about implementation. Thus, following the guidelines of an expert in compensation, and his experiences from conflicts such as Kosovo, Iraq, and others, restitution and compensation for property loss were grouped. The idea was that if restitution took place, it may not be realistic to think that the refugee owner of a deed in Israel may be able to execute the deed and displace occupants from the property. Hence, compensation would follow. Figure 9.5 gives a decision tree examining the possibilities of a refugee who is the owner of a deed in Israel.

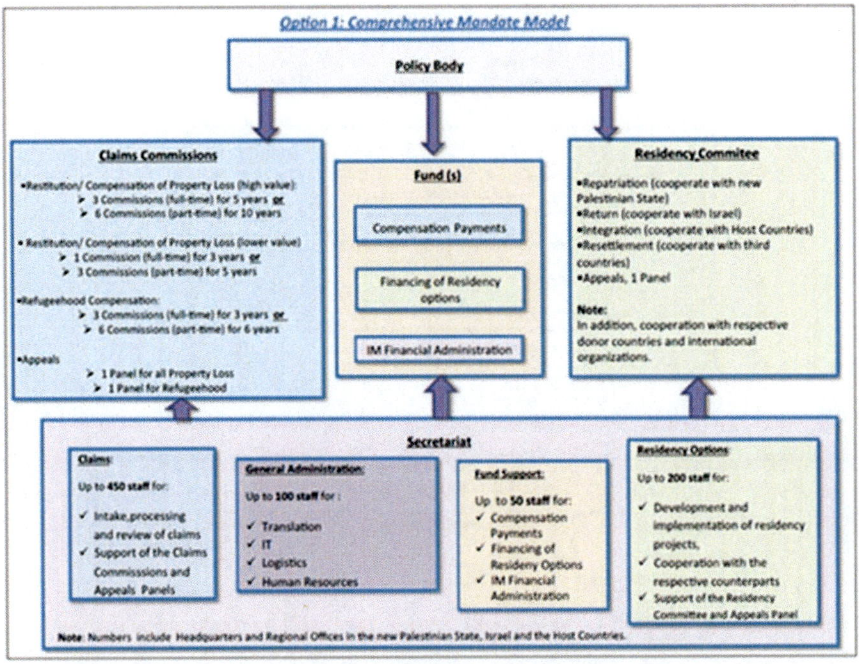

Fig. 9.3 A comprehensive mandate model. Source: An IOM Facilitated Dialogue on Solutions to the Palestinian Refugee Problem, Wühler (2012)

To understand this problem, the participants prioritized restitution (R), claims-based compensation (compensation based on an existing claim properly filed) (C-B), and status-based compensation (compensation based on being a refugee without filing a claim) (S-B) with respect to the impact criteria of acceptability, sustainability, well-being, and status. The results are given in Table 9.7. They show that there is divergence with respect to the criterion acceptability. For the Palestinians, the implementation of restitution is very important (0.7968); for the Israelis, it does seem to be a pressing need (0.0495). To keep both parties synchronized, rather than separating restitution and compensation, we kept them together. Figure 9.6 shows the hierarchy used for the implementation of restitution/compensation.

To simplify the exposition, we show in Table 9.8 the final priorities obtained from the restitution/compensation hierarchy given in Fig. 9.6. The priorities from this hierarchy indicate that funds could be allocated as follows:

- Restitution/compensation of property loss (Big claims): 10.67%
- Restitution/compensation of property loss (Small claims): 34.94%
- Refugee compensation: 54.40%.

Of course, the funds available will have to be dedicated not just for restitution/compensation. There are other programs that need to be addressed, such as economic development, narrative, and choice of residence (See Fig. 9.1).

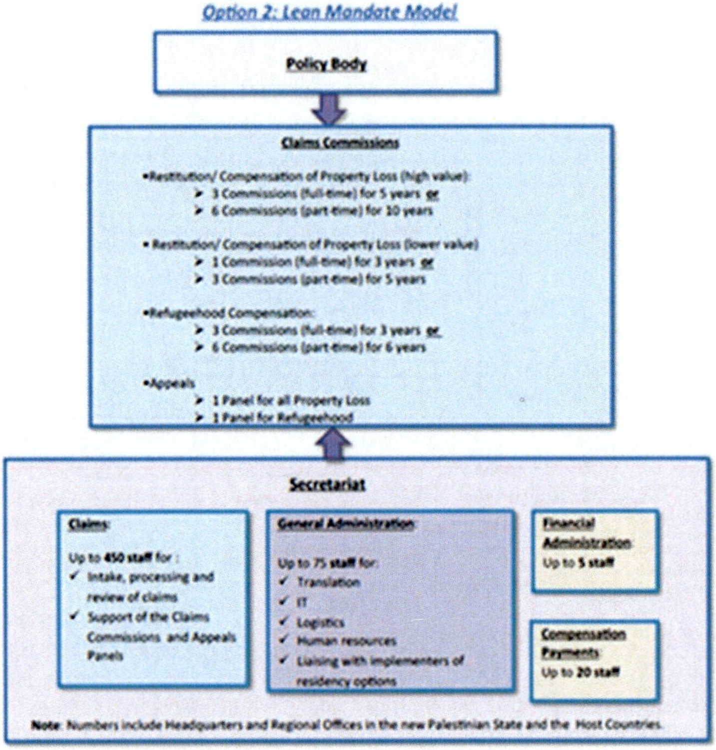

Fig. 9.4 A lean mandate model. Source: An IOM Facilitated Dialogue on Solutions to the Palestinian Refugee Problem, Wühler (2012)

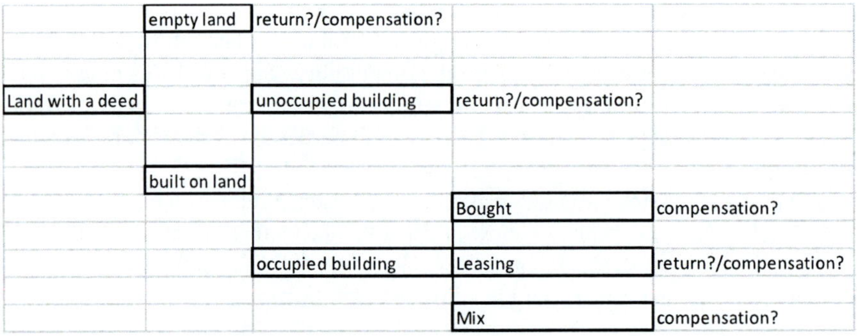

Fig. 9.5 Restitution of a refugee owner of a deed

The Palestinian Authority commissioned a study (Senechal, 2008a):

. . . a quantification of the aggregate value of losses incurred by Palestinian Arab refugees as a result of their forced displacement from what is now known as Israel, following military

Table 9.7 Prioritization of criteria, restitution and compensation

Israelis' Perspective

	Acc	Sust	M-W	Status	Priorities
Acceptability	1	0.5	5	5	0.3492
Sustainability	2	1	3	5	0.4437
Well-Being	0.2	0.33333333	1	0.2	0.0682
Status	0.2	0.2	5	1	0.1388

Acceptability	R	C-B	S-B	Priorities
R	1	0.11111111	0.1111111	0.0495
C-B	9	1	3	0.6419
S-B	9	0.33333333	1	0.3086

Sustainability	R	C-B	S-B	Priorities
R	1	0.11111111	0.1111111	0.0436
C-B	9	1	0.1428571	0.2053
S-B	9	7	1	0.7511

Well-Being	R	C-B	S-B	Priorities
R	1	0.33333333	0.2	0.1047
C-B	3	1	0.3333333	0.2583
S-B	5	3	1	0.6370

Status	R	C-B	S-B	Priorities
R	1	1	1	0.3333
C-B	1	1	1	0.3333
S-B	1	1	1	0.3333

	Synthesis
Restitution (R)	0.0900
Claims-based Compensation (C-B)	0.3792
Status-based Compensation (S-B)	0.5308

Palestinians' Perspective

Palestinians	Acc	Sust	M-W	Status	Priorities
Acceptability	1	3	0.2	7	0.3032
Sustainability	0.333333	1	5	5	0.2832
Well-Being	5	0.2	1	0.142857	0.2092
Status	0.142857	0.2	7	1	0.2043

Acceptability	R	C-B	S-B	Priorities
R	1	9	9	0.7968
C-B	0.111111	1	5	0.1514
S-B	0.111111	0.2	1	0.0518

Sustainability	R	C-B	S-B	Priorities
R	1	0.3333333	0.2	0.1047
C-B	3	1	0.333333	0.2583
S-B	5	3	1	0.6370

Well-Being	R	C-B	S-B	Priorities
R	1	0.3333333	0.2	0.1047
C-B	3	1	0.333333	0.2583
S-B	5	3	1	0.6370

Status	R	C-B	S-B	Priorities
R	1	1	1	0.3333
C-B	1	1	1	0.3333
S-B	1	1	1	0.3333

	Synthesis
Restitution (R)	0.3613
Claims-based Compensation (C-B)	0.2412
Status-based Compensation (S-B)	0.3975

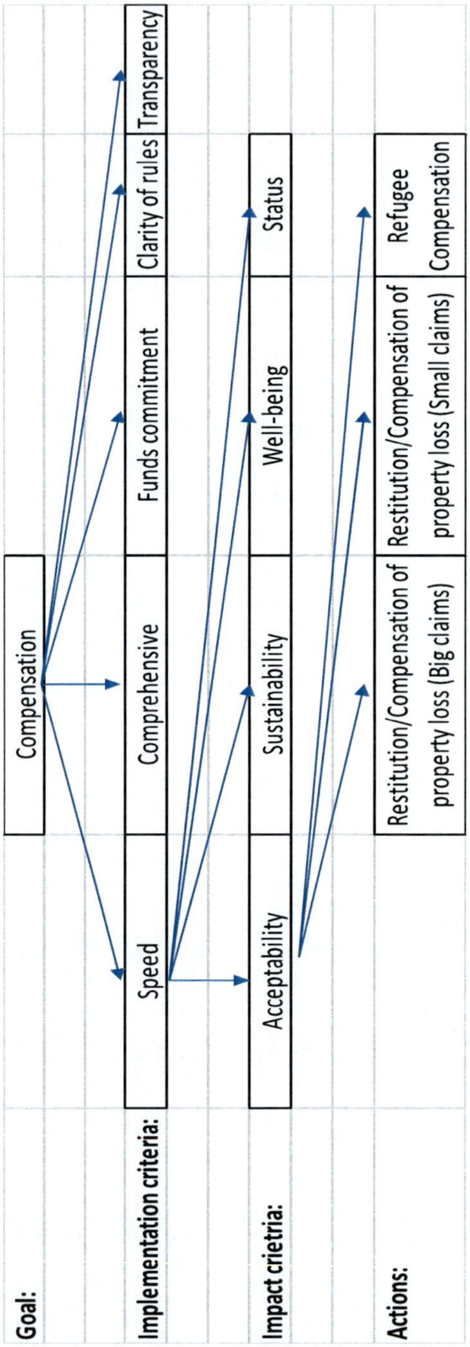

Fig. 9.6 Restitution/compensation hierarchy

Table 9.8 Restitution/compensation priorities

	Compensation				
	0.2504	0.1330	0.2875	0.1140	0.2151
	Speed	**Comprehensive**	**Funds commitment**	**Clarity of rules**	**Transparency**
Acceptability	0.3279	0.2752	0.1813	0.2172	0.4522
Sustainability	0.1087	0.2494	0.3689	0.3445	0.2977
Well-being	0.3421	0.2815	0.3712	0.1919	0.1812
Status	0.2214	0.1939	0.0786	0.2464	0.0689
	0.2928	0.2697	0.2907	0.1467	
	Acceptability	**Sustainability**	**Well-being**	**Status**	
Restitution/Compensation of property loss (Big claims)	0.0778	0.0778	0.0480	0.3333	
Restitution/Compensation of property loss (Small	0.4353	0.4353	0.1912	0.3333	
Refugee Compensation	0.4869	0.4869	0.7608	0.3333	
	0.1067	0.3494	0.5440		
	Restitution/Compensation of property loss (Big claims)	**Restitution/Compensation of property loss (Small claims)**	**Refugee Compensation**		

> action during the years 1947 and 1948. We aimed to provide a comprehensive view of a full range of financial losses suffered by approximately three quarters of a million Palestinian people so displaced. ... our objective has been to provide Palestinian negotiators with a reasoned, realistic and independent aggregate financial valuation.

In this study, the losses were classified into:

Individual (Urban and rural land—Urban land, houses, buildings. Rural land is related to the valuation of various agricultural activities and properties (cereal growing and fruit plantations); personal property—Movable assets such as household and personal effects, livestock, cars, moveable financial assets including cash in hand and foreign assets, bank accounts, and other securities—Cash accounts, safe deposit boxes, financial assets held in financial institutions, bearer bonds, shareholdings in income-generating businesses, and items held abroad. There is little information to propose a thorough valuation of such loss type; loss of employment and livelihood—Loss of wages or salaries of refugees, loss of livelihood because of the 1948 war by losing a source of direct or indirect earnings to sustain their livelihood.)

Business (Loss of income-producing property—Loss of industrial and commercial capital, factories, hotels and restaurants, workshops... (food, textiles, metals and machinery, woodwork, leather, printing and paper, chemicals, stone and cement, diamonds, ...), loss of income and profits.)

Communal (Communally owned property—Bush, grassland, and land that has collective ownership, Negev land, water, and mineral water. The following categories shall be distinguished as different valuation principles may be applied: Agricultural land; non-agricultural land (mostly used for grazing); and uncultivable land/desert land. In this valuation, communal land and buildings are valued in the urban and rural land sections.)

Religious (WAQFS or religious endowments—This category is related to the following loss types: public properties such as roads, railways, seaports, airports, schools, clinics, hospitals, laboratories, public buildings, irrigation networks.)

This evaluation is based on the principles of conciseness, flexibility, simplicity and consistency, auditability, and verifiability. It follows international valuation standards, and it is based on market valuation, and when market valuation is not possible, it provides guidelines to value properties. All types of loss should be supported with suitable documentation. Historical records are a legitimate source of information as well as past valuation work, best evidence vs. secondary evidence, and audit trail of evidence.

There have been several estimates of the total loss incurred by the Palestinians between 1947 and 1949 (Senechal, 2008a, p.24). In the report by T. Senechal, the estimated losses are given in Table 9.9 (Senechal, 2008a, p.185). These values need to be translated into actual US dollars. There are different ways of doing this (Senechal, 2008b). Table 9.10 shows the 2020 US dollar values of the estimated losses at different rates.

Note that the average monthly interest rate, the discount rate for the USA from 1950 to 2020, is 4.32 (Economic Research, 2020). At that level, the estimated

Table 9.9 Summary of aggregate findings

Loss Category	**Value in £P * in 1949**	**Value in $US in 1948 @ 4.0319/£P**
Rural land	398,221,800	$1,605,590,475
Urban land	126,830,885	$511,369,445
Holy places	1,602,280	$6,460,233
Loss of employment and livelihood	122,739,012	$494,871,422
Personal property and movable assets	44,853,524	$180,844,923
Business losses	85,516,266	$344,793,033
Ara share of state-owned property	37,062,985	$149,434,249
Total	816,826,752	$3,293,363,781
* £P - Palestinian pounds		

Table 9.10 2020 estimates of estimated losses

1948 USD	$ 3,293,363,781	
Rate	(1+rate)^72	2020 USD
1%	2.047099312	$6,741,842,731
2%	4.161140375	$13,704,148,999
3%	8.400017267	$27,664,312,625
4%	16.84226241	$55,467,697,003
5%	33.54513415	$110,476,329,848
6%	66.37771515	$218,605,962,938
7%	130.5064551	$429,805,232,502
8%	254.9825118	$839,750,169,294
9%	495.1170154	$1,630,600,445,837
10%	955.5938177	$3,147,118,068,651

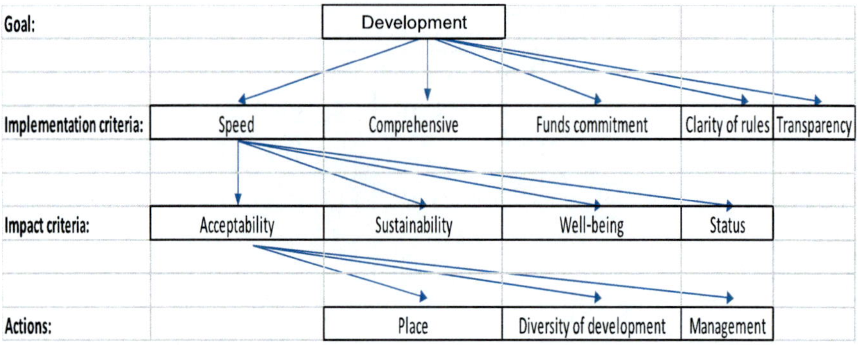

Fig. 9.7 Economic development hierarchy

amount needed in 2020 dollars is equal to USD 69,199,881,209. A significant amount that would have to be gathered to address the compensation program.

Economic Development

Economic development was decomposed into place, diversity of development, and management (Fig. 9.7).

The priorities derived for this hierarchy are given in Table 9.11. Whatever funds are allocated to programs in economic development, the place of development should receive 23.31%, the type of development—diversity of development—should receive 40.40%, and 36.29% should be allocated to managing economic development. Of course, how much is allocated to economic development depends on what point of view one chooses to take. From Table 9.6, we can see that the Israeli point of view allocated 36.45% to economic development, while the Palestinian point of view allocates 16.60%. This divergence will have to be addressed later if the agreement is implemented.

Narrative

The next group of programs was dedicated to address the narrative of the conflict. Although there are many writings on this topic (West, 2003), our intention was to see how our participants perceived the subject. They developed the hierarchy given in Fig. 9.8, but they only prioritized the implementation criteria (see Table 9.12). These criteria emphasized the need for a clear (0.2023), transparent (0.2866), and comprehensive (0.3360) narrative. The narrative had to address (1) how to guarantee the status for citizens, (2) acknowledgment of responsibility—by both parties—for some of the events that led to the refugee problem, and (3) contain an element of

Table 9.11 Economic development priorities

	Development				
	0.1059	0.1802	0.3919	0.1248	0.1972
	Speed	**Comprehensive**	**Funds commitment**	**Clarity of rules**	**Transparency**
Acceptability	0.3768	0.1605	0.1711	0.2856	0.1626
Sustainability	0.1549	0.4549	0.4990	0.3222	0.6279
Well-being	0.3474	0.3226	0.2471	0.1580	0.1778
Status	0.1208	0.0619	0.0829	0.2342	0.0317
	0.2036	0.4580	0.2465	0.0919	
	Acceptability	**Sustainability**	**Well-being**	**Status**	
Place	0.4239	0.1111	0.1840	0.5499	
Diversity of development	0.1826	0.4444	0.5842	0.2098	
Management	0.3935	0.4444	0.2318	0.2402	
	0.2331	0.4040	0.3629		
	Place	**Diversity of development**	**Management**		
	Palestine	Social	Int'l Commission		
	Israel	Economic	WB		
	Host countries	Physical	Donors		
	Third countries	Environmental	Goverments		

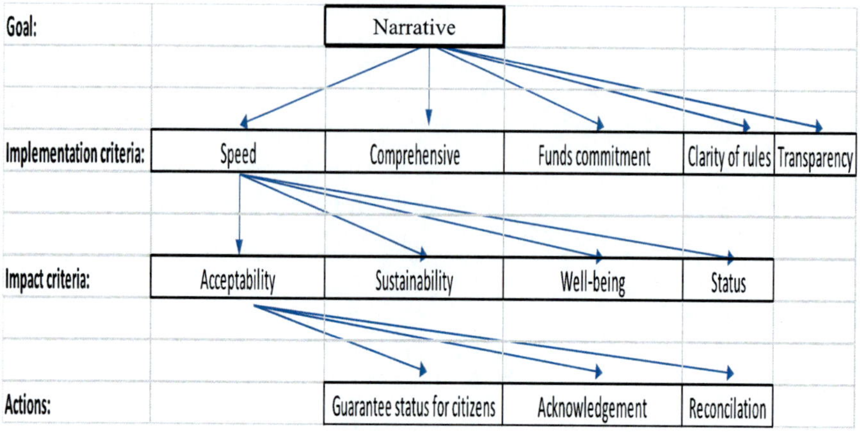

Fig. 9.8 Narrative hierarchy

Table 9.12 Priorities of implementation criteria for narrative

Narrative	Speed	Comprehensive	Funds commitment	Clarity of rules	Transparency	Priorities
Speed	1	0.2	0.333333333	0.2	0.2	0.0503
Comprehensive	5	1	3	2	1	0.3260
Funds commitment	3	0.333333333	1	1	0.333333333	0.1349
Clarity of rules	5	0.5	1	1	1	0.2023
Transparency	5	1	3	1	1	0.2866
					CR	0.032

reconciliation. This topic may be the thorniest of all the problems in this conflict. However, a look at Table 9.6 shows that narrative is almost equally important to both parties, 8.39% for the Israelis, and 7.76% for the Palestinians. Hence, perhaps there is no insurmountable difference between them. This subject will have to be explored in the future.

Choice of Residence

The final set of programs addressed the choice of residence of the refugees. Figure 9.9 shows the hierarchy used to prioritize these programs.

First, the impact criteria (acceptability, sustainability, well-being, and status) were prioritized with respect to the implementation criteria (speed, comprehensive,

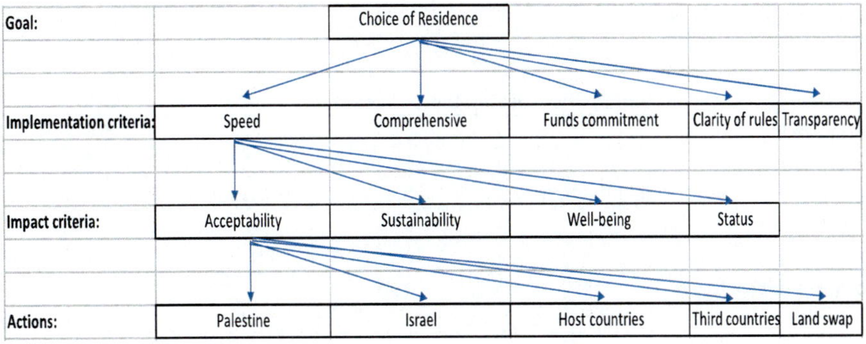

Fig. 9.9 Choice of residence hierarchy

funds' commitment, clarity of rules, and transparency). The resulting priorities are given in Table 9.13.

Next, the choice of residence programs (where to live—Palestine, Israel, host countries, third countries, and land swap) was prioritized with respect to the impact criteria. The results are given in Table 9.14.

The composite priorities (see Table 9.15)—most preferred location to reside—according to the participants in the exercise are Palestine (39.35%), land swap (27.63%), Israel (14.51%), host countries (13.68%), and third countries (4.84%). Table 9.16 gives the priorities of all the programs with the Israeli's and Palestinian's perspectives side by side for comparison purposes.

Conclusions and a Starting Point

We separated the preferences for the programs into the two perspectives, Israeli's and Palestinian's points of view. Recall that in Table 9.6, reproduced below, we gave the priorities both parties assigned to the programs: restitution, compensation, economic development, narrative, and choice of residence.

Table 9.13 Priorities of impact criteria with respect to implementation criteria

Speed					
	Acceptability	Sustainability	Well-being	Status	Priorities
Acceptability	1	5	3	1	0.3668
Sustainability	0.2	1	5	0.166666667	0.1318
Well-being	0.333333333	0.2	1	0.166666667	0.0632
Status	1	6	6	1	0.4381
				CR	0.2051
Comprehensive					
	Acceptability	Sustainability	Well-being	Status	Priorities
Acceptability	1	2	2	0.5	0.2693
Sustainability	0.5	1	3	0.5	0.2119
Well-being	0.5	0.333333333	1	0.333333333	0.1088
Status	2	2	3	1	0.4100
				CR	0.0578
Funds commitment					
	Acceptability	Sustainability	Well-being	Status	Priorities
Acceptability	1	1	0.5	1	0.2073
Sustainability	1	1	2	0.5	0.2422
Well-being	2	0.5	1	0.5	0.2128
Status	1	2	2	1	0.3376
				CR	0.1253
Clarity of Rules					
	Acceptability	Sustainability	Well-being	Status	Priorities
Acceptability	1	7	7	3	0.6299
Sustainability	0.142857143	1	3	1	0.1484
Well-being	0.142857143	0.333333333	1	1	0.0851
Status	0.333333333	1	1	1	0.1366
				CR	0.0993
Transparency					
	Acceptability	Sustainability	Well-being	Status	Priorities
Acceptability	1	5	5	3	0.5684
Sustainability	0.2	1	2	0.5	0.1313
Well-being	0.2	0.5	1	0.5	0.0924
Status	0.333333333	2	2	1	0.2078
				CR	0.0262

Table 9.14 Priorities of choice of residence programs with respect to implementation criteria

Acceptability						
	Palestine	Israel	Host countries	Third countries	Land swap	Priorities
Palestine	1	5	3	7	2	0.4395
Israel	0.2	1	0.5	3	0.5	0.1052
Host countries	0.333333333	2	1	3	0.333333333	0.1423
Third countries	0.142857143	0.333333333	0.333333333	1	0.2	0.0479
Land swap	0.5	2	3	5	1	0.2650
					CR	0.0332

Sustainability						
	Palestine	Israel	Host countries	Third countries	Land swap	Priorities
Palestine	1	7	3	9	5	0.5308
Israel	0.142857143	1	0.333333333	3	0.2	0.0624
Host countries	0.333333333	3	1	5	0.333333333	0.1405
Third countries	0.111111111	0.333333333	0.2	1	0.2	0.0351
Land swap	0.2	5	3	5	1	0.2312
					CR	0.0941

Well-being						
	Palestine	Israel	Host countries	Third countries	Land swap	Priorities
Palestine	1	0.2	2	3	1	0.1660
Israel	5	1	2	2	5	0.4497
Host countries	0.5	0.5	1	3	0.5	0.1364
Third countries	0.333333333	0.5	0.333333333	1	0.333333333	0.0817
Land swap	1	0.2	2	3	1	0.1660
					CR	0.1594

Status						
	Palestine	Israel	Host countries	Third countries	Land swap	Priorities
Palestine	1	3	5	7	1	0.3671
Israel	0.333333333	1	0.333333333	3	0.333333333	0.0953
Host countries	0.2	3	1	3	0.2	0.1289
Third countries	0.142857143	0.333333333	0.333333333	1	0.142857143	0.0415
Land swap	1	3	5	7	1	0.3671
					CR	0.0784

Table 9.15 Choice of residence priorities

	Choice of residence				
	0.1489	0.1084	0.5041	0.1249	0.1138
	Speed	**Comprehensive**	**Funds commitment**	**Clarity of rules**	**Transparency**
Acceptability	0.3668	0.2693	0.2073	0.6299	0.5684
Sustainability	0.1318	0.2119	0.2422	0.1484	0.1313
Well-being	0.0632	0.1088	0.2128	0.0851	0.0924
Status	0.4381	0.4100	0.3376	0.1366	0.2078
	0.3316	0.1982	0.1496	0.3206	
	Acceptability	**Sustainability**	**Well-being**	**Status**	
Palestine	0.4395	0.5308	0.1660	0.3671	
Israel	0.1052	0.0624	0.4497	0.0953	
Host countries	0.1423	0.1405	0.1364	0.1289	
Third countries	0.0479	0.0351	0.0817	0.0415	
Land swap	0.2650	0.2312	0.1660	0.3671	
	0.3935	0.1451	0.1368	0.0484	0.2763
	Palestine	**Israel**	**Host countries**	**Third countries**	**Land swap**

Table 9.16 Perspectives of both parties about programs

Goal	Find a solution for the Palestinian refugees wihin the broader context of a Peace Agreeement			
Stakeholders:	**Israelis**	**Palestinians**	**Host countries**	**International Community**
Criteria:	**Acceptability** By whom? what? how?	**Sustainability** Implementation Monitoring Verification Arbitration & guarantees feasibility	**Well-being** Socio-economic benefits	**Status** Legal benefits

Programs:	**Restitution/Compensation**			**Development**			**Narrative**		**Choice of Residence**		
I perspective		0.2831			0.3648			0.0839		0.2682	
P perspective		0.4270			0.1660			0.0776		0.3294	
	Restitution/Compensation of property loss (Big claims)	0.1067		Place	0.2331		Guarantee status for citizens		Palestine	0.3935	
I perspective			0.0302			0.0850					0.1055
P perspective			0.0455			0.0387					0.1296
	Restitution/Compensation of property loss (Small claims)	0.3494		Diversity of development	0.4040		Acknowledgement		Israel	0.1451	
I perspective			0.0989			0.1474					0.0389
P perspective			0.1492			0.0671					0.0478
	Refugee Compensation	0.5440		Management	0.3629		Reconcilation		Host countries	0.1368	
I perspective			0.1540			0.1324					0.0367
P perspective			0.2323			0.0602					0.0451
									Third countries	0.0484	
											0.0130
											0.0159
									Land swap	0.2763	
											0.0741
											0.0910

Limiting Priorities		
	Israelis	Palestinians
Israel	0.1571	0.3211
Palestinians	0.0865	0.1202
Host countries	0.2666	0.1390
Int'l community	0.4898	0.4197
Acceptability	0.0811	0.1486
Sustainability	0.8506	0.7352
Well-being	0.0288	0.0470
Status	0.0395	0.0691
Restitution	0.0608	0.1454
Compensation	0.2223	0.2816
Economic Development	0.3648	0.1660
Narrative	0.0839	0.0776
Choice of residence	0.2682	0.3294

Table 9.16 shows the global perspectives of both parties for all the programs. We highlighted the major issues in which the parties appear to disagree:

	Restitution/Compensation of property loss (Small claims)	0.3494		Diversity of development	0.4040	
I perspective			0.0989			0.1474
P perspective			0.1492			0.0671
	Refugee Compensation	0.5440		Management	0.3629	
I perspective			0.1540			0.1324
P perspective			0.2323			0.0602

From the Israeli's point of view, refugee compensation (15.40%), diversity of development (14.74%), and management of economic development (13.24%) are the key issues to solving the refugee problem. From the Palestinian's point of view, refugee compensation (23.23%) and restitution/compensation of property loss (small claims) (14.92%) seem more critical. This seems to indicate that a starting point for a dialogue could be talking about "refugee compensation."

References

Economic Research. (2020). Interest rates, discount rate for United States. *FRED Economic Data*. Accessed June 4, 2021, from https://fred.stlouisfed.org/series/INTDSRUSM193N

Saaty, T. L. (1980). *The analytic hierarchy process*. McGraw-Hill Intl.

Saaty, T. L., & Vargas, L. G. (2013). *Economic, political, social & technological applications of the analytic network process (ANP): Benefits, opportunities, costs and risks* (2nd ed.). Kluwer Academic Publishers.

Senechal, T. J. (2008a). *Valuation of Palestinian Refugee Losses: A study based on the National Wealth of Palestine in 1948*. Accessed June 4, 2021, from http://www.ajtransparency.com/files/2767.pdf

Senechal, T. J., (2008b). *Present day valuation in international arbitration: A five principle-based framework for awarding interest (April 2, 2008)*. Available at SSRN: https://ssrn.com/abstract=1122584 or Accessed June 4, 2021, from https://doi.org/10.2139/ssrn.1122584

Shlaim, A. (2001). *The Iron wall: Israel and the Arab world.* Penguin.

West, D. L. (2003). *Myth and narrative in the Israeli-Palestinian conflict.* World Peace Foundation, Report 34. Harvard University.

Wühler, N. (2012). *An IOM International Organization for Migration facilitated dialogue on solutions to the Palestinian refugee problem.*

Chapter 10
Strategic Communications: Communicating Internally and Externally

Over the course of both official and unofficial (Track II) negotiations, one of the most critical points of controversy has been the articulation, or lack of, regarding the desired end goal. This is true with respect to both overarching strategic negotiations and tactical implementation negotiations whose purpose was to resolve on-the-ground issues. The challenges are relevant to communicating with different audiences and publics. One of the most challenging aspects of the negotiating process—whether strategic or tactical—was recognizing the seminal importance of communication. To address this issue, this chapter is divided into the following sections: 1. Introduction; 2. National Leadership; 3. Drafters–Implementers Communication; and 4. Final Thoughts.

Introduction

The failure to fully appreciate the impact and significance of communication discussed in this chapter highlights the need to give this issue far greater attention should the parties re-engage in the future. While the substantive differences between Israelis and Palestinians must not be minimized, the importance of a strategic approach to communication demands the attention of decision makers on different levels of authority and responsibility (Gregory, 2005). The retrospective analysis below of the period immediately following the announcement of the Oslo Accords, including the way national leaders approached/addressed the question of communication with distinct publics, and the subsequent lack of interaction between Oslo drafters and on-the-ground implementers, demonstrates the degree to which communication was not considered a relevant consideration (see, e.g., Bigler 2007). The failure to fully appreciate the relevance of communication—whether strategic or tactical—rings loudly through this chapter. Its relevance is magnified when we consider what we observed (as discussed below) in the meetings/sessions we conducted. One of the most important takeaways, both from the post-Oslo process

T. L. Saaty et al., *Overcoming the Retributive Nature of the Israeli-Palestinian Conflict*, https://doi.org/10.1007/978-3-030-83958-1_10

and in the meetings we organized, is the need to develop significantly more sophisticated lines of communication among those involved. While we understand deep differences exist between the sides, it is clear that absent recognition of the importance of communication—manner and substance—the two sides will not be able to effectively resolve the conflict (Zaharna, 2014). That is not to minimize the complexity of the substantive issues demanding resolution, but it is to note the centrality of communication—in its different levels—to the process.

There are distinct layers of interaction (internal and external alike), requiring different expertise, background, and disciplines which, as we shall see below, were either missing or insufficiently emphasized (Gregory, 2005).

To that end, we examine different vectors of communication, whether internal (among Israelis) or external (between Israelis and Palestinians, on a national level or on the ground level). In retrospect, on both levels, there were lapses whose impact was significant. In addition to the failings addressed in this chapter, we also note an example of effective on-the-ground communication that enabled resolution of a significant, geographical specific crisis. One of the most compelling takeaways when engaging in this retrospective is that insignificant attention was paid to the importance of communication. Whether that reflects a lack of understanding regarding communication or an assumption that things will fall into place (magically) is unclear. What is clear is that decision makers in the Oslo Accord process failed to appropriately address the question of communication in an undertaking as complex as seeking to resolve the Israeli–Palestinian conflict.

It is an aspect of the negotiating process that never received the attention, or systemic (or systematic) approach it demanded. That reflects a failure on the part of Palestinian and Israeli leaders, over the years (with one exception) to compellingly communicate with both their own and each other's publics. To best understand the question of communication we began with an overview of how national leaders communicate with their public in general. That is distinct from how leaders communicate with each other and how negotiators (drafters and implementers alike) communicate with each other.

There are five layers of communication integral to the Israeli–Palestinian negotiations. These five layers of communication can be either bidirectional or unidirectional. To illustrate this distinction, we should consider how different groups talk to each other. For example, Israeli leaders can talk to the Israeli public, but the Israeli public cannot respond. At least not directly. Conversely, Israeli on-the-ground implementers should set up channels of communication between Palestinian on-the-ground implementers. This distinction is important to consider the power dynamics inherent in every level of communication. Keeping these power dynamics in mind can help negotiators at every level to determine the best course of communication. To illustrate how negotiators should consider the way information flows at the various levels, arrows will be used. Arrows pointing in one way suggest a flow of information from a leader to subordinates, whereas arrows pointing two ways suggest information flowing between peers.

1. Israeli leadership → Israeli public.
2. Palestinian leadership → Palestinian public.
3. Israeli leaders → Palestinian public/Palestinian leaders–Israeli public.
4. Israeli negotiators ←→ Israeli implementers.
5. Israeli on-the-ground implementers ←→ Palestinian on-the-ground implementers.

While not our intention to allocate grades, were we to do so the only group that successfully communicated was the fifth category. The other categories did not communicate in a manner reflecting foresight or sophisticated understanding of the importance of communication, with one individual exception. As discussed in detail below, the success of the fifth category can be ascribed to a number of factors, most importantly common professional language and a mutual recognition-understanding of a specific problem, requiring resolution (Gregory, 2005, pp. 7–14).

National Leadership

Our analysis focuses on the period in the immediate aftermath of the signing of the Oslo Accords, when Yitzhak Rabin was Prime Minister; Shimon Peres, Foreign Minister; Benjamin (Bibi) Netanyahu, head of the opposition; and Yasser Arafat the first President of the Palestine Authority. We do not examine the actual negotiations conducted in Norway that resulted in the Oslo Accords. Similarly, while we briefly reference Netanyahu's policies as Prime Minister, our primary focus is his role as head of the opposition after the agreement was announced and signed.

The focus on Rabin–Peres–Netanyahu–Arafat when examining communication in the context of the Israeli–Palestinian conflict is deliberate, reflecting particular realities. First and foremost, until Oslo (1993) there had not been direct interaction between the leaders of both sides (US Dept. of State, 1993). While there had been talks, earlier meetings between Israelis and Palestinians, including the Madrid–Washington talks, those never reached the level of the Oslo talks, not carrying the same weight and consequences (Friedman, 1991). This was, after all, the first-time Palestinian and Israeli leaders met in person and signed an agreement. More than that, the Oslo talks were intended to result in the establishment of the Palestinian State, reflecting the most far-reaching and determined efforts to resolve the conflict between the two (U.S. Dept. of State, 2000).

While many reasons have been offered over the years for the ultimate failure of the Oslo Process, the failure to effectively communicate with the broader public is, undoubtedly, one of the most important. That is not to gainsay the importance of additional factors, including Palestinian terrorism, the assassination of Israeli Prime Minister Yitzhak Rabin, the subsequent election of Benjamin Netanyahu as Israeli Prime Minister, the intransigence of Palestinian President (Re'is) Yasser Arafat, and historical enmity between the two sides, fighting over a small piece of land with deep historical, religious, and cultural ties (US Dept. of State, 1993). It is not an exaggeration to suggest that Rabin–Peres did not accurately assess the significant opposition that was clearly articulated by the Israeli political right whose suspicion of Arafat and deep distrust of the Palestinians were a reality (Tessler, 1986). In that context, Rabin–Peres did not effectively communicate with the broader Israeli public.

With respect to Arafat, the following story (believed to be accurate) is telling in the context of communication: Rabin told Arafat that until there is an "Altalena" there will be no Palestinian state (Landau, 2018). To Rabin's great surprise, Arafat pleaded ignorance as to the reference. When Rabin explained that the "Altalena" was a ship that sought to bring in arms for the Jewish underground—against the specific orders of Israeli PM David Ben-Gurion—and that Rabin (at Ben-Gurion's direct orders) opened fire at the ship, killing 16 Jews, Arafat reacted, "I could not do that" (Green, 2015). In response, Rabin said "then there will never be a Palestinian state" (Landau, 2018). The point, from Rabin's perspective, was that unless Arafat directly confront Palestinian extremism and extremists there will never be a Palestinian state. From the perspective of tragic historical irony, Rabin was assassinated by Jewish religious extremism as he had never been able to overcome their fervent opposition to the agreement.

Our analysis is based on both assessment and personal experience of one of the authors. In addition, our observations of Israelis and Palestinians during the numerous sessions we conducted give us unique insights into the way Palestinians and Israelis communicate on issues at the crux of the conflict. While we did not conduct simulations where participants role-play particular positions, we observed how individuals (Palestinians and Israelis) communicated both internally and externally. Therefore, we are able to provide—at the conclusion of this chapter—recommendations applicable to various levels of Palestinian and Israeli leadership, drafters, and negotiators.

We begin our retrospective analysis of communication with national leaders because of the primacy of their respective roles. We primarily focus on Israeli leaders with one reference to Arafat, premised on a reported interaction with Rabin. The ultimate failure of Rabin–Peres to successfully communicate with the broader Israeli public must serve as an important warning for any Israeli political leader intent on negotiating with Palestinians. Netanyahu's playbook will be far less challenging to duplicate for a future Israeli politician opposed to any peace plan with the Palestinians: highlight dangers, reject compromise, incite-delegitimize those seeking accommodation with the Palestinians.

Distinct from Rabin–Peres who presented a way forward (from their perspective), Netanyahu adopted (successfully from his perspective) the position of negativism. There was, in his approach, no counterproposal reflecting a reasoned alternative to Rabin–Peres. The effectiveness of communicating dangers-risks-threats, from the perspective of political pragmatism, poses far less challenges than presenting an alternative to the status quo. Communicating alternatives requires a skill set that, in retrospect, neither Rabin nor Peres possessed. In addition, they did not have the rhetorical skills of Netanyahu.

Rabin and Peres were unsuccessful in communicating with the Israeli public beyond the center-left political camp as they could not broach audiences beyond the echo chamber. The consequences of this failure were most significant: those in support of the negotiating process were already convinced, whereas those opposed remained opposed. While their efforts were hampered by Palestinian terrorism, they were unable to overcome a visceral, hate-filled, incitement-based campaign for which Netanyahu, as the head of the opposition, is responsible. Netanyahu's "anti" campaign was more successful than Rabin–Peres' "pro" campaign; the former was fear and hate based, the latter more rational and logical based, seeking to resolve a profoundly complex conundrum (Levy, 1997).

No other Israeli leader has the ability to communicate as effectively with a specific target audience as Netanyahu. That ability does not translate into effective communication with his political opponents. Netanyahu's skills are important when considering the extent to which "his" public consistently rejects calls for resolution of the conflict and the establishment of a Palestinian state (Tessler, 1986). As Netanyahu's core belief is consistent opposition to a two-state solution—the Bar-Ilan speech notwithstanding (Jerusalem Post, 2009)—we must view his effectiveness through that window (Tessler, 1986). His sole purpose when discussing the Israel–Palestinian conflict is convincing his base that a Palestinian partner does not exist, and that the Palestinians are unwilling to resolve the conflict (Lazaroff, 2019).

In communication with the base, Netanyahu did not offer a counterproposal, preferring the theme-message of "no" to any means reflecting a way forward. In a deeply divided political culture like Israel, rarely does communication cross boundaries, between distinct camps and perspectives. When Rabin announced to the Israeli public that Israeli and Palestinian negotiators had met secretly in Norway and an agreement was in the offing, public reaction reflected the deep split in Israeli society (Lustick, 1997a).

Those in the "peace camp" felt vindicated; after years of calling for resolution of the conflict, the occupation (per their terminological understanding) of the West Bank and Gaza Strip would shortly end (Lustick, 1997b). The opposition camp responded with direct attacks against Rabin–Peres and the agreement. The mood in Israel was angry, dark, and violent. Blame can—and must—be laid squarely at Netanyahu's door. After all, even before Rabin was assassinated (November 1995) public opinion polls predicted a loss for the Labor Party, of which Rabin was the head. After the assassination, in May 1996 Netanyahu was elected Prime Minister (in Israel's only direct election in its history), defeating Peres. Historians are left to debate what would have been the results of a Rabin–Netanyahu election. Tragically, that was denied the voter because of the assassination.

Rabin, his stellar military career notwithstanding, was unable to convince a majority of the Israeli public to support the Oslo Agreement. Does that mean he failed as a communicator? If the test is measured by the ability to convince opponents to cross the proverbial street and agree to a position previously objected, then we would conclude that Rabin failed. If the test is measured by the ability to convince the convinced (the so-called echo chamber), then we would conclude that Rabin was effective. However, as one of the tests of a national leader is the ability to sway public opinion, while preserving the public good in accordance with that leader's perspective, Rabin–Peres ultimately failed.

The caveat that might be offered in response is that Rabin's efforts were cut short by the assassination and Peres' efforts were dramatically impacted by a sharp rise in suicide bombings, from which Netanyahu directly benefitted (Schmemann, 1996). In the immediate aftermath of the assassination and prior to the suicide bombings, Netanyahu significantly lagged in the public opinion polls. His ability to platform the suicide bombings, a direct reaction to the successful targeted killing of the Hamas bomb maker Yech'ya A'yash (the "engineer"), in January 1996 reflects well on his ability to communicate with the public (Ephron, 2015).

In addition to viewing communication through the lens of domestic politics, we need to also inquire the extent to which the leader of a country communicates with the other side's public and its leadership. In the Israeli–Palestinian paradigm, it is not an exaggeration to note that Rabin felt overwhelming antipathy toward Yasser Arafat (Ephron, 2016, pp. 27–28). That was fully evident at the Rose Garden ceremony in September 1993. When Rabin shook Arafat's hand, the look of utter disdain was apparent to all (Ephron, 2016, pp. 27–30). Peres and Arafat enjoyed a warmer relationship, for which Peres was mocked by the Israeli political right (Weiner, 1996).

Neither Peres nor Rabin spoke Arabic and had no engagement with the Palestinian public; the same holds true for Arafat who did not speak Hebrew and had no interaction with the Israeli public, though over the years he met with members of the Israeli peace camp. The unwillingness to reach out to the other side's public, perhaps perceived as a political risk one step too much, was, in retrospect, a missed opportunity. That is not to suggest that by directly communicating with the Palestinian public Rabin–Peres would have swayed all skeptics or were Arafat to have spoken on Israel TV all opposition to Oslo would have melted, but the effort, in retrospect, might have had a positive impact. It is hard to imagine negative consequences to such an effort.

In sum, then, the communication efforts of the four relevant national leaders can be categorized as follows:

- In analyzing their ability to sway undecided opponents of the Oslo Peace Process, Rabin and Peres were only minimally successful in swaying undecided opponents. Conversely, in galvanizing opposition to the peace process, Netanyahu was very successful.
- In recognizing the need to galvanize domestic support for the Oslo Peace Process, Rabin and Peres had a minimal understanding of the need for support. Conversely, Netanyahu understood the significance of the need for support.
- From the Palestinian perspective, whether Arafat was successful or unsuccessful in playing both the right (Netanyahu) and the left (Rabin and Peres) against the middle is a matter of one's perspective.

Drafters–Implementation Interaction

Over the course of several years, one of us was deeply involved in on-the-ground implementation of the Oslo Peace Process. In this section, two examples are offered addressing the issue of communication: the first between drafters and implementers and the second between implementers. Important lessons can be learned from both examples.

The implementation process was largely defined by an unexplainable-unfathomable lack of interaction between the "implementers" and the drafters of the Oslo Agreement. While the reason for this extraordinary failure is not clear, its consequence and importance cannot be overstated. Whether the Israeli team who convened in Oslo felt their work was completed with the Rose Garden signing ceremony is unclear. Were that to be the case, then it is not an exaggeration to accuse them of malfeasance, reflecting an extraordinary misunderstanding of how agreements are implemented. Whether this was a deliberate oversight or simple negligence is irrelevant. In reality, it meant that those entrusted with implementing the agreement received no guidance or insight from those responsible for the agreement. It is assumed (at risk) that this failure was not deliberate and was not made consciously with an intention to deprive implementers of relevant insight and background. A caveat is in order: it is not known (to this writer) whether Palestinian implementers met with Palestinian drafters, in contrast to Israelis tasked with implementation. Anecdotal evidence suggests this disconnect applies to both sides.

Case in point: one of us was asked (Fall, 1994) to meet with a Palestinian official (after the signing of the Gaza-Jericho Agreement, May 1994 in Cairo) to negotiate the Safe Passage Agreement facilitating Palestinian traffic between the Gaza Strip and West Bank through Israel, in accordance with language from the Oslo Agreement. In response to the request for instructions-guidelines, none were given; not because of a lack of cooperation, rather because none were available. Environmental scanning—intelligence—was not provided to negotiators, thereby totally handicapping any possibility to define a communication strategy. The most practical consequence was a complete inability to identify common grounds given the lack of guidance from those best positioned to provide any. Guidelines that should come from decision makers were not shared with the negotiators; therefore, whether implementation measures reflected the true intent of the drafters is anyone's guess.

The guiding instruction was succinct, "we trust you." Needless to say, those are not instructions and provided no guidelines whatsoever. It became quickly apparent that the Palestinian counterpart was similarly in the dark regarding guidelines as to the Palestinian position. Accordingly, the implementers charged with a negotiating mandate were deprived of an understanding regarding the drafter's intent. This is but an example, from which much can be learned, regarding disassociation in the context of communication. While there is much to be said for on-the-ground expertise (more about that below), weight must also be given to the articulation of expectations, goals, and parameters that depends on direct interaction between distinct "layers" of involvement. The consistent failure to facilitate interaction between "implementers" and "drafters" reflects a deep misunderstanding regarding communication in the implementation process.

After two initial meetings, it became abundantly clear to those involved that negotiating implementation would be, primarily, a local undertaking with little, if any guidance, from senior command. In retrospect, this is extraordinary for even a casual glance at a map would unequivocally indicate the geopolitical significance of Safe Passage. While the intentions of the drafters were (and are to this day) unclear, from an operational-security-public safety perspective the ramifications had great importance. Whether the drafters understood the practical importance of Safe Passage is an open question as the (for lack of better word) casualness with which the Israeli negotiators at Oslo agreed to this clause is astounding.

Implementing mechanisms whereby Palestinians could travel through Israel required intensive negotiations which, as we came to learn, reflected two diametrically distinct understandings of the word, "safe." From the Israeli perspective the word meant that Palestinians driving through Israel (West Bank–Gaza Strip/Gaza Strip–West Bank) would not pose a security threat to Israel and Israelis; to Palestinians the word safe meant that their travel would be safe from heavy-handed Israeli security measures and impediments.

The two distinct interpretations came to light, almost accidently, in an intimate meeting in Tel Aviv between two senior officers (Palestinian and Israeli) and a legal advisor. It was at that meeting, more than two years after the initial meeting that the sides understood the significant gap regarding their interpretation of one word, "safe." The failure to define the critical word, "safe," reflects either deliberate obfuscation by the Oslo negotiators or a failure to pay attention to critical details, assuming that implementers could address matters of interpretation and nuance. While that approach—hypothetically speaking—is not beyond the realm of possibility, implementers (on both sides) would have benefitted from direct communication with drafters on this critical issue.

Putting this dispute—of extraordinary importance—under the microscope of communications suggests the two sides tasked with implementing a critical aspect of the Oslo Agreement stood behind the proverbial eight ball from the beginning. The failure, as became clear that evening in Tel Aviv, was overwhelming. Not only had the sides spent two years seeking to negotiate implementation with guidance, but the most basic discussion point was never clarified. Worse than that, for three years, the Israeli side negotiating Safe Passage never met with any government official (or drafters), meaning that sole responsibility rested with Israel Defense Forces officers, including one of the authors. This was a closed world (the only exception were meetings with Foreign Ministry officials who had no particular insight as to the drafter's intent), whereby—for lack of a better term—those involved were left to their own interpretation and understanding. While ultimately the Safe Passage Agreement was signed, that occurred only after a government official (albeit not a drafter) became involved five years after the negotiating process began. From the perspective of "lessons learned," much can be suggested were the parties to re-engage in the future, particularly regarding lines of communication between different levels of participants. This was a distinct failure, for which blame must be assigned primarily to the Oslo drafters. While it is not clear what were the lines of communication between the drafters and senior IDF command, the fact that the only instruction was “we trust you, your English is excellent” is astounding in its utter disregard from establishing lines of communication and instructions. As became quickly apparent, that same failing marked the Palestinian side. The fact that an agreement was signed must not, in any way, be understood as mitigating the overwhelming disregard for the need to establish (and implement) channels of communication between different levels of participants.

The second example we explore reflects resolution of a particular crisis that, perhaps, can be understood as “crisis management.” Distinct from the Safe Passage discussion, the circumstances below were contained to a geographical specific security crisis in the Gaza Strip, resolved when two commanders, equal in rank, met face-to-face to address the particular matter. The physical circumstances of the meeting are no less important than the content: the Israel Defense Force commander (a Colonel) met his Palestinian counterpart at the particular location which had proved particularly problematic from a security perspective. The Palestinian commander accepted the invitation of the IDF commander, hopped into his jeep (the COL drove), and three officers (the IDF commander, a Judge Advocate General Corps officer, and the Palestinian commander) drove together to the location. The two commanders assessed the situation from the perspective of shared language (more about that below) and then asked the legal advisor to draft a security memorandum specific to the location and the security dilemma posed. The document was written in English (as the accepted language of record) and agreed upon by the two commanders.

What made this possible? Why was it possible in the course of 30 min for two commanders (of equal rank) to collaborate, cooperate, and resolve a vexing issue? What can we learn from this example in the context of communications as applied to the Israeli–Palestinian conflict? We begin with the following, trite as they might seem: the Israeli commander spoke Arabic which significantly facilitated the interaction; the two commanders had a common professional language (security); the two had a vested interest in resolving the particular issue at hand (Palestinian terrorism), and both felt empowered by their commanders to resolve the specific problem. The professional commonality—a shared security background—greatly facilitated their ability to identify the danger at hand and the means by which they, together, could address the particular matter without assuming that the resolution applied to other areas of the Gaza Strip. That is, in the context of strategic communications, both understood they had the means, authority, and skills to resolve the issue. While the decision to include a Legal Advisor to draft the agreement was suggested by the IDF commander, the Palestinian commander readily agreed. Drafting disagreements were resolved (literally) in the jeep and a one-page (hand-written) agreement was signed by the two commanders.

While the agreement, on the face of it, was not of enormous strategic significance, its importance must not be underestimated. Given its timing—shortly after the signing of the Oslo Agreement and the (literally) microscopic attention paid to implementation of the security agreement between Israel and the Palestinian

Authority—any successful terrorist attack would be perceived by Israeli opponents of the agreement as reflective of the PA's inability to control Hamas. Accordingly, the Palestinian commander had a vested interest in calming the waters and was intent on doing so in conjunction with his Israeli counterpart. Failure to resolve the particular, then, could have had significant negative repercussions, extending well beyond the reach of the commanders and the particular territory for which they had command responsibility.

If we parse this successful resolution in a broader context, what do we learn in the context of the Israeli–Palestinian negotiating history? Without overstating, or engaging in mythmaking, the interaction is instructive on a number of different levels, large and small alike, from which we can learn much regarding communication:

1. The two commanders spoke in a common language, Arabic and professional (security-military).
2. The two commanders identified a common goal (crisis management) and common enemy (Palestinian terrorism) (Chapman, 2016).
3. The two commanders were entrusted by their commanding officers to resolve on-the-ground tensions.
4. The two commanders agreed on how the agreement would be memorialized (written agreement).
5. The importance of small human gestures (the IDF commander drove the jeep, rather than his driver, whereby enabling both commanders to sit in the front, rather than one in the front, the other in the back).
6. Both commanders openly demonstrated warmth and respect to each other, thereby sending an important message to their subordinates and by extension larger audiences.

The agreement held, outlasting the tenure of the Israeli commander. While that cannot be said, regarding many of the agreements (large and small) signed in the aftermath of the Oslo Agreement, it is an effective manifestation of communication, as outlined above. While personalities played a role (the conversation was professional yet congenial with humor), both commanders understood the risks at hand. Their decision to meet, and to quickly reach an agreement, reflects their recognition that the threat posed by a mutual enemy (Hamas) required their joining forces to minimize the dangers posed, both in the area under their operational control (a tactical consideration) and also recognition that the impact of a terrorist attack in the initial stages of the post-Oslo era could have long-term strategic implications.

Final Thoughts

The communication failures as described in this chapter are telling, demanding the attention of future decision makers. Otherwise, they, too, will fall short in the all-important requirement of articulating intentions, aims, and goals (Leibstone, 2005). That failure impacts both levels of communication, internal and external.

The inability to effectively engage with one's domestic audience directly impacts a subsequent ability to interact with the other side (Brown & Glaisyer, 2011). More than that: to truly communicate one must have the ability to cut across all relevant sectors and populations (Simons, 2019). As made clear above, with the exception of Netanyahu, the relevant national leaders failed in their communication efforts. The failure to do so reflects insufficient attention attached to the art of conveying intentions, aims, and goals. The inability to articulate to one's domestic audience the true intention of a particular policy directly impacts the subsequent ability to interact with the other side (Gregory, 2005).

More than that: to truly understand communication one must develop cross-over perspective, cutting across all relevant sectors and populations (Simons, 2019). This was, as we have seen, clearly missing post-Oslo; it is as if no consideration was given to this most important issue. The failure to do so had significant consequences; because there is no vacuum, Netanyahu was able to fill the unintended vacuum created by Rabin–Peres. However, while doubtlessly unintentional, their inability to address the portion of the Israeli public whose reaction to the agreement ranged from skepticism to opposition had significant consequences. In many ways, Netanyahu's consistent opposition, over 25 years later, largely defines contemporary Israeli politics. The center's (the Israeli left is significantly weakened) inability to cohesively, coherently, and consistently find a path forward (2020) is the defining reality of those favoring resolution of the Israeli–Palestinian conflict. The Palestinians post-Oslo, as discussed in previous chapters, are split between Hamas in the Gaza Strip and the Palestinian Authority in the West Bank (Israeli Defense Forces, 2020). Resolution of this split does not appear to be in the offing.

Notwithstanding the current stalemate reflecting preservation of the status quo between the two sides, our experience over the years has provided us with insight regarding the way communication plays an integral role in the negotiation process. As we have explored, communication—to be most effective—must have dual focuses, internal and external (Gregory, 2005). While "internal" might be the instinctual answer regarding which is more important, the external is no less important. To focus exclusively on the internal would suggest that the needs and realities of the other side are not important. Nothing could be further from the truth. Therefore, drawing on our experiences from the innumerable interactions we have conducted-facilitated over the past years, we recommend paying particular heed to the manner in which policies are articulated.

This, as we have come to learn, depends on, among other considerations, the speaker's rhetorical skills, intended message, understanding of the other side, and recognition that the primary undertaking is communicating directly in an effort to convey one's intention. More than that: the direct communication which we believe is essential to any future undertaking must be cross-vector, cutting across different publics and distinct levels of engagement, authority, and decision-making responsibilities. The examples we have offered in this chapter provide a window into how those responsible—national leaders, drafters, implementers—can apply lessons learned in any future effort to resolve the Israeli–Palestinian conflict. While, presently, the "naysayers" have the upper hand, the checklist below is intended to provide a negotiation communication road map that would facilitate progress, if not resolution. While, as discussed in earlier chapters, many of the parameters of the Israeli–Palestinian conflict are known, we have been repeatedly surprised during the course of our engagement to come to the realization that matters seemingly apparent were unknown or not sufficiently understood and recognized as important to the other side. This notwithstanding the fact the two sides live in immediate proximity and have not infrequent interaction. Nevertheless, as we have learned, geographical closeness does not guarantee a true understanding of the ways, norms, and cultures of the other, with all due respect to assumptions and presumptions, which more often than not are incorrect. We have been repeatedly confronted with this reality.

Therefore, premised on the primary requirement to understand the "other" we proffer the following for future negotiators. While our focus is the Israel–Palestinian conflict, we believe understanding, emphasizing, and directly engaging these points when considering the "other" are relevant to many negotiating undertakings. We suggest that everyone consider these 14 points when negotiating peace. This includes history, culture, traditions, politics, religion, domestic considerations, ethnic tensions, linguistic nuance, leadership tensions, posturing, economic pressures, geopolitical implications, military capability, and "under the radar" needs and desires. All 14 of these points can be distilled down to one overarching goal: to effectively negotiate with people, you must understand those people. You must understand who they are and what drives them. You must understand how they view their place in the world; this will be informed by their history, culture, tradition, politics, religion, and language. You must understand the issues they will face when negotiating; this includes ethnic tensions within their borders, geopolitical implications, and other "under the radar" needs and desires like food shortages, the ability to portray the negotiation as a "win" instead of a compromise, or other hardships that might tax their resources and lead to distrust of their leaders. Negotiators fail when they do not understand what is driving those they are negotiating with and the pressures they may face. It is also necessary for negotiators to consider the pressure the other's public might put on them. For instance, while the negotiator sitting at the table may not think that religion is important in negotiation, if the public that they serve does, then failing to address it may lead to long-term failure of the negotiated compromise.

To truly engage in effective communication, it is incumbent to understand the needs—whether tangible or intangible—of the other side (Bigler, 2007). Devoid of this insight, regardless of whether the needs are deemed worthy or unworthy, any negotiating process is deemed to fail for it will be afflicted, or encumbered, by a dialogue of the deaf. While the importance of understanding the "other" is undeniable, significant effort must—simultaneously—be given to understanding and addressing domestic audiences and politics (Bigler, 2007). Similarly, clear lines of communication must be developed, and implemented, between those involved in the negotiation process, whether drafters or implementers. Otherwise, the failures that largely define the Oslo Process are all but guaranteed to repeat themselves.

References

Brown, T., & Glaisyer, T. (2011). Strengthening U.S. statecraft through public diplomacy. *The Fletcher Forum of World Affairs, 35*, 47–59.

Bigler, G. E. (2007). Strategic communications and the decline of US soft power. *International Law Studies, 83*, 217–234, M.D. Carsten (Ed.).

Chapman, B. (2016). Geopolitics of the 2015 British defense white paper and its historical predecessors. *Geopolitics, History, and International Relations, 8*(2), 42–63.

Ephron, D. (2015, October 16). *How Israel's most fervent peacemaker squandered his best chance*. The Washington Post. Accessed June 3, 2021, from https://www.washingtonpost.com/opinions/how-israels-most-fervent-peacemaker-squandered-his-best-chance/2015/10/16/598f0840-72ac-11e5-8248-98e0f5a2e830_story.html

Ephron, D. (2016). *Killing a king: The assassination of Yitzhak Rabin and the remaking of Israel*. W.W. Norton & Company.

Friedman, T. L. (1991). *The Middle East talks: A step ahead in Madrid; At last, all the players in the Middle East have sat down and talked to each other*. A version of this article appears in print on Nov. 4, 1991, Section A, Page 1 of the National edition. Accessed June 3, 2021, from https://www.nytimes.com/1991/11/04/world/middle-east-talks-step-ahead-madrid-last-all-players-middle-east-have-sat-down.html?searchResultPosition=1

Green, D. B. (2015, June 21). Altalena arms ship reaches Israel, and is attacked with friendly fire. *Haaretz*. Accessed June 3, 2021, from https://www.haaretz.com/jewish/.premium-1948-altalena-arms-ship-sunk-by-friendy-fire-1.5373581?_ga=2.91544986.1272692862.1608460312-357720147.1605890506

Gregory, B. (2005, August 31). Public diplomacy and strategic communication: Cultures, firewalls, and imported norms. *American Political Science Association, Conference on International Communication and Conflict*.

Israeli Defense Forces. (2020). *Short history of Gaza*. Accessed June 3, 2021, from https://www.idf.il/en/minisites/Hamas/Hamas/short-history-of-Hamas-in-gaza/

Jerusalem Post. (2009). Full text of Binyamin Netanyahu's Bar Ilan speech. *Jerusalem Post.*, June 14. https://www.jpost.com/Israel/Full-text-of-Binyamin-Netanyahus-Bar-Ilan-speech. Accessed June 6, 2021.

Landau, N. (2018, June 9). Rabin's man in Oslo analyzes what went wrong – and right – with the 1993 Accords. *Haaretz*.

Lazaroff, T. (2019, April 8). Netanyahu: A Palestinian state won't be created. *The Jerusalem Post*.

Leibstone, M. (2005). Strategic communications – Global security & being understood, North America outlook. *Military Technology, 29*, 6–6.

Levy, Y. (1997). After Rabin and Peres: The personal dimension of Israel's turn to peace. *Security Dialogue, 28*(4), 465–478.

Lustick, I. S. (1997a). The Oslo agreement as an obstacle to peace. *Journal of Palestine Studies, 27*(1), 61–66.

Lustick, I. S. (1997b). Ending protracted conflicts: The Oslo peace process between political partnership and legality. *Cornell International Law Journal, 30*, 741–755.

Schmemann, S. (1996, February 26). Bombings in Israel: The overview; 2 Suicide Bombings in Israel Kill 26 and Hurt 88, highest such toll. *The New York Times*. Accessed June 3, 2021, from https://www.nytimes.com/1996/02/26/world/bombings-israel-overview-2-suicide-bombings-israel-kill-25-hurt-77-highest-such.html

Simons, G. (2019). Digital communication disrupting hegemonic power in global geopolitics. *Russia in Global Affairs, 17*(2), 108–130.

Tessler, M. (1986). The political right in Israel: Its origins, growth, and prospects. *Journal of Palestine Studies, 15*(2), 15–55.

U.S. Dept. of State. (1993). *The Oslo accords*. Accessed June 3, 2021, from https://2001-2009.state.gov/r/pa/ho/time/pcw/97181.htm

U.S. Dept. of State. (2000). *The Oslo accords and the Arab-Israeli peace process*. Office of the Historian, Foreign Service Institute. Accessed June 3, 2021, from https://history.state.gov/milestones/1993-2000/oslo

Weiner, J. R. (1996). An analysis of Oslo II agreement in light of the expectations of Shimon Peres and Mahmoud Abbas. *Michigan Journal of International Law, 17*(3), 667–704.

Zaharna, R. S. (2014). *Battles to bridges: US strategic communication and public diplomacy after 9/11*. Palgrave Macmillan.

Chapter 11
Looking Ahead

As these lines are written (between December 2020 and January 2021), Israel was planning its fourth election in two years. The election, held on March 23, 2021, can be boiled down to one, primary, issue: "Bibi yes/Bibi no." The reference is to Prime Minister Netanyahu and whether he will continue to be Israel's Prime Minister, regardless of the fact he is under indictment for bribery, violation of public interest, and fraud. To date, he has not been investigated for his role in a far more serious matter, involving the sale of German nuclear submarines to Egypt. Israeli law does not require an indicted Prime Minister to resign.

While predicting election results, particularly in a parliamentary democracy where the question is which party can form the government is "fool's gold" it is reasonable to assume whether Netanyahu is Prime Minister or not, the Israeli political center-right will continue to dominate Israeli politics in the foreseeable future. The left/center-left significantly lag in public opinion polls, regardless of which party is deemed "the flavor of the day."

While Israel is faced with significant challenges and issues, the dominance of the Bibi dilemma ensures that all other pressing questions take a back seat. That includes questions related to the economy and COVID, which would rate a close second after the Bibi question which is the sole reason for the endless cycle of elections. That is even more so regarding questions of national security, with one exception that reflects political needs and realities. The Palestinian question as it relates to resolving the Israeli–Palestinian conflict, the future of the West Bank settlements, and tension with Hamas is not on the Israeli political radar. The only blip on the radar is related to specific events, whether rockets fired from the Gaza Strip or the death of a "hilltop youth" which results in demonstrations against the police (The Times of Israel, 2021).

However, even such events capture media attention; they must not be understood as reflecting widespread public concern regarding efforts to resolve the Palestinian conflict. As discussed below, there are two somewhat related national security questions that Netanyahu views as important: Iran and normalization with Arab countries, the former because of concern regarding Iran's nuclearization efforts and

T. L. Saaty et al., *Overcoming the Retributive Nature of the Israeli-Palestinian Conflict*, https://doi.org/10.1007/978-3-030-83958-1_11

the latter in an effort to forge agreements with the Sunni world aimed at weakening Iran. The Palestinian Authority and Hamas are, in a word, irrelevant to both. However, before turning our attention to the complicated Hamas–PA–Israel triangle, examining broader geopolitical developments is essential.

When convenient, and suiting a particular moment, Netanyahu is quick to raise the Iran question, particularly regarding the development of their nascent nuclear capability. During the Trump Administration, Netanyahu felt there was a direct link between Washington and Jerusalem regarding Iran, as evidenced by the US decision to withdraw from the Iran nuclear deal (NYTimes, 2018a). It is unclear if President Biden intends to rescind President Trump's decision. Arguably more than any other foreign leader, Netanyahu was instrumental in Trump's decision. The basis for the caveat is the Abraham Accords (U.S. Dept. of State, 2020), an agreement fostered by the USA between Israel and the UAE. The Accords, which subsequently led to an agreement between Israel and Bahrain, reflect the ancient aphorism in the Middle East: "the enemy of my enemy is my friend."

That is, there is—at least from the perspective of the Trump Administration—a natural convergence between Israel and Arab Sunni countries who share a common enemy, Iran which is Shi'ite. Whether the Accords will ultimately result in an agreement between Israel and Saudi Arabia is a matter of much speculation. Close relations between President Trump's son-in-law, Jared Kushner, and Prince Mohammed bin Salman (MBS) were integral to the Trump Administration's relationship with Saudi Arabia and other Gulf countries (NYTimes, 2018b).

These agreements included the sale of sophisticated US military equipment, including F-35 fighter planes, to the UAE and Bahrain. Concerns whether this violated the US obligation to Israel regarding the preservation of a qualitative military advantage (JVL, 2008) were set aside in the name of the agreement. In addition to agreements with Gulf states, Israel also signed an agreement with Morocco that included US recognition of Moroccan sovereignty over Western Sahara (Riboua, 2020).

While these developments reflected a geopolitical alignment between Trump and Netanyahu, on the question most germane for our purposes, "mixed bag" is an apt moniker. Netanyahu's much criticized, lacking in detail, not cohesively presented plan to annex parts of the West Bank faced, as expected, strong opposition in Europe and among members of the Democratic Party and liberal US Jews (The Times of Israel, 2020b). What was not expected, and what ultimately torpedoed the plan, was the Trump Administration's opposition, particularly Kushner's maneuvering (Aljazeera, 2020). Whether Kushner's opposition reflected his close relationship with MBS or because of a belief that moving forward threatened to undermine Kushner–Trump's "deal of the century" (The Guardian, 2019) is a matter of conjecture. Regardless of the reason, Netanyahu's assumption that the Trump Administration, especially in an election year, would fully support the annexation plan was misguided and reflected either poor intelligence or a misread of President Trump (The Times of Israel, 2020a).

As the curtain closed on the Trump Administration, Netanyahu with the exception of annexation can largely be satisfied: (1) the USA moved its embassy to

Jerusalem (from Tel Aviv), thereby recognizing Jerusalem as the capital of Israel; (2) the two leaders saw eye to eye on Iran; (3) most importantly (for Netanyahu) there was no pressure to engage with the Palestinians as with the exception of the poorly received (understatement) Kushner Plan; (4) the question of a Palestinian state was never on Trump's radar, and (5) the Trump Administration, in contrast to its predecessors, rejected the notion that Jewish settlements in the West Bank violate international law (NYTimes, 2019).

From Netanyahu's perspective this provided him important political cover in a never-ending election cycle; simply put, the lack of Trump engagement in the Palestinian dilemma enabled Netanyahu to position himself as protecting Israeli interests in the West Bank. For "hard-core" Likud (the party Netanyahu heads), the continued building of Jewish settlements in the West Bank is of prime importance as is ensuring that a Palestinian state is not created. While the latter clearly did not occur, Netanyahu's right-wing critics bristle at the lack of building in the West Bank (The Jerusalem Post, 2021).

Where does all this leave the Palestinians, much less resolution of the Israeli–Palestinian conflict? The litany above, capturing important (or at least seemingly important) developments in the Sunni world's engagement with Israel and the USA had one target, Iran. Seemingly left behind or at least not included in the various agreements are the Palestinians. The word "Palestinian" is deliberately used, in contrast to "Palestinian Authority" or "Hamas." This refers back to our discussion in Chap. 1 when we explained that our efforts focused, at the request of the Palestinian participants, exclusively on the West Bank and that Hamas is not to be a part of the discussion. We made the decision to honor that request and accordingly over the course of our innumerable interactions, stretching over many weeks, we deliberately ignored the Gaza Strip and Hamas. While we did not question what were, clearly, internal Palestinian considerations and realities, the reality is that Gaza–Hamas is the elephant in the room. However, the Gaza Strip was very much in the minds of the participants as Principle 2 states:

> Israel must respect the integrity of the West Bank and Gaza by allowing free and safe passage between the two areas, and the Palestinian State must guarantee that any agreement reached with Israel will be accepted and supported by the majority of the Palestinian people both in Gaza and the West Bank.

While it would be a stretch to suggest this is the reason the US–Gulf States–Israel did not include the Palestinians in the agreement, or at least incorporate them in the discussion, the reality as expressed by a former senior PA official to one of the authors bears repeating: "*... until the Palestinians get their own house in order, moving forward will be extremely difficult.*" The ongoing split between Hamas and the PA casts significant doubt regarding the viability of a two-state solution; it is considered highly unlikely a PA leader would agree to the establishment of a Palestinian state that would not include Palestinians who live in the Gaza Strip. It is not far-fetched to assume, then, that until the internal conflict is not resolved, moving forward to create a Palestinian state would be deemed a non-starter.

Over the years there have been efforts, primarily by Egypt, to mediate a resolution between the two parties. Those efforts have largely been unsuccessful. It is an open question whether the Sisi government has continued interest-willingness in this role. Absent Egyptian engagement, there does not seem to be another Arab or Moslem country willing to accept this role, with the possible exception of Turkey, albeit that is a long shot. The fact that Morocco, the UAE, and Bahrain were willing to normalize relations with Israel—without including the PA/Hamas—-speaks loudly as to the diminished status of the Palestinians. Even though Saudi Arabia has yet to sign an agreement with Israel, it is widely understood that absent Saudi agreement—passive or otherwise—UAE and Bahrain would have normalized relations with Israel.

In years past, the oft-repeated mantra in the Middle East (writ large) was that the most important issue to resolve was the Israeli–Palestinian conflict: absent establishment of a Palestinian state and removal of all Jewish settlements in the West Bank, normalization with Israel would be a non-starter. While Egypt (1979) (CBS News, 2012) and Jordan (1994) (MEE, 2018) violated that "sacred" pledge, the recent normalization agreements spoke loudly regarding, for lack of a better word, the diminished status of Palestinians in the eyes of the Arab world. There had long been a "whispered" sense among Palestinians that decades-long promises of the Arab world regarding Palestine were nothing more than lip service, intended to pacify the Arab street.

What we learned in the aftermath of the agreements is, from a Palestinian perspective, sobering promises of years past were, indeed, empty sloganeering, without substance or impact. While an argument might be made that COVID has distracted the "street" and that events outside the immediate environment carry less significance, the truth is the Arab world has long abandoned the Palestinians. The only exception, in a very limited manner, is Iran that has provided Hamas arms, albeit on a limited basis. However, Iran has played no role in efforts to reconcile the PA and Hamas; in addition, any Iranian effort to participate in the resolution of the Israeli–Palestinian conflict would be a non-starter for all the obvious reasons.

So, where does that leave the parties? The easy answer, oft-repeated, is that resolution of the conflicts (plural intended), Hamas–PA and Palestinian–Israeli, will require the parties to convene around the table, devoid of external participation-influence-pressure. The role of third parties—primarily but not exclusively the USA—has not proven to have a lasting, positive effect. The imposition of the world's sole superpower in negotiations results in the parties engaged in indirect interaction with each other, in a sense "playing" to the USA, seeking to curry favor. In the long run, that has proven less than successful, various efforts over the years by different Administrations notwithstanding. That is not to minimize the efforts expanded over the years or to gainsay some achievements from the perspective of those committed to conflict resolution. However, those gains have not translated to a just and lasting peace that satisfies the numerous stakeholders.

The Oslo model might be offered as duplicable, gathering the parties under a presumed neutral "umbrella," creating an environment cohesive to negotiations. That would be distinct from experience with US negotiators who were actively involved-intervened in the negotiation process. However, whether it is an Oslo US model the primary question is whether the sides – intra-Palestinian and Israeli–Palestinian—are truly committed to resolving both conflicts. It is to that we turn our attention; we do so not in a blame-game, finger-pointing manner but rather suggesting a mechanism to unlock the stalemate. There are three assumptions that demand acknowledgment and resolution:

1. The international community (writ large) has disengaged from the conflict.
2. The Biden Administration will primarily focus on China, absent specific hot-spots that endanger US national security.
3. There are the parties—Israel, PA, Hamas—to this conflict, and in spite of historic, political, social, and cultural baggage resolution demands, all three have a seat at the table.

It is not an exaggeration to suggest that current (December 2020) leadership among all parties has not exhibited a willingness to move beyond the status quo that defines the current situation. It has been suggested that Netanyahu and Abu Mazen, the President of the Palestinian Authority, are engaged in a mutually beneficial symbiotic relationship whereby neither national leader is required to make difficult decisions with political (domestic) consequences that are, from their perspective, unnecessary. In that context, the two leaders are a comfortable fit for each other, not interested in resolution, not interested in escalation. While the Palestinians expressed anger in response to the normalization agreements referenced above, the response was muted by leadership and public alike.

Whether that reflects an understanding of the current geopolitics or an unwillingness to engage Saudi Arabia (perhaps the two are related), the reality is the Palestinian voice has been muted. With regard to Hamas, reliance on Iran as a "patron" is akin to standing on shaky ground, which can turn into quicksand. As made clear in the aftermath of the killings of two Iranians—General Soleimani (BBC, 2020a) and Mohsen Fakhrizadeh, a top nuclear scientist (BBC, 2020b)—Iran presently seemingly has neither the means nor the capability to respond, beyond statements best described as mild and measured, more intended for a domestic audience than anything else.

Recognizing the impact of a limited Iranian response is of great importance when Hamas considers how, if at all, to resolve the conflict with the PA. Much like the Israeli–Palestinian conflict is best defined as status quo, perhaps that definition can be equally applied to the Hamas–PA conflict. Absent a third party and/or the willingness of the sides to engage in serious efforts to resolve their differences, the practical consequences are that the situation will remain "as is" in the immediate future. This has an impact both on the intra-Palestinian conflict and on the Israeli–Palestinian conflict. The two, then, are inexorably linked, similar to an umbilical cord. There is, then, a triangle that must be unknotted; the challenge is how to proceed.

While we were sensitive to the request of our Palestinian colleagues to ignore Gaza–Hamas in our meetings, perhaps we were mistaken in doing so. An argument can be made that by doing so we created a false narrative whereby Israel need only negotiate with the PA to resolve the conflict. While perhaps convenient given the nature of the PA–Hamas relations and Hamas's consistent threats against PA leaders, the conflict can ultimately only be resolved were Hamas to have a seat at the table. The adage "you don't make peace with your friends but with your enemies" applies in this case. This adage applies to both Hamas's relationship with the PA and its relationship with Israel. Much like "official" Israel ignored Arafat until the Oslo process, Israel and Hamas have been locked in battle since the organization was formed in 1987 during the First Intifada (1987–1993). In subsequent decades, much blood has been spilled both in the Gaza Strip and in Israel as a result of Hamas attacks, whether KASAM missiles or suicide bombings. Similarly, the conflict between Hamas and the PA has been violent, albeit not to the same degree as Hamas–Israel. The status quo of the triangle (which we deliberately ignored in our meetings) can be summarized as follows: violent confrontation between Hamas and Israel; violence–reconciliation efforts cycles between Hamas and the PA; studied/deliberate ignoring between Israeli and PA officials; and occasional acts of violence by Israelis and Palestinians alike. Those acts, however, do not have geopolitical impact.

In that spirit, were we to re-engage with the relevant parties we would recommend incorporating representatives from Hamas. While this poses logistic if not legal challenges, for Israelis participants, creating a platform whereby direct interaction occurs would make a significant contribution to developing a deeper understanding of the parties' respective positions and the limits of flexibility and compromise. We are aware of the challenges such an undertaking would present; however, there is much to be gained from mutually addressing the points of conflict. While that does not, obviously, guarantee resolution, it would enable an "airing of grievances" from which national leaders would greatly benefit.

The relevance of a tripartite undertaking is enhanced when examined in the context of the Biden Administration. Based on statements—on and off the record—by officials, it is reasonable to predict that the administration's foreign policy priorities will primarily be Russia, China, and climate issues with the Middle East a distant second, or third. There is, as we have learned in the past years, both positives and negatives in this predicated reality. The positive: it forces the party, should they be desirous of conflict resolution, to directly interact. The negative: absent a figurative "adult figure" pushing the parties together, resolution will be as distant tomorrow as it is today.

Which brings us to the following practical recommendations, based in part on the Pittsburgh Principles but, in reality, going beyond what we accomplished over the course of several years. That is not to minimize the achievements of our participants but rather to build what we have learned, both in our intensive interactions with them and in additional forums and circumstances. The list below should not be understood as replacing the PP but, rather, an addition to what has been previously agreed upon with one significant distinction: Hamas's voice is heard, with recognition logistics and politics presenting significant challenges which we readily acknowledge.

In addition, the recommendations are based on recognition that present Israeli (Netanyahu) and Palestinian (Abu Mazen) leadership is not equipped-capable of engagement to resolve the conflict. While the results of the March 2021 election leave uncertain who the Prime Minister will be, it is assumed that regardless of who the PM is, the government will be a center-right government. Similarly, as these lines are written, Palestinian succession is unclear following Abu Mazen. The same uncertainty holds true for Hamas. Therefore, the recommendations below must be understood as not leader dependent but rather as a road map for future leaders, regardless of their identity and political affiliation and identity. The core premise of the recommendations is that third parties will not be involved, reflecting both USA and Arab world disengagement from the Israeli–Palestinian conflict, as outlined above.

The proposed "steps forward" are predicated on a desire of the respective parties' leaders to end the conflict and an acknowledgment that the current "status quo" is not a sustainable model. That does not mean that warm relations are obligatory but does represent recognition that continued conflict, regardless of intensity, does not benefit the respective populations and that a degree of economic–trade–commerce interaction benefits all involved.

Before outlining our recommendations, there is an additional issue that demands our attention which was addressed, in large part, in Chap. 10. In a nutshell, the question is how will Hamas, PA, and Israeli decision makers address both their own publics and each other's publics, much less how will they engage on a personal level and what instructions will they give to their negotiators and on-the-ground implementers. As discussed in Chap. 10, internal and external communications was one of the major failings of the Oslo Agreement. For our purposes (in this chapter), it is irrelevant whom is to blame as there is no benefit from that.

The question is what lessons were learned and what fundamental adjustments will be made. There is little doubt that the lack of attention to communication and failure to understand the need to communicate was a major reason for Oslo's failure. While it was, obviously, not the only reason, its prime importance must be recognized. For decision makers to proceed forth, when parties traditionally associated with resolution efforts are disengaged, an even greater onus is placed on the manner in which communication is conducted as the ability to "play" to a third party will not be available.

This will require negotiators to speak directly to each other; understandably, this will pose a challenge to all involved. However, in examining previous negotiation undertakings, there is no alternative but to do so. The direct communication must apply across the board: Israeli leaders to the Israeli public, PA to the Palestinians in the West Bank, and Hamas to Palestinians in the Gaza Strip. Public opinion polls suggest this will be a difficult undertaking given significant domestic resistance to resolving the conflict. It is a challenge that leaders must accept; otherwise, the effort will be a non-starter from the beginning. That same burden applies to the way the other's public is addressed; as noted in Chap. 10, Rabin, Peres, and Arafat thoroughly failed to undertake even a minimal effort. The emphasis, then, on communication is not by chance; it is there that we begin our list of recommendations:

1. Every leader must directly communicate with his/her public.
2. Every leader must directly communicate with his/her negotiators.
3. Every leader must directly communicate with on-the-ground implementers.
4. Every leader must directly communicate with publics of the other side/s (the plural refers to three-way negotiation).
5. There will be need for mutual recognition and agreement for "end of hostilities."
6. There will be need for Hamas and PA to unify under one flag unless the intention is to create two different Palestinian states, one Islamic, the other secular.

However, the extremist stance of Hamas toward Israel and Palestinians who do not adhere to their covenant makes it almost impossible to consider it as a peace partner. Then if Hamas is not part of the future, what are possible future scenarios for that region? Here are some extreme situations. The order provided does not represent what is more likely:

1. Hamas creates an Islamic state.
2. The Palestinian people choose for themselves to create the State of Palestine without religious considerations and rejects Hamas as their leader.
3. Israel annexes all the territories regardless of who lives in them and exiles the occupants who do not cooperate to eliminate enemies from within.

Just these three scenarios can make one tremble of the repercussions to the losing party. The only scenario that has more future not for the politicians but for the people is a cooperation scenario between the Palestinian people and the Jewish people. This is what this book advocates, a future for the children of Palestine and the children of Israel.

References

Aljazeera. (2020, August 17). Kushner: US will not approve Israeli annexations for 'some time'. *Aljazeera*. Accessed June 4, 2021, from https://www.aljazeera.com/news/2020/8/17/kushner-us-will-not-approve-israeli-annexations-for-some-time

BBC. (2020a, January 3). Qasem Soleimani: US kills top Iranian general in Baghdad air strike. *BBC News*. Accessed June 5, 2021, from https://www.bbc.com/news/world-middle-east-50979463

BBC. (2020b, November 30). Mohsen Fakhrizadeh: Iran scientist killed by remote-controlled weapon. *BBC News*. Accessed June 5, 2021, from https://www.bbc.com/news/world-middle-east-55128970

CBS News. (2012, August 21). Israel says Egypt violating peace treaty in Sinai. *CBS News*. Accessed June 5, 2021, from https://www.cbsnews.com/news/israel-says-egypt-violating-peace-treaty-in-sinai/

JVL. (2008). Legal requirements to maintain Israel's qualitative edge. *Jewish Virtual Library*. Accessed June 4, 2021, from https://www.jewishvirtuallibrary.org/legal-requirement-to-maintain-israel-s-qualitative-edge

MEE. (2018, November 7). Why Jordan cancelled part of its peace treaty with Israel. *Middle East Eye*. Accessed June 5, 2021, from https://www.middleeasteye.net/opinion/why-jordan-cancelled-part-its-peace-treaty-israel

NYTimes. (2018a, May 9). Trump abandons Iran pact he long scorned. *New York Times.* Printed Edition, p. A1.

NYTimes. (2018b, December 9). Wooed by Saudis, Kushner Became influential friend. *New York Times.* Printed Edition. Accessed June 4, 2021, from https://www.nytimes.com/2018/12/08/world/middleeast/saudi-mbs-jared-kushner.html

NYTimes. (2019, November 19). In reversal, U.S. Sides with Israel on settlements. *New York Times.* Printed Edition, p. A1. Accessed June 4, 2021, from https://www.nytimes.com/2019/11/18/world/middleeast/trump-israel-west-bank-settlements.html

Riboua, Z. (2020, December 24). How Moroccans reacted to normalization with Israel. *Atlantic Council.* Accessed June 4, 2021, from https://www.atlanticcouncil.org/blogs/menasource/how-moroccans-reacted-to-normalization-with-israel/

The Guardian. (2019, June 26). Jared Kushner's 'deal of the century' fails to materialize in Bahrain. *The Guardian.* Accessed June 4, 2021, from https://www.theguardian.com/world/2019/jun/26/jared-kushner-deal-of-the-century-israel-palestine-bahrain

The Jerusalem Post. (2021, January 13). Israel to advance West Bank building 3 days prior to Biden inauguration. *The Jerusalem Post.* Accessed June 5, 2021, from https://www.jpost.com/israel-news/israel-to-advance-west-bank-building-3-days-prior-to-biden-inauguration-655207

The Times of Israel. (2020a, January 30). Annexation, stalled: How Trump, Netanyahu fell out of step on core part of deal. *The Time of Israel.* Accessed June 4, 2021, from https://www.timesofisrael.com/annexation-stalled-how-trump-netanyahu-fell-out-of-step-on-core-part-of-deal/

The Times of Israel. (2020b, June 11). Mapping Netanyahu's annexation plan: Experts explain a charged, complex process. *The Times of Israel.* Accessed June 4, 2021, from https://www.timesofisrael.com/so-you-want-to-annex-the-west-bank-map-experts-weigh-in-on-netanyahus-plan/

The Times of Israel. (2021). Accessed June 3, 2021, from https://www.timesofisrael.com/topic/hilltop-youth/

U.S. Dept. of State. (2020, August 13). The Abraham Accords Declaration. *U.S. Department of State, Bureau of Near Eastern Affairs.* Accessed June 4, 2021, from https://www.state.gov/the-abraham-accords/